'Naomi Jacobs and Emily Richardson know that example is the best teacher, testimony the best advocate, but argument, persistence and reframing are needed if change is to come about. They long for a Church that looks more like God and a society that inhabits God's reign, and they provide relentless examples, moving testimonies and compelling arguments for what would change and how things could be if the voices and lives of people with disabilities were permitted to reshape the culture of communities. This is an elegantly structured and profoundly argued case for a very different but much holier and more faithful Church.'

Samuel Wells, Vicar of St Martin-in-the-Fields, London

'Churches should be inclusive and accessible for everyone, and sadly all too often barriers still remain in place. I am pleased that this book has drawn on the lived experience of disabled people, and I hope it can act as a turning point to encourage churches to ensure they do everything in their power to be inclusive for all of us.'

Marsha de Cordova, MP for Battersea

'*At the Gates* is a phenomenal journey. It transports the reader into the world of the disabled person who loves Christ. It then points to a world and a Church which attempts to disable the image of Christ in so many. The book exposes the ableist tendencies many institutions and individuals perpetuate. Through strong theological rigour and a variety of gifted storytellers, we learn to encounter God within all, we are asked to provide access with all, create bespoke tables to accommodate all, and design liturgies which include all. It points forward with many practical and necessary steps, for a renewed Church within our world.'

A. D. A. France-Williams, priest, author of *Ghost Ship*

'*At the Gates* brings together stories from more than fifty disabled Christians as a much-needed prophetic call to churches to repent of the ableism that prevails. Refreshingly, this collection allows disabled Christians to share our own experiences, offering a tender and heartbreaking invitation to open the gates of exclusion. A mix of modern-day parables, compelling research, and first-person narrative, this timely work of disability theology demands justice that will leave readers transformed.'

**Amy Kenny, disabled scholar, author of
*My Body Is Not A Prayer Request***

'In centring the diverse voices, stories, experiences and theologies of disabled people, both within and beyond the Church, *At the Gates* offers profound and powerful insights into being human, being Church, the gospel and God, that come together in a call not for inclusion but for transformation: a radical re-centring among those who have for so long been marginalised and excluded by the narrow ableism of both world and Church, and a repentance that leads to the justice and liberation of the Kin-dom of God. This book is Spirit-breathed good news for the Church: prophetic, challenging and life-bringing!'

Al Barrett, vicar, co-author of *Being Interrupted: Re-imagining the Church's Mission from the Outside, In*

'Naomi and Emily have given us a precious gift – the voices of disabled people. Interwoven with the statistics, facts and failings of society, politics, and church structures, disabled voices have shone through and told the story of hope. Have no doubts, this book is also a challenge. Don't read it, sit back and say "now I am better informed and understand their experiences – what a blessing". Read, weep, lament for the injustices. Repent, re-adjust, and change the culture. Collaborate with us, the disabled people (some of whom are already on the inside). Pay attention to this prophetic book and its contributors. Join in.'

Kt Tupling, priest, author, disability activist

'This is a book of hope and prophecy; the authors and those whose stories they share are not looking for sympathy or pastoral care or even to inspire others but to claim their baptismal status as equal children of God. They challenge the Church to open its eyes to see and actively embrace the gifts of disabled people and to allow itself to be transformed, to enter into its divine calling to be the place of justice and equality in a world that is a hostile place for so many.

'Written from the margins, this is a practical book for all who love God and love the Church and desire to see it become what God called it to be.'

Hannah Lewis SCL, Chaplain amongst the Deaf Community, Diocese of Oxford

AT THE GATES

Disability, Justice and the Churches

Naomi Lawson Jacobs and
Emily Richardson

DARTON·LONGMAN+TODD

First published in 2022 by
Darton, Longman and Todd Ltd
1 Spencer Court
140 – 142 Wandsworth High Street
London SW18 4JJ

ISBN: 978-1-913657-18-5

A catalogue record for this book is available from the British Library.

Printed and bound in Great Britain by Bell & Bain, Glasgow

Dedicated to Professor John M. Hull, blind theologian, who saw disabled people 'not so much as pastoral problem as prophetic potential', and called the Church to see us as witnesses and leaders of renewal. With thanks to him for helping us to find our place in the prophetic life of the Church.

CONTENTS

ACKNOWLEDGEMENTS   9

INTRODUCTION   13

CHAPTER 1   Our Stories   35

PART ONE   Closed Gates: Access, Participation and   41
             Leadership

CHAPTER 2   Knocking on the Church Gates: Disabled   43
             People Accessing Church Buildings

CHAPTER 3   A Transformed Table: Accessible   65
             Church Cultures

CHAPTER 4   Distinctive Gifts: Disabled People's   99
             Service and Ministry

PART TWO   Opening the Gates: Disabled Prophets   129
             Speak

CHAPTER 5   Theology at the Gates: Disabled People   131
             Telling Our Own Stories

CHAPTER 6   Fearfully and Wonderfully Made: 159
             Disabled People's Stories of Healing

CHAPTER 7   Church on the Edge: Disabled Christian   190
             Community Beyond the Church Gates

CHAPTER 8   Church in COVID-19 and the Prophetic   215
             Witness of Bed-Based Prophets

CONCLUSION   233

APPENDIX 1   Storytellers' Stories   241

APPENDIX 2   Glossary   265

APPENDIX 3   Abbreviations   277

APPENDIX 4   Resources for Churches on Disability,   279
             Access and Justice

ENDNOTES   283

ACKNOWLEDGEMENTS

Naomi would like to thank...

First, and most importantly, we are indebted to the disabled Christians who have shared their lived experience with us, without whom this book could not have been written. You have been generous, bold and courageous in speaking out for justice. You are the disabled prophets the Church needs. These are your stories. Thank you.

Thank you also to Erin Raffety for the insight that the storytellers in this book are evangelists.

Thank you to Emily, for recognising how much these stories need to be heard, and joining the effort to share them more widely with the Church. As disabled Christians ourselves, writing a book like this has been very painful at times, joyful at other times, and having a co-writer to share the load has been invaluable. I'd like to thank the disabled-led Christian communities who have encouraged us to share their stories, including those with whom we have worshipped and shared fellowship. I'm grateful to the St Martin-in-the-Fields/Inclusive Church annual conference on disability and church, especially Fiona MacMillan, and all the members of the conference community who generously shared their stories. Thank you to Wave Church and its members, who welcomed me into their community and told me why it matters to them. Many thanks also to the leaders of YouBelong, Disability and Jesus, and Struggling Saints, for sharing their stories of church on the edge. The growing disabled Christian movement in the UK has been a force behind this book, and it's a privilege to share your stories here.

We're so grateful to Dr Rachel Holdforth for creating a beautiful print of a blind Christ leading a sighted disciple for our front cover image. It is a joy to be able to use an illustration which so perfectly encapsulates the themes of the book: the prophetic, pioneering role of disabled Christians leading and discipling others.

Many thanks to our publishers at Darton, Longman and Todd, particularly David Moloney, who have encouraged us in writing a challenging book. I'd also like to thank colleagues who looked at early versions of this book and shared helpful advice and encouragement: thank you to Rev Dr Erin Raffety, Krysia Waldock, Fiona MacMillan and Rev Kate Harford. I'm grateful to my PhD supervisor, Dr Sîan Hawthorne, for invaluable guidance during the original research project, and to the St Luke's College Foundation for part-funding the original research, so that I could offer storytellers a contribution for their valuable time and expertise. Many thanks also to the disabled Christians who made up the Research Advisory Group, who helped set the direction for my PhD research. I am also grateful to representatives from the Church of England, the Methodist Church and the Baptist Church, for sharing data about their disability ministries.

On a more personal note, I want to thank my spouse Shai for infinite patience and practical support while I've been writing, and for encouraging me ever to swim against the tide.

Emily would like to thank...

My first thanks must go to Naomi, for the invitation to collaborate on this project. It has been a joy to help bring these stories to a wider audience. Working on a book with the added complications of COVID lockdowns, not to mention the everyday setbacks that come with living with chronic illness, has been a challenge but it was made easier knowing I had a co-writer who more than understood what I meant when I said I was 'having a rough day'! Thank you, too, to David Moloney at DLT for his support and encouragement throughout.

I am thankful to Fiona MacMillan for her continued wisdom and ability to bring out the gifts in others. I have learned so much about disability justice and *edgy* theology through my involvement with the

ACKNOWLEDGEMENTS

Living Edge conferences. Fiona drew me deeper into the heart of the conference and exposed me to so many new and exciting voices which have inspired me when writing.

Personal thanks go to my friends and family for their love and support. I would like to thank especially the Whaites and the McPhees for their continued prayers and encouragement. Thank you to my friends at the Moot Community (and to the staff at Host Cafe for keeping me caffeinated) as well as the Parish Office and congregation of All Saints Fulham. The Zoom Morning Prayer Club have been a particularly grounding and sustaining presence. Finally thank you to Mum and Ellen for their love and endless supply of tea, hugs and painkillers.

Writing this book has been a sacred experience (most of the time!) and that is only because of the knowledge that I am sharing the stories of those who are so often ignored or belittled. So my final thanks must go to the people who shared their stories with us and allowed us access to their hurts, their pain and disappointments, their desires, their hopes and their longings. I hope what we have produced will be just the beginning of an important and long-avoided conversation.

INTRODUCTION

'There is a part of the body of Christ that is unseen and if we can make our voices heard then we might get our needs met by our fellow brothers and sisters in Christ. We may not be physically able but I believe we still have gifts to share with the rest of the Church if they could only accommodate us!' Faith

This is a book about justice.

Fern has often found herself on the edge of church communities. Told by other Christians that chronic illness and autism are the result of sin in her life, she has also had to deal with such poor access to churches that she has mostly stayed away. She has often become a target for those wanting to pray for her cure, without ever asking her if that is what *she* wants. It is no wonder that it has taken Fern a long time to understand that God loves her, just as she is. In her own words, her experiences at church have left her feeling 'in all honesty, less than human'.

Hazel and Victor have been attending their church for many years. Yet the couple, who are both blind, are often forgotten in a community where every aspect of church life is designed for sighted people. They cannot sing with their congregation when words are projected onto a screen; rarely do worship leaders remember to email lyrics to them in advance. Registering for church events means signing up via an inaccessible website, so that joining in with church social life has become all but impossible for them. Victor once hoped to lead Alpha, but he was disappointed when pastors could only imagine the problems a blind man would have in a leadership role. The couple remain on the edge of their church, enjoying the worship and teaching there, but excluded as disabled people.

These are stories of a Church that has closed its gates to disabled people.[1]

> **❛I have often found navigating the church experience difficult … I think being disabled in the church, it is common to feel extremely alone and othered.❜ Fern**

As long as there has been a Church, disabled people have been part of the Church. Jesus's mission to the marginalised brought him close to those who knew the stigma that came with illness and impairment, those we would now call disabled. Yet for many disabled people today, the Church is a tower built in the shadow of disability injustice. The Church has been 'a "city on a hill"' for us, as disability theologian Nancy Eiesland writes, 'physically inaccessible and socially inhospitable'.[2] In spite of Jesus' command to the powerful to give us a seat of honour among the Body of Christ,[3] disabled people have more often found ourselves waiting at the gates.

In this book, based on a decade of research with disabled Christians in the UK, we share disabled people's stories of churches. Many of their experiences echo the words of Fiona MacMillan, Chair of the Disability Advisory Group at St Martin-in-the-Fields Church in London:

> The Church of the twenty-first century frequently fails disabled people, hearing echoes of an understanding that links sickness with sinfulness, mental health issues with possession, and disability as being in need of cure. Pounced on by street evangelists, spoken about rather than listened to, regarded as difficult or demanding,

costly or time-consuming, it's not surprising that many disabled people are put off going to church – even if we can get in. Access is often focused on getting in – ramps and lifts, hearing loops and loos – rather than joining in, with participation seen as a step too far. We are more likely to be known by our needs than celebrated for our gifts.[4]

In the generous, vulnerable stories shared in this book, storytellers tell us about the ways that they have been failed by churches. Disabled people are failed by churches that make no room for us, as leaders lament financial limits – while managing to find money for the projects and people they value. We are failed by churches where we cannot participate, because we are not imagined in the pews or the pulpits. We are failed by churches that see disabled people as a 'pastoral problem'[5] rather than as partners in transformation; who talk about us, but rarely ask us about the stumbling-blocks that churches put in our way. Disabled people are failed by a Christian tradition that uses ableist language and metaphors, without examining the values at the heart of oft-repeated hymns and stories.[6] And we are failed in churches that have seen disabled Christians only as objects of others' ministry, where our gifts and leadership potential have gone unrecognised.[7] In some of the stories in this book, we hear of disabled people so harmed by damaging theology, so frustrated by churches that will not engage with ableism, that they have walked away from churches altogether.

Yet none of them has given up on the Church. The disabled storytellers in this book are prophetic voices, speaking out against ableism in churches. They are showing churches what it means to live out God's Kingdom justice.

‘ I have this fight [for disability access at church] ... I try very hard to do it through education, through talking, through creating a cause ... But I have cried bucket loads over it, because I do feel completely invisible and violated. ’ Brianna

AT THE GATES

Ableism has a social context beyond the Church. In the twenty-first century, the 14.4 million disabled people in the UK remain deeply marginalised,[8] with real-world consequences for our health, our participation in society, and for whether we live or die. We are twice as likely to live in poverty as non-disabled people;[9] two-thirds of those referred to the UK's food banks are disabled.[10] Disabled people are still feeling the effects of an austerity agenda that began in the 2000s, when cuts to government services and support were excused by public narratives that condemned us as 'shirkers and scroungers',[11] while today, a punitive benefits system has been implicated in our deaths.[12] Disabled people are less likely to be in employment than non-disabled people, and when we are, we earn significantly less than our non-disabled colleagues,[13] all while dealing with the staggering extra costs that come with disability.[14] We are victims of crime more often than non-disabled people; the grim statistics show that disabled women are twice as likely to be sexually assaulted as non-disabled women[15] and that all disabled people are doubly at risk of domestic abuse,[16] while rising rates of disability hate crime put thousands of us at risk every year.[17] Disabled people are over-represented in prisons[18] and under-represented in education; we are more likely than our non-disabled peers to leave school with no qualifications.[19] The UK's social care crisis is leaving hundreds of thousands of disabled and older people without the help they need to wash and dress.[20] And since 2020, the coronavirus pandemic has deepened the disability inequalities that were already rife, in the UK and across the globe.[21] This is systemic ableism: structural injustice against disabled people.[22] It took root in society only a few hundred years ago, when a demanding capitalist system came to value people for their ability to be productive, and a physically, mentally 'normal' vision of humanity was privileged over all other ways of being human.[23] Today, ableism 'tells us some bodies [and minds] are valuable and some are disposable'.[24] It paves the way for daily discrimination against disabled individuals, or *disablism*.[25] In a society that could afford to act justly towards disabled people, we know how little we are valued when the ugly reality of ableism characterises every aspect of our lives.

Where is the Church? disabled people are beginning to ask. Where were churches when Connor Sparrowhawk drowned in the bath at an NHS assessment centre, one of thousands of people with learning disabilities who have died of medical neglect in the UK?[26] Where were churches when fifteen disabled people died in the fire at Grenfell Tower, because the landlord had put no evacuation plans in place for them, instead telling them to 'stay put'?[27] Why is the Church silent in the face of disability injustice?

For many disabled people at the sharp end of ableism, Christianity is 'not seen as part of the answer but part of the problem', in disability theologian John Hull's words.[28] Ableism is not just an issue 'out there' in the world. It is at work in churches, with deep roots in Christian thought about disabled people.[29] Far from seeing the Church as the answer to injustice, Hull says, disabled people have more often seen the Christian faith as 'a major source of the social and economic disadvantage they suffer'.[30] The same power structures that marginalise us in the world are also at work in the churches. And for the most part, the ableism in our Christian tradition has gone unexamined and uncritiqued by the Church's leaders.

Until churches come to understand their own ableism, they cannot speak out as prophetic voices against disability injustice in society.

Listening to the stories of disabled Christians

' Many, many books are written about disabled people and the Church, but our own voices are not heard. ' Jemma

In the Christian conversation on disability, church leaders have more often spoken *about* disabled people than they have listened to us. Nearly thirty years ago, disabled pioneer and prophet Nancy Eiesland raised the cry for churches to listen to the voices of disabled Christians.[31] But little has changed since. Church tradition has more often seen disabled people as a niche issue of pastoral care than as prophetic voices.[32] Most church disability ministries in the UK are still *for* disabled people, rather than led *by* disabled people.[33] We see in churches a mirror of society's unequal power relationships between disabled people and non-disabled professionals, who have the power to make decisions about our access, our participation, and our right to speak. This is *pastoral power*, rooted in churches' traditional role of caring for the 'needy'.[34] To borrow the words of theologian Rachel Muers, disabled Christians know what it is to live a 'life shaped by the silence imposed by another'.[35]

As the many of the stories in this book will show, churches have been especially reluctant to listen to disabled Christians' cry for *justice, not charity*.[36] Today, there are still Christian thinkers who downplay the role of power, privilege and injustice in the lives of disabled people to whom the gates of the Church have been closed. Christian teaching on disability tends to be *about* us, 'from the centre looking out,' written by those with privilege in churches.[37] Books tend to focus on welcoming disabled people into churches.[38] But the power to open the church gates is in the hands of those who hold the keys. Through our painful experiences of rejection from churches, it is disabled people who know best how churches have failed to welcome us, just as we are.

Christian theology often discusses disabled people from a distance, whether it is calling disability a social fiction,[39] arguing that disability does not exist,[40] or asking whether concepts of disability or rights are relevant to churches at all.[41] While a few theologians are beginning to talk about ableism,[42] there is more often a well-meaning emphasis on how we are all one in Christ. It is true that we are all limited in comparison with God.[43] But, in some very real ways, some of us are disabled and some are not. 'There is not a level playing field that all bodies occupy,' writes disability theorist David T. Mitchell, 'and calling for a universalizing recognition of insufficiency will do little to accomplish meaningful systems change.'[44] In a focus on the ways we are all the same, the Church has often failed to engage with disabled people's lament at the ableism that marginalises us.[45]

When Andrew tells us how he left his church for the want of subtitled sermons, when Nicki tells us how her need for an accessible toilet was never remembered at her church, and when Fern tells us how she was 'pounced on' by strangers praying for her healing when she had not asked for it, they tell us that *disability is real*, and that churches need to understand it. The language of disability rights may be new to churches, but the Bible speaks the language of *justice*.[46] The disabled people in this book take up the Bible's cry for justice for those on margins, echoing it back to the centre – to the churches.

Churches, disability and justice

' Disability – it's just part, for me, of the whole theology of the church. That Jesus came to turn values upside down, with the Beatitudes. The Church needs to be turning their theology upside down. Jesus came for the broken. Not for the rich and the able. ' Rhona

For disabled people praying for change in churches, there is hope. In recent years, in the UK context, we have seen the beginning of long-overdue conversations on justice in Christian churches, most recently in the Church of England's report on racial justice, *From Lament to Action*.[47] But prophetic calls for justice have always come first from the edge of the Church. Discussions on racial inequality have only begun because of the faithful witness of Black and Global Majority Heritage Christians,[48] who have been speaking out for decades against racial injustice in churches.[49] With LGBTQ+ Christians, and many other marginalised groups who have been on the receiving end of injustice, these voices on the margins are asking, 'Can the Church of Jesus Christ be politically, socially, and economically identified with the structures of oppression and also be a servant of Christ?'[50]

Disabled people's experiences are part of this broader picture of injustice in churches. And yet the Church has been slow to understand disability as a social justice issue, with some denominations showing firmer commitments to their disabled members than others.[51] Many churches have little to say about how they are addressing ableism and disability exclusion. In 2022, at a fringe event at the Church of England's General Synod, disabled priest Tim Goode joined with other disabled Christians to celebrate the work of one disabled-led conference.[52] He spoke of a 'systemic failure to live out our baptismal promise' to disabled Christians, in a Church that has too often denied disabled people's dignity, diminished our gifts, and closed the gates on our access. He called the Church to affirm a commitment to disabled people. It was a cry for justice, joining a chorus of prophetic voices that has been 'calling from the edge'[53] for at least a decade.

In this book, we centre the stories of other disabled Christians calling from the edge, from the margins. Renewal in the Church comes from the edge, from those the Church has marginalised, as theologian Samuel Wells argues.[54] Through our lived experience, disabled people are all too aware of the injustice and ableism that may be invisible to majority non-disabled congregations. As the Church has honoured the rich, the powerful and the 'normal' over those on the margins, it has been caught up in the ableist values of the world, becoming 'a mirror of normal society'.[55] But disabled people bring the gift of another way of being church, another way of understanding God. As Hull puts it:

> Disabled people are not so much a pastoral problem as prophetic potential. We need to ask not how the church can care for disabled people but to ask what is the prophetic message of the church in our culture and how disabled people can make a unique contribution to that renewal ... [and] become witnesses to and leaders of it.[56]

In this book, disabled people call churches' attention to the ways they value one way of being human over others. They call for churches to care about the flourishing of all, not just the non-disabled.[57] Theirs is a Kingdom theology of *metanoia* – repentance, that leads to justice. Listening to our stories and experiences is no tokenistic act. It is part of the work of repentance for ableism; it is the first step in reconciliation with the disabled people whom churches have rejected. This is not 'inclusion,' in which the powerful seek to welcome outsiders into the centre of churches.[58] This is transformation.[59] The disabled Christians in this book are crying out, not just for a seat at the edge of the old, inaccessible table, but for a reimagined table that truly makes space for everyone who is part of God's good creation. As churches listen to these prophetic voices, they may learn to turn their understanding of mission and ministry upside-down.

No longer a mirror of society's values, these Christian communities will become a truer reflection of the diverse, just Kingdom of God.

Christian ableism: Whose story is it?

God made me and God makes nothing wrong, therefore there's nothing wrong with being disabled. Granted, pain and disability are often unpleasant, but what makes them so difficult is the lack of support and understanding. Jane

'Bad theology is deadly,' writes Jarel Robinson-Brown.[60] Christian stories about disability can make space for disabled people to enter church buildings, participate in church life and lead Christian communities – or they can close the gates to us. As non-disabled people have told most of the stories about God, they have unintentionally shared a gospel for non-disabled people.[61] The Church needs to hear the perspectives of disabled people, like the storytellers in this book, if it is to ensure 'that the Bible reveals its riches to everyone' and not just to the non-disabled.[62]

Christianity has always struggled to make sense of different bodies and minds in the diversity of God's creation. A Christian fiction of perfection is at the root of much of our modern ableism.[63] Icons of Jesus paint him as powerful and physically healthy.[64] Christians are comfortable with this 'hallucination of wholeness,' says disability theologian Sharon V. Betcher;[65] we imagine that only 'perfect' bodies and minds, without impairment, are whole and holy enough to approach God. Disabled Christians have told a very different story about God. Eiesland's story of a Christ resurrected with enduring wounds, rooted in disabled people's experience of rejected bodies,[66] is a story that points us back to a God of justice. This is a disabled God, who becomes one of the marginalised, and affirms that disability is holy. For disabled people, this can be a powerful, redemptive story. But it remains a marginal story. Christians have rejected this vision of the resurrection, believing that a powerful, holy God cannot also be disabled, says disability theologian

Lamar Hardwick.[67] In churches that value an imagined perfection above all other ways to be human, disabled people's different *ways of being* have become a theological stumbling-block. Our storytellers tell a different story, from within their own lived experience. They share a theology of justice that honours the image of God in disabled people.

In a Christian faith that struggles to accept disability, disabled people have become little more than plot devices,[68] either to show God's power at work in miracles, or to teach lessons about charity and good works.[69] That can leave real disabled people on the wayside, silenced by language and symbols that exploit us, but do not allow us to speak. As Christians read biblical stories about disabled people, we read our modern ableist values into the Bible.[70] So we may interpret the Gospel healing stories as evidence that disability is *deficit*, or a lesser way of being human, in need of 'fixing' by God. This belief has echoes of a powerful 'sin-disability conflation' that runs through Christian tradition, Eiesland argues – a belief that disability and sickness are the result of sin, and that disabled people cannot be holy until we are made non-disabled.[71] It is ableism that keeps these stigmatising beliefs alive, even though there are many other reflections of disability in the pages of the Bible.[72] In this book, storytellers will tell us about the personal impact of these ableist Christian traditions, which imagine disabled people not as a diverse part of God's good creation, but as Fallen mistakes waiting to be cured.[73] Their experiences stray far from the vision of *Kingdom healing* in the Gospels, through which Jesus announced justice and reconciliation for us all.[74] Yet many of our disabled storytellers believe there is a difference between healing and cure. They have discovered God's authentic healing in the midst of impairment and illness. Radically, many affirm, with Nancy Mairs, that 'the bodies we inhabit and the lives we carry on need not be perfect to have value'.[75] These storytellers share a theology of bodily justice that recognises all of God's creation as 'fearfully and wonderfully made'.[76]

For our many storytellers who are longing to lead and serve in their churches, Christianity's 'hallucination of wholeness' makes them a particular problem. Millennia after people with stigmatised bodies were kept out of the holiest parts of the Temple,[77] the stories in this book show how churches continue to exclude disabled people from service and leadership. Storytellers share the ways they have been seen as objects for the ministry of others, when a Christian *pastoral model* can only imagine disabled people as those who receive from churches' care and mission. Disabled priest Tim Goode has spoken of his encounters with fellow priests who cited ancient laws from Leviticus as a reason why he should never have been ordained.[78] The Church of England still has a canon law that asks disabled ordinands to prove that their 'infirmities' do not prevent them from ministering, when the Church might instead be asking itself what barriers it puts in the way of disabled people's ministry.[79] For many storytellers, there was a sense that the *ideal* priest is non-disabled. It was an expectation that closed the gates to their ministry. Their experiences should be a prophetic call to churches to dismantle barriers to disabled people's leadership.

Grace for an ableist Church comes from the edge. In this book, disabled Christians share their own stories about God, faith and disability, their own 'frontier theology'.[80] As they speak back against ableist readings of the Bible, these storytellers have often been inspired by *disability liberation theology*.[81] They draw strength from other disabled people's stories about God, even if they do not always know the names of the theologians who first told those stories. For the sake of the gospel, disability liberation theology seeks the transformation of an ableist Church and world. It speaks out against sins of ableism, and embraces a God who is wounded and yet still perfect, in defiance of society's normative values that keep disabled people from flourishing.[82] This is theology *by* and *for* us, and by allies who centre disabled people's stories; Shane Clifton calls it *crip theology*.[83] For Deaf liberation theologian Hannah Lewis, *liberation* is redemption, as God frees us to become the people were created to be:

> For me, social liberation as a Deaf person means above all the freedom to develop as a 'first class Deaf person' rather than constantly playing catch up as a 'second-class hearing person' in today's world... [This is] liberation from whatever deprives human beings of the opportunity to realize as fully as possible their own God-given potential.[84]

As the Spirit liberates all of us from the social sin of ableism, we are shown the first glimpses of God's anti-ableist Kingdom, where we can celebrate the image of God in ourselves and each other. In a world and church that has sought to 'fix' or even eradicate disabled people, God's future is different. The storytellers in this book imagine 'crip futures ... "desirably disabled" worlds that are not founded on the normalization of disabled people'.[85] As disabled people are empowered to share our stories, our liberation becomes everyone's liberation.

This is the Kingdom theology that storytellers share in this book. These are disabled people's own stories, which they can only tell because they are disabled people. Their 'hopeful reimagination' is shaped by marginalisation, injustice, suffering, joy, creativity and difference.[86] Theirs are stories with the power to transform a Church that has come to value the powerful and the 'perfect' over those with different, stigmatised bodies and minds.

The power to name ourselves

❛ When we look at God from a different angle, i.e. the angle of people who are disabled ... we will learn stuff about God that we might not ordinarily see. ❜ Tim

Disabled people are speaking back. The slogan of the disabled people's movement, 'Nothing about us without us',[87] is vital for churches to remember, if they are to hear our stories. Disabled people have been calling for 'justice, not charity' for more than a century, but it was about fifty years ago when a small, grassroots network of disabled people's groups gave us one tool to fight against disability oppression: the *social model* of disability.[88] It says that in a world that was not designed for us, people with impairments are disabled by *barriers* – physical, attitudinal and social barriers, from inaccessible communities to degrading benefits systems.[89] The social model has been liberatory for many disabled people; it shows us that it is society that is broken, not us. But it was never intended to tell the full story of disability. It has sometimes led disabled people to emphasise social injustice over all other aspects of our lives.

That can erase the reality of those of us who experience pain, fatigue and illness, and 'the often-disabling effects of our bodies', says disability scholar Alison Kafer.[90] Disabled writers have gone deeper, exploring illness and pain,[91] society's reactions to our stigmatised bodies,[92] and all the ways that 'disability is about both barriers to 'doing' and barriers to 'being'.[93] This book draws on wisdom from these disabled writers and their allies in disability studies. The authors share Kafer's view that disability is both political and relational.[94] In the face of the horrors of ableism, we refuse to depoliticise disability. But we also want to honour the 'mixed blessing' of the bodies and minds of our storytellers, when they echo Disability Justice activist Leah Lakshmi Piepzna Samarasinha:

> I do not want to be fixed. I want to change the world. I want to be alive, awake, grieving, and full of joy. And I am.[95]

These are some of the ways disabled people have been speaking back against ableism in society for decades. The Holy Spirit is at work outside the church walls too, especially when churches are silent. In the churches, it has been harder for disempowered disabled Christians to raise prophetic voices against injustice.

But the Spirit is moving on the edge of the Church. In the UK, through a small but growing disabled Christian movement, disabled Christians are beginning to form our own communities and networks, raising our voices together.[96] In this book, more voices join that chorus of liberation for disabled people who belong not at the edge, but at the heart of the Body of Christ. As these storytellers – these disabled evangelists – call for churches to transform into anti-ableist Kingdom communities, they are making the gospel accessible. Despite some historical Christian thought, we disabled people do not have a special blessing from God to be saints or prophets.[97] But our lived experience makes us uniquely placed to call from the edge, together, for a more diverse, just vision of the Reign of God. That's the kind of prophetic calling of disabled people that John Hull called the Church to recognise.

For those who have not been enabled to speak, the power to name ourselves is a gift from God.[98] In this book, when we speak about 'disabled people', we use *identity-first language,* terminology that is widely used by UK-based disability campaigners.[99] Not all disabled people use the same language, and we have respected storytellers' choices in how they define themselves. But when, as authors, we use the term 'disabled people,' we affirm that this is who we are. We cannot leave disability at the church door, nor do we believe God wants us to try. We are used to euphemisms, like 'people with dis/abilities,' from those who are uncomfortable with the stigma of disability.[100] But what we name reflects what we value.[101] It is the first step towards naming disability injustice.

That word, 'we,' is also important to us. Authors Naomi and Emily are part of the community we write about. We are disabled Christians, and *we* are activist researchers and writers. Disabled Christians cannot distance ourselves from the conversation about us: our own bodies and minds are at stake.[102] Many of our storytellers have been alienated by a flood of theology that speaks *about* them, which tends to call disabled Christians 'they'. At the same time, we are not trying to claim that all disabled people are the same, nor that disability is easy to define.[103] Disability has fuzzy borders, and not everyone who fits legal definitions will identify as disabled.[104] We hold the term 'disabled community' loosely, but we use it to identify our shared experiences with many who are waiting at the gates of the Church. We share a personal, political and theological heart-cry for disability justice in churches with the disabled storytellers in this book.

In the Kingdom of God, there will be no privilege of one group over another. There will be no ableism. Then, as Paul argues in Galatians, will we need no definitions of disabled or non-disabled, Black or white, working class or middle class, nor of any other marginalised and privileged groups. That's when we will be one in Christ Jesus.[105] But we cannot jump to the end of the story without taking a hard look at the realities of disabled people's experiences in churches in the face of ongoing ableism. As the stories in this book will show, the Church has a long way to go before justice is a reality for disabled Christians. A journey towards reconciliation can only start with repentance for ableism and exclusion of disabled people.

How this book was written

This book is based on over a decade of research with more than fifty disabled Christians in the UK, exploring their experiences of churches and Christianity. To honour those who have shared their vulnerable, powerful gift of lived experience, we have called them *storytellers*.

There are many untold stories of disabled Christians. There is very little social research that explores disabled Christians' experiences of access, participation or leadership, particularly in the UK.[106] This missing research is one sign that disabled people's stories are not being heard in churches. We do not know how many churches in the UK have disability access and justice statements, nor how many have carried out access audits with expert advice from disabled people. We don't know how many churches have accessible facilities, nor which kinds. For the most part, we do not know how many disabled priests there are, nor how many disabled people are turned away when discerning a call to ordination or leadership.[107] We *do* know that there is at least one disabled person in every Church of England congregation,[108] but we know almost nothing about their experiences. This book is based on qualitative research, which explores stories in depth. It cannot answer all these questions; it can only help to start a conversation about the experiences of disabled people in churches. To tell some of the untold stories.

The story of the research begins with Naomi's PhD, and interviews with 35 disabled Christians from the UK, with several more conversations in disabled-led communities.[109] Naomi reached out to Emily, a theologian and participant in the research, to collaborate on sharing these stories more widely. We spoke to more disabled Christians between 2020 and 2021.[110] In this book, we write about 31 storytellers in detail, but we draw on the experiences of all 54.[111] We are grateful to them all for sharing their stories, when speaking back against ableism in the churches can come with risk.

One book cannot represent all disabled people. But our storytellers are a diverse group of people, from many church backgrounds, lay and ordained, aged from 23 to 82, and with many different impairments.[112] All of them are covered by the legal, Equality Act definition of disability: they have a physical or mental impairment that has a 'substantial' and 'long-term' effect on their ability to do everyday activities.[113] Most, but not all, identify as disabled people. We heard stories from people with chronic illness and chronic pain, those who experience mental and emotional distress, and many others whose impairments are invisible. We spoke to neurodivergent people, including autistic storytellers and those with ADHD and dyslexia. We heard from wheelchair users and mobility-impaired people, through illness and injury, and blind and deaf people. Many storytellers have more than one impairment. Naomi also spent time with and interviewed members of Wave Church, a Christian community 'with not for' those with learning disabilities.[114] Some storytellers asked us to use pseudonyms to protect their anonymity, often when sharing very painful experiences in churches, while others chose to use their first names. Chapters 7 and 8 include expert interviews with leaders of disabled people's Christian groups, who write and speak publicly. Several of these leaders asked us to use their full names in these chapters, to give them ownership of their stories and theology.[115]

Most of these diverse storytellers have one overwhelming experience in common: ableism. Many are longing to be full, active members of churches, but until ableism is addressed and disabling barriers are dismantled, not all of them can be. Some have had more positive experiences, in churches that have valued them, just as they are, but most tell very mixed stories. Many have been longing for solidarity with a community of disabled Christians; they have not always found it easy to hear the stories of the disabled people of God.[116] It was one reason why so many storytellers wanted us to share these stories with the Church. There are many disabled people waiting at the Church gates. None of us is 'the only one'.[117]

There were people we could not include in this research. Despite our efforts to reach out to Black Christians and others of Global Majority Heritage, the majority of our storytellers are white.[118] This is a failing based in our privilege, one that we need to address in future research with disabled Christians. It is also worth noting that we spoke to many more women than men. We do not know why fewer men wanted to share their stories, but we know that disability is a gendered experience.[119] In churches where a legacy of patriarchy persists alongside ableism, some of our women storytellers may have been disempowered in specific ways. Finally, this book is only able to share stories from the UK; churches can look very different in other global contexts. But some of the most interesting Christian critique of ableism is coming from disabled people beyond the UK, and we have much to learn from international conversations about disability and churches.[120]

As we share the stories of disabled Christians, we bring disability studies and social research into conversation with theology. The words of Jesus and the witness of the prophets against injustice are eternally relevant, but theology does not always have the tools to explore disability and ableism.[121] From the inside, it can sometimes be difficult for churches to see the power and privilege at work in their midst, when they are human social communities, as much as they are also the Body of Christ. Wisdom from beyond the church walls can amplify voices that have often gone unheard in Christian communities.

Terms we use in this book

We hope a wide audience will be able to read this book. We have done our best to cut down on jargon, but we sometimes use terms from disability studies, sociology or theology. When a term is written in italics, we define it in a glossary at the end of the book. Where we mention academic theories, we give more details in endnotes.

These are some of the terms we use in the book:

- *Disabled people*, not 'people with disabilities'; the more common term used in the UK.
- *Neurodivergent people*, a group that includes autistic people, ADHDers, and people with Tourette Syndrome, dyslexia and/ or dyspraxia, among others, who celebrate our divergent ways of thinking and being, as compared with accepted norms.[122]
- *People with mental and emotional distress*. A term often used by people with psychiatric labels to de-pathologise their distress. Where our storytellers preferred to speak about *mental health problems*, we have honoured this.[123]

- *People with learning disabilities.* The term used by Wave Church, a community of people with and without learning disabilities, whose stories we share later in the book. Learning disability 'affects a person's development and ... means that they may need help to understand information, learn skills and live independently'. This term is also widely used in the UK.[124]
- *Deaf people.* We have one storyteller who defines as a *Deaf person*: a member of the Deaf community – a cultural and linguistic minority – who uses British Sign Language (BSL). Another storyteller uses the term *deaf,* with the lower-case 'd,' to show that she does not use BSL.[125]
- *Blind* and *visually impaired people.* Some storytellers preferred one of these terms over the other, but many people who define as blind have some vision.
- *Justice for disabled people.* We try not to overuse the term 'disability justice'. The Disability Justice movement is an intersectional movement to end ableism together with other forms of oppression, understanding that ableism, white supremacy and capitalism have grown from the same twisted roots. Emily and Naomi are inspired by the movement's commitment to collective access and liberation, and we draw on their framework for understanding ableism. But we cannot claim to be part of the movement, which is led by the most marginalised disabled people.[126] Independently, some churches in the UK have been using the term 'disability justice' since the early 2000s, seeing justice as central to the story of God's people.[127]
- *The Kin(g)dom* or *Reign of God.* We use these terms interchangeably, knowing that some people prefer words that honour our equality in God's now-but-not-yet Reign.[128] But the familiar term 'Kingdom of God' was used by several of our storytellers, as they called for the justice that Jesus announced through his ministry on the margins.
- *Church.* When we write Church with a capital C, we are talking about the whole Church of Christ, the *ecclesia.* When we speak about individual churches, we use a small c.

The structure of this book

Shaped by disabled Christians' own stories, each chapter of this book looks at a different aspect of disability in churches.

In Chapter 1, Naomi and Emily tell our stories, reflecting on how our lived experience as disabled Christians led us to write this book.

The rest of the book is divided into two parts.

Part One: *Closed Gates: Access, Participation and Leadership*

- In Chapter 2, we talk about *access*. We share disabled Christians' stories of crossing the thresholds of often-inaccessible church buildings and worship environments. We reflect on the ways that church design can push disabled people to the edge of communities. We begin to ask how, through empowering decisions about the ways they use their buildings, churches can show that they value disabled people, and that they can imagine us in their communities.

- In Chapter 3, we take a closer look at *access* and how it enables *participation*. We think about what it means to create *cultures of access* in churches, challenging all the ways we 'do church' that exclude disabled people. We share stories of access and participation denied to disabled worshippers. And yet storytellers imagine radical hospitality that would make it possible for disabled people to participate in churches, not as permanent guests, but as full, active members and leaders.

- In Chapter 4, we share disabled Christians' stories of *service and leadership,* in churches where we have more often been seen as objects of others' care. Disabled laypeople share stories of communities that have failed to recognise their gifts; disabled leaders tell us about barriers placed in the way of their ministry. Yet storytellers show how, through disabled people's ministry, churches can be transformed into truly interdependent communities, where the gifts of every part of the Body of Christ are recognised and valued.

Part Two: *Opening the Gates: Disabled Prophets Speak*

In this second half of the book, disabled storytellers share their own lived disability theologies of Kingdom justice, as keys to open the gates of the Church.

- In Chapter 5, storytellers talk about *theology*. They speak back to a Church that has often told disabled Christians' stories for us, rather than enabling us to speak for ourselves. Storytellers share their own Kingdom theologies, rooted in their lived experience as disabled people. They tell distinctively disabled stories of God – God who is with us, God who is like us, and God who is for us. These are stories that can transform the Church.
- In Chapter 6, we look at the complex relationship between *disability and healing*, as disabled Christians respond to churches that have seen them as broken and in need of 'fixing'. We share storytellers' own understanding of God's Kingdom healing, which often goes far deeper than simple cure, as they declare that they are 'fearfully and wonderfully made'.
- In Chapter 7, we share the stories of a disabled Christian movement in the UK, speaking back from the edge. We hear from disabled-led church groups and communities that have been forged through shared experiences of isolation or marginalisation from traditional churches. These storytellers call on churches to learn from disabled people's own models of participation and justice.
- In Chapter 8, we look at the recent COVID-19 pandemic and the rise of online ministry, exploring its effects on the ways we worship together, and how these have been both a help and a hindrance to disabled Christians. At a time of change for us all, disabled people share what the churches can learn from our experiences of new ways of doing and being Church, where we are embodied together online.

The storytellers in this book are calling for an accessible, hospitable Church. A Church that loves disabled people as God loves us, and shows that love by listening to our calls for transformation, and enabling our access, participation and leadership. A Church that values us, *just as we are*. A Church where no disabled person is ever left waiting at the gates.

We pray that their voices will be heard.

‘ **Maybe the Church needs to understand the needs of the disabled community better and to see them as equal, to see people like me as equal and real people ... Disability rights shouldn't be an issue in 2020, but they are. In the church they really shouldn't be, but they still are.** ’ Nicki

CHAPTER I
Our Stories

Naomi's Story

I am fearfully and wonderfully made.[129]

Among all the many things that make me unique, I have two different *ways of being*. I think differently: I am autistic, dyspraxic and an ADHDer. And I have a genetic condition that causes pain, joint problems, fatigue and mobility difficulties.

And I am fearfully and wonderfully made, and God made no mistakes with my design.

Growing up, my life was good, not least because of my privileges – I am white, middle class, and educationally privileged. But it was the 1980s, when awareness of neurodiversity and my physical condition were both poor. I had no language for my differences, but I *knew* I was different. I struggled to understand a world that made little sense to me. I had difficulties regulating my emotions and my attention. Social rules were a mystery to me – every time I thought I understood one, I'd encounter a terrifying exception. I had the uneasy sense that I was 'hard work' for friends and family. I was broken. A burden. *Wrong.*

Gradually, trying to survive in a hostile world became traumatic. Misdiagnosis and mental distress shadowed my life for many years. Anxiety was a constant companion. To make things more complicated, the chronic illness that had been lurking in the background for years became overwhelming in my late twenties. Friends drifted away, confused by my new wheelchair and the changes in my life. The world began to bar my way to life – everywhere I went, I was stopped up short by locked gates, flights of steps, hostile stares.

I never asked God the reason for my suffering. My prayer was that the Church and society would no longer see me as something less than human, less than whole. I did not wonder why the Potter had made a fragile pot; I wondered why the world seemed determined to break it.

The Church had few, if any, answers for me. I could never take for granted that I would be able to make it through a church door or up to the altar. I would sit in my wheelchair at the back, kept apart from the Body of Christ, feeling profoundly alone. Church was a confusing sensory nightmare, with too-loud music, sudden changes of order in the service, stressful small talk over coffee. Friendly, frightening hands kept reaching out to touch my easily-injured, reactive body. And every Sunday, as I listened to Gospel healing stories and sang about the leaping lame, I felt like all eyes were on me, watching for a miracle that I did not need.

It was becoming all too clear that the Church, too, saw me as broken. And I would look down at my beautiful, difficult body, and my fascinating, frustrating mind, where I could see the fingerprints of God emerging from my unique genetic code. And I'd think, 'Can't I go to heaven and still be *myself?*' Sunday after Sunday, I tried to leave disability at the church door. But the only way to do that was to deny the person God created me to be.

I was still young when I learned that disability is about justice. That understanding was a gift from God. When I needed hope in an ableist world, I came to understand that I wasn't broken – the world was. Over long years, as I learned from the wisdom of many disabled people, I came to celebrate my neurodivergent self, my disabled self. But I stumbled upon these revelations beyond the church walls. It would be a long time before I saw myself reflected in Christian teaching. In the Church, no one told me that God made me exactly as I am.

One summer, at a Christian festival, I ran into a raised pipe between my accessible camping area and the bustling activity of the gathering. There was no way my wheelchair was getting over that pipe.

It barred my way to the rest of the Body of Christ. *We have thousands of people to help*, staff said. *We'll get to your access issue eventually*. While I waited, listening to others sing and celebrate, I thought about Jesus the Liberator, who tears down barriers. The God who does not bar my way to life.

I didn't go back to church for seven years.

In those seven years in the wilderness, I could not walk away from a calling. I longed to hear the stories of the disabled people of God. The answers I was seeking would unfold through a decade of research, initially for a PhD, as more than fifty generous disabled Christians shared their painful, joyful stories with me. A chorus of voices was singing in harmony with my song. Crying out for the Church to open the gates. Sharing new revelations about God and God's diverse creation. Emily Richardson was one of those research participants. Knowing her talent as a theologian and communicator, I invited her to help me share these stories with a Church that needs to hear them.

The many disabled Christians I have met in the past decade have been Christ to me. They are everyday theologians, showing me the truth I needed to hear: that I am fearfully and wonderfully made. We are Church on the edge together, meeting in sacred spaces on the margins. That's where I've found the disabled people of God.

I am fearfully and wonderfully made. After years of ableism in the Church, that's still hard to say. But it doesn't make it any less true. It's true of you too. I hope that, as you listen to the disabled prophets who speak in this book, you'll see God in a new light, shining through the prism of their disabled experience. In their stories, I hope you'll see that there is room for all of us in the diverse Reign of God. We are fearfully and wonderfully made.

Emily's Story

Growing up, it was always my 'mind' that was praised. I was bright, sharp, good at my studies and taught that my intellect was my strength. That was a bonus, since my body was less reliable. Prone to falling, with poor coordination, weak muscle tone and the low hum of constant pain (something I didn't even realise wasn't normal), this was given the rather vague diagnosis of 'mild cerebral palsy'. Mild was always the stressed word, giving encouragement that it was not so bad. With the right support I could be just like everyone else. I got through school with helpers to write my work: I dictated my words to someone else who could get them onto the paper. My brain could bypass my body and I could, for the most part, ignore its inconveniences.

As a model student in a church school I was brought up with familiarity to the Christian faith, with varying degrees of engagement. My home church was low Anglican and provided me with memories of church as being a fun place to be, but the personal aspects of faith I didn't discover until my late teens, when a Baptist youth group became a life giving source of friendship and, ultimately, faith. This is where I also became immersed in Christian culture, eagerly listening to the latest WOW[130] releases and spending my pocket money on Bible study guides in my local Christian bookshop.

The natural progression was to a theology degree at university, allowing me to combine my twin personalities of 'model student' and 'model Christian'. My application form to university quoted St Anselm, which tells you all you need to know about me. I wanted to follow my faith with my best asset: my *mind*. This endeavour worked. Initially. It got me to a top university. It took me possibly as far away from my home as it could – Aberdeen was too cold so I found myself in St Andrews. I found myself as a disabled student, as well. The 'mild' cerebral palsy, which had meant very little to me until then, suddenly became a valuable key to unlocking student support, with funding for a new laptop and a notetaker at lectures (including a poor person who had to take notes in Hebrew).

All going rather well. I had everything I needed. Support in place. A happy life in a beautiful town, surrounded by friends and opportunities for learning from some exceptional thinkers. And then I began to notice some bumps in my normally smooth life. The quiet hum of pain was becoming louder. My concentration was failing me as I became more and more tired. My mood suffered as I couldn't rely on the coping mechanisms that had previously worked. The usual approach of 'pushing on' was no longer an option as I reached a seemingly impenetrable brick wall. I collected a list of specialists and medications as symptoms were added to the list. I left university as my normally safe backup of 'brains' could no longer allow me to ignore my increasingly unhappy body.

To cut a very long story short, the answer to my problems was discovered in my hands. Finally showing a rheumatologist my bendy, extremely painful, hands I was deemed to be 'hypermobile'. This rather confusing word was in fact the key to everything, the missing piece. Suddenly my life made sense in reverse, as symptoms fell into place. My unstable joints, my frequently dismissed 'growing pains', the increasing health problems with the onset of puberty, including gastrointestinal, neurological and musculoskeletal abnormalities, all of this was suddenly obvious when viewed through the lens of growing up with hypermobility-type Ehlers Danlos Syndrome.

Throughout this long period of waiting for and then processing my diagnosis, my faith continued to evolve. Sometimes strong, with periods of fervent prayer and diligent observance and sometimes faintly as the hard realities of living in an increasingly unreliable body became too hard to process. I still sought to 'understand' with my mind, reading theology, listening to sermons and an emerging practice of writing and journaling. My experience of churches widened as I became aware of different traditions, mainly with the advent of Twitter, and I participated in online megachurch services in the US in the early 2010s. I was, and still am, a spiritual nomad, finding treasure in many different traditions. Alongside exploring faith and spirituality, Twitter was a space for exploring my health problems and, indeed, after diagnosis it was social media I turned to for advice and support in learning to live with EDS. It was in these online spaces that I found people like me, asking the same questions about life and even asking those questions in relation to faith.

As the networks grew, I became more connected both in the online and 'everyday' worlds. Online research into new monasticism led me to find a contemplative community that nurtured my faith and gently challenged me to reject the ways I divided my life into 'mind and body' or 'sacred and secular'. Online bloggers like Rachel Held Evans and Sarah Bessey and podcasts such as The Liturgists challenged me to see God in the everyday. The trouble is, every day for me was pain, fatigue and seeming mundanity. It was not the romantic theology that teenage me had aspired to, but this crucible of suffering, confusion and questioning was what turned me into a 'proper theologian'. I was working out my beliefs in the midst of life. At this time, concepts like incarnation became actual rather than abstract concepts: 'If Jesus became human, then the body is good. What does that mean when I try to act as if my body is not important or, indeed, a burden?'

I wrestled with these questions in Twitter threads, in the comments sections on blogs, through podcasts and with the ongoing prayer practices I had learned in my community. I went to conferences; I took part in PhD studies (which led to this book!). The online space was a safe and welcoming place. Alongside this social media seminary I also grew in the practices of the faith: contemplative prayer, liturgy, journeying with a spiritual director. In all my exploration, I learnt again and again that none of this could be done apart from my physical, lived experience. The more I gave voice to my actual lived reality, the more 'real' my faith became. A vital part of this process was my involvement in the Living Edge conferences, as I moved from attending as an interested delegate, to a storyteller to becoming involved in the planning process. One of the first conferences I worked on behind the scenes was 'Just As I Am'. That is the arc of my spiritual and creative experience, learning and practicing what it means to be called *just as I am,* in all my achy places, with all my tired days and with all the frustrations that come with being me. Just as I am.

PART ONE
Closed Gates: Access, Participation and Leadership

CHAPTER 2

Knocking on the Church Gates: Disabled People Accessing Church Buildings

'My experiences of Christian events and conferences have mostly been bad. Access is a total afterthought!' Jemma

Churches are designed for normative bodies and minds. Bodies that can sit in pews without pain; minds that are not overwhelmed by bright lights or loud music. Bodies that can read words on a projector; minds that can understand what happens in a service. What about those of us with more divergent bodies and minds? We don't fit so easily. In buildings that are designed around the 'normal' body and mind of an ideal worshipper, church communities can struggle to accommodate disabled people.[131]

Church buildings are a mirror of a community's values and attitudes towards disabled people. 'A church's architecture usually reflects the attitude (and the pocket-book) of the congregation's leadership and members,' writes disability theologian Kathy Black.[132] Of course, worship priorities guide decisions about the layout of many church buildings. But access to churches is also shaped by *normalcy* – society's expectation that we will all have the same kinds of bodies and minds.[133] In a church with steps up to the altar, if you can climb those steps without difficulty, you may have always experienced communion as an uninterrupted ritual, designed for your body to *fit*. But those who cannot easily reach the altar become the square peg struggling to fit into the round hole of the church building. We *misfit*, in this central liturgical moment of the service.[134] We may become very aware of our different bodies. We may wonder if we belong in church at all. So it is, too, for autistic people in worship spaces where bright lights are too painful to bear, and for deaf people in churches with no hearing aid loops. Disabled people cannot fit in churches that were not designed for us, where other needs are higher up the list of design priorities than we are. In moment after moment where we do not fit in churches, we come to understand that our bodies, minds and *ways of being* are not valued there. The church gates are closed to us.

Access is about power, privilege and (in)justice.[135] The non-disabled Church has the power to decide whether or not to open the gates to disabled people. Communities shape their buildings around those they imagine as being 'in' or 'out,'[136] as they make 'political and power-laden choices'[137] that reflect their beliefs about who belongs. As disability theologian Mike Walker puts it, 'many Christians with disabilities inhabit a *place* without much *grace* in the institutional Church, because we are not ... "intended" participants. The place of people with disabilities in the *ecclesia* often lacks God's abundant love because it has been created with only one set body type – the ideal – in mind.'[138] There is no 'grace in a place' for us in church buildings that are not designed for disabled people, where we are not imagined as part of the Body of Christ.[139]

This is *structural* exclusion. Churches often truly *want* to include disabled people, but communities cannot always recognise the barriers that keep us from entering, participating and leading in churches. Church leaders and congregations often speak positively about their desire to welcome disabled people. They offer what we might call a *rhetorical welcome,* in sincere words and good intentions. But when disabled people arrive at church buildings and find that these are painful places for us to be, where our bodies and minds do not fit, there is no *embodied welcome* for us. That's when inaccessible church buildings tell disabled people a different story – that we are an exception to be accommodated. We are a problem to be solved, not an expected part of the community.[140]

Any church that leaves disabled people waiting at the gates, however unconsciously, is an ableist church.

Access is not participation,[141] but it is a necessary first step towards it. In the Christian conversation on disability, well-meaning writers sometimes skip ahead to participation, implying that churches are all already physically accessible. However, the occasional sight of a ramp up to a church door, or a yellow strip marking out a step, does not mean that it is easy for people with mobility difficulties or blind people to get into any church. For many of our storytellers, getting into church buildings was a struggle. For others, once they made it into the building, inaccessible worship spaces could leave them feeling like second-class members of churches. Disability justice must go far beyond buildings, as we discuss in Chapters 3 and 4. But if a disabled person cannot get through the doors or stay through a Sunday service, then they have little chance of participating fully in church life.

In this chapter, disabled people share their stories of access to churches. We heard from storytellers with many different impairments about buildings and worship spaces where the gates were closed to them: chronically ill people, wheelchair and crutch users, blind people, and neurodivergent people, among others. They told us about the barriers they faced to getting into church, and the ways they were pushed to the edge of church buildings by poor access. They shared their experiences of being taken where they do not want to go, segregated into side aisles and to the back of church. They told us how a single feature, such as an accessible toilet, could allow them to participate in a community. And they related stories of exclusion from the Eucharist, in church buildings designed for only one way of sharing communion. For those storytellers who were blessed to find churches they could access equally, it transformed their experience of faith communities. But for many, accessing churches was a difficult, marginalising, and even humiliating experience.

We believe that these often painful stories, shared as prophetic resistance to ableism, hold the keys to transformation. They are a roadmap that can show how, through equal access, churches can tell the story that disabled people are valued and expected in churches. Because when disabled people are missing from churches, the Body of Christ is diminished.[142]

Accessing Church Buildings and Environments

Barriers to getting into church

‘I was honestly very afraid of church in a wheelchair.’ Fern

Fern's new wheelchair was giving her hope. For a long time, chronic illness had limited Fern to the four walls of her house. Her wheelchair was transforming her life. It was a tool for freedom, giving her precious access to the world, even when she was tired or in pain. Yet that was far from the way Fern's wheelchair was seen at church:

> When I first became a wheelchair user it enabled me to ... start attending church services in person again. However, for a long time I didn't attend. It was, from a mental point of view, much harder to enter a church in a wheelchair than it was for me to go for a coffee, meet up with people, go out and about.

Fern was shocked, at first, when members of her church saw her wheelchair as a sign of her personal failure to be healed, a symbol of her fall from a non-disabled state of grace. It was a stark contrast to Fern's own attitudes to her mobility aid:

> To attend church in a wheelchair, while actually being a tool to get me (in theory) through the door and give me freedom, was also a symbol I felt that would lead to me being judged and condemned as a failure, who shouldn't be seen.

The more she encountered these marginalising attitudes, the more Fern began to dread using her wheelchair, in any church. 'I was honestly very afraid of church in a wheelchair,' she told us. Fern's wheelchair should have opened the Church gates to Fern. Instead, they were closed to her.

Eventually, Fern gathered enough courage to attend a church where

KNOCKING ON THE CHURCH GATES

she was not known, hoping unfamiliarity would bring fewer negative reactions from the congregation. She went to the church's website, scouring it for evidence that the church building might be accessible to her. *Wheelchair accessible,* the church's website said, reassuring Fern enough to make the journey there. And then:

> We turned up on the day to be met with A LOT of stairs at the entrance. 'No problem,' said the greeters, 'we are accessible, we have a ramp, wait here.' Twenty minutes later they returned with what was just two long planks of wood… I had never been so mortified. My mum struggled to push me up what felt like a 180 degree staircase on two planks of wood, while a crowd gathered to watch me slowly and wobbly (and with hindsight, extremely dangerously) make my way up these bits of wood.

Embarrassing comments from the crowd of onlookers made getting into church an even more humiliating experience for Fern. There were probably good intentions behind the access misinformation on the website, from a church that wanted to welcome disabled people, but this did not make Fern's 'welcome' any less a dangerous and traumatic experience.

Fern never returned to the church.

Fern was only one of many storytellers who struggled to get into church in spite of leaders' good intentions and claims that their churches were accessible. Well-meaning church leaders, thinking from a place of privilege, may assume what accessibility means – but without listening to disabled people's lived experience of accessing churches, those with the power to make decisions about access cannot always conceive of the barriers that they are creating.

Rhona, who is visually impaired, dealt with her own architectural barriers to getting into and around her Methodist church building. She often arrived at church already tired from a struggle with poor access on public transport and on the streets, long before she reached her church. There, she had to overcome yet more disabling barriers, all because the building had not been designed with her access needs in mind:

47

AT THE GATES

I go to a modern church, which is just riddled with problems
for me. The doors are all half glass and half wood. Which makes
it, for me, a nightmare. Because if it's all glass or all wood I can
understand that far more. It was thought an absolutely fabulous
idea to put the light switches for the foyer down the bottom end
[of the corridor]. And so, if I'm the first in, I have to walk through
the dark.

The age of a church is not the issue, when it comes to disability access;
what matters is whose bodies and minds the building was designed for.
Nor is design the end of the story. Simple decisions about building use
could have transformed Rhona's access, from those with the power to
remember Rhona and imagine her as part of their community. The church
doors were often closed to Rhona, she told us; just leaving them open,
or leaving the lights on, could have helped her to access the church. Even
after architectural barriers are in place, churches make powerful choices
about how they use buildings.

Day-to-day decisions about uses of the church building could be
either disempowering or humanising for Isabelle, who has mobility
impairments as a result of multiple sclerosis (MS). 'Our church has
basic access,' she said. She could get into her church's building, but the
recently-redesigned main door was difficult for wheelchair access. The
accessible toilet door had to be approached from outside, and was kept
locked, so that Isabelle was often left waiting out in the cold:

What you have to do is go round and the outside door is not
accessible from the outside. Someone has to go round and open
it ... I know it's fine. Someone should go and do it for you. But
there's something about having to ask.

'They don't see that as a problem,' Isabelle told us, hinting at how the
church was ignoring power imbalances. Pastoral power kept power in
the hands of leaders. And yet when she was listened to about her access
needs, Isabelle was enabled not just to get into church and around the
building, but to participate and serve in the community. In the end, that
was what mattered most to her. She reflected that churches tend to

ask, 'Can you get into the building?' rather than, 'Can you serve in all capacities in the church as a full member?' Access opened the gates to Isabelle's participation, as a valued member and leader of her church.

For some of our storytellers with physical access needs, good access was important, but only as important as being part of a community that valued them. Stephen, who has ME/chronic fatigue syndrome, is only able to attend churches with step-free access, where his mobility scooter can be accommodated. When he moved to a small village, positive attitudes and good access together made him welcome at the local Church of England congregation:

> [In the past] I would possibly be in church twice a year. [But] I've recently moved to a small village ... And the local church is just down the road, very close by, and is very easy to access, very welcoming and calm and traditional. And so it's been very easy to attend services there much more regularly than I ever have done since being ill.

'They've been absolutely brilliant,' Stephen said of the church's attitudes towards him and his wife, who is also disabled. He contrasted that sense of welcome with his experiences at his previous church:

> The church that I used to go to was a very rich church, lots of people there, lots of money and they really struggled [with disability]. They had a reordering of the church pretty soon after I fell ill, where they removed the pews, and there was a lot of talk about inclusivity and making sure that everything was accessible. So they got these chairs that they could stack up and make spaces for people. But as soon as anyone went there with a wheelchair or a scooter or anything like that it was as if the church had caught fire and everyone was horrified. 'What are we going to do?' Whereas the church here is full of locals, lovely people who don't care at all what state you're in. And who welcome you and who do their best to accommodate whatever you've got. And they're wonderful. And I don't imagine they've had special training.

For Stephen, access was a necessary first step to belonging in a church community, but it was only the first step. Once he was physically inside the church, it mattered just as much to him that his community was not just paying lip-service to 'inclusivity,' but welcomed him no matter how unwell he was on a Sunday. Stephen found a community where justice for disabled people was woven into church life. The church may not have had the resources that his previous community did, but they were committed to opening the gates to him – starting with access.

As these stories show, access and attitudes work together to close the gates to disabled people, in church buildings where our bodies and minds do not fit. Through closed doors, steep steps and poor lighting, physically inaccessible churches communicate their values, telling disabled people with physical access needs whether or not we are invited and expected. For some storytellers, like Fern and Rhona, the message *You are not welcome here* was clear as soon as they crossed the threshold of a church building – or tried to. As the church buildings pushed them to the edge, inaccessibility reinforced other messages they already heard about how their bodies did not *fit* in Christian communities. For others, like Stephen, churches opened the gates to storytellers' participation by learning about their access needs and offering 'grace in a place'.

Pushed to the edge

‘ It was a long time before they really began to make access easy. ’ Jane

In churches that do not give enough thought to accessibility, disabled people often find ourselves pushed to the edge. When our storytellers *misfit* in church environments, they were segregated to the side or the back, where they would not 'spoil' worship for non-disabled people.[143] Others met with second-rate access, through the literal back doors and back alleys of churches. It gave them the message that they were second-class members of churches. Poor access made them *partial participants,* as Titchkosky puts it; she tells us that disabled people are often 'only partially included in work, leisure, *and love*.'[144] While none of our storytellers expected church buildings to be perfect, many were longing for more complete access, on an equal level with the rest of the Body of Christ. They were praying for the kind of access by which churches would show them that they were completely loved.

For Maria, who has fibromyalgia and mental health problems, the church environment could be deeply inaccessible when she was unwell. During services, she was often forced to retreat to the kitchen:

> This last Sunday is a classic example. I was in the kitchen during the worship time because [in the main church] it's too hot and it's bright and it's too loud, and I just can't cope at all. So I'm hiding in the kitchen. There's a step ladder there which I use as a seat ... I meet some very nice people in the kitchen. There's other people hiding out there as well [who] can't cope with the service.

In her church kitchen, Maria ended up in what disability theorists call a *liminal* space – a place on the margins, where disabled people may find ourselves when everywhere else is inaccessible to us.[145] Out on the edge, Maria found others who could not cope with the normative ways churches 'do church'. But that solidarity on the edge did not make up for being pushed out from the central space of worship and teaching. Maria longed for more flexibility in service times, as she put her body and mind under strain in order to stay half-present at church, keeping herself awake with coffee. If her church had found ways to embrace what disability theorists call *crip time* – time that disabled people bend to fit our needs, rather than having to harm our bodies to fit schedules made for non-disabled people – Maria might have been able to attend church at times when she was less fatigued, when she could cope better with the environment.[146] She might have found herself pushed to the edge-space of the kitchen far less often.

Sarah told us a similar story of church buildings that pushed her to the edge, even all the way out of the gates. Like many autistic people, Sarah is sound sensitive. While taking a break from her church for a few weeks, she returned to find they had installed a new heating system that was so noisy, it was distressing for her:

> So they went from a heating system that was very passive, because it was bars that heated up, to one that blows air. And I've

51

basically not been able to go back to church since ... I just felt so uncomfortable and I couldn't cope and I was close to tears, and I began to realise what the problem was... I basically came to the conclusion that I wasn't going to be able to attend the service, and I hated that. I didn't feel like I could say anything to them because they fundraised for this.

Not wanting to cause – or be – a problem in her community, Sarah left her church without raising the issue. When church communities fail to consider access for disabled and neurodivergent people when they develop or reorder their buildings, the result can be our quiet exclusion. The rest of the church carries on, just as it ever did. From the church's perspective, there is no need to transform to make room for people they do not even know are missing from the pews.

Other storytellers were pushed to the edge of churches by second-rate access. Storyteller Kt, who has cerebral palsy and uses crutches, was frustrated by the poor access at one church she often visited:

[St F's Church] is held like a paragon church of the New Wine network, which it is. But to get in you've got to go up I think it's 30 steps, solid stone steps on the outside. Or, you can use the lift which is past all the recycling bins, past all the kitchen bins ... into this lift that feels like you're in the back of beyond. 'And you probably ought to be in a bin bag, because that's what it's used for. Which comes out right into the very busy main foyer.' And you sort of step into a sea of bodies. It's like, yeah, that's really welcoming. If [the lift] is working.

Kt was describing access that is technically compliant with the Equality Act, but that does not offer equity to disabled people. We commonly find this second-rate access out in society; it is dispiriting to find it in churches, too. As Kt ironically pointed out, her body was side-lined and segregated into the worst parts of this church building, leaving her feeling like literal rubbish. It was a dehumanising experience, in communities that had not imagined or expected her. Other storytellers had to wait outside for accessible doors to be opened, in the cold and the rain, as Jane told us:

It was a *long* time before they really began to make access easy, such as leaving the churchyard gate open for car access to church doors, and unlocking the level access door without having to be asked.

Second-rate access left our storytellers dependent on the whims and memory of those with the power to open the gates – sometimes literally. While many storytellers knew their communities wanted to include them, they could not deny the emotional impact of poor access, which did not make them feel like loved, expected members of churches.

And yet many storytellers were willing to compromise and wait for access improvements, in an expression of love for church communities that did not always have the resources to create ideal or immediate access. Nicki, who is a wheelchair user, was happy to sit at the back while her community redeveloped their building, even though temporary access was far from perfect, and kept Nicki segregated from church life:

> The only problem is the main auditorium is down some wooden steps … There are some old ladies, as well, that use wheelchairs. They tend to sit at the back, so we all tend to sit together. In some ways, I'd prefer it not to be like the wheelchair department at the back, but … it doesn't bother me enough to make a fuss about it.

Knowing a redevelopment was coming at her church, Nicki was patient and gracious about the short-term access issues that pushed her to the edge, and she was touched that the church community was making every effort to help her fit in their temporary worship space. But Nicki did not want to be left waiting at the back of church forever. Today, she is praying for the time when better access in the renovated building will bring her out from the back, returning her to the heart of her church community. In the meantime, she has been advising leaders on access in the new building. She is helping to build a church that imagines disabled people among the congregation and dismantles the barriers in their way.

Without an embodied welcome into the centre of their churches, many storytellers were only partial participants in their communities. While we wait at the edge and at the gates, disabled people are missing from churches.[147] Instead, storytellers had a Kingdom vision of equal access that would return disabled people to the heart of church communities. Theirs was an eschatological hope[148] – a Kingdom hope, to be fully loved. They imagined churches that, through dignified access, signalled to disabled people that they aspired to be places of grace and justice.

'Where can I put you?'

> **❝'Where can I put you?' Don't put me anywhere because it won't go well.❞** Zoe

Where disabled people sit in church reveals a great deal about a church's attitude to disability, says disability theologian Lamar Hardwick. Powerful people have always given the seats of honour to those they value, something that Jesus himself rebuked.[149] Seating in church may not seem consequential for those who enjoy access to the best seats to see, hear, and sit comfortably in. But for disabled people, whether we find ourselves segregated to the side of the church building, or a place is made for us in the centre of the congregation, it tells us whether a community has simply invited disabled people, or done the hard work of transforming to include us.[150] When storytellers' different bodies and minds did not fit in churches, they became little more than an inconvenience to be relegated to the back, out of sight. And there is no need to change the layout of a church if you simply move disabled people out of the way.[151]

As she sat in the 'wheelchair area' at the side of an aisle, in her cathedral church, Brianna was separated from her husband and set apart from the rest of the congregation. As if that was not disempowering enough, Brianna and other disabled people were literally 'in the way' at the cathedral:

> The very first time I arrived in the cathedral, we just put the wheelchair in an aisle at the side, which seemed like a good place to go. And as the service started, somebody from behind me pulled my wheelchair back and actually manhandled my wheelchair and said 'I've got to move you, because the choir won't get past ...' Now, since then, I have had to witness other people go through that same hideous ordeal ... At big services

I'm constantly seeing people arriving with nowhere to go, and the seats already filled up. What the stewards then have to do is ask people to move: 'Would you please go and sit elsewhere?' This poor person in the wheelchair is going, 'I'm so sorry, I'm so sorry to cause this fuss and I'm so sorry.'

Seeing wheelchair users as a disruption to the smooth running of the service, Brianna's church leaders moved them aside, with little sensitivity for their needs or agency, leaving these disabled people distressed and apologetic for causing – and being – a 'problem'. As the church prioritised liturgical order over access, it signalled the insignificance of disabled people in the liturgical life of the cathedral. They were not expected or imagined in the congregation, and there was no welcome for their disabled bodies. As Brianna put it, no one at the cathedral *thought* about how to include people with mobility impairments, but they could have. And yet, disabled people's disruption can be a prophetic call to churches to transform the ableist ways they 'do church'.[152] Brianna spoke up in her church against the way mobility-impaired people were treated there. She knew that the one sheep is at least as important as the ninety-nine who would prefer disabled people not to be 'in the way' of the processing choir.

It was not only mobility-impaired people who were segregated into side-spaces in church, for the convenience of the non-disabled majority. In a church where she was known to be visually impaired, Rhona found that other people assumed where she needed to sit, deciding what was best for her without asking:

You know when people grabs you by the arm and says, 'Well you can't see, sit here.' I hate it … Disabled people should be comfortable to be where they want to be.

Rhona's agency was removed when she was corralled into spaces that were not ideal for her needs – taken, in Jesus' words, where she did not want to go.[153] It is not uncommon for blind people to be grabbed against their will,[154] but Rhona hoped to feel more empowered at church. Shona, who is deaf, had similar experiences of being told where to sit, though she had a lifetime's experience of knowing for herself where she needed to sit to lip-read. In failing to listen to their lived experience and respect them as the experts on their own access needs, these storytellers' churches made disempowering assumptions that kept them from being able to participate fully in liturgy and worship.

Relegated to the worst seats at the side or the back, many storytellers found that their need to see and participate in the Body of Christ was neglected. But when storytellers experienced full physical inclusion in a church, they found a welcome for their bodies and minds, as well as their souls, just as they are. Simple improvements in accessibility could transform their experience of worship. Brianna told us about a visit she made to another church, one Sunday when she was tired of feeling like an outsider at her cathedral church:

> So we went to our local church. And, oh my word, the welcome! There were wheelchair spaces, and it's a hodgepodge building, but there were two other wheelchair users in a congregation of about 30 … It made me think, 'Right, maybe I should just give up on the cathedral and go to the local church, because I will feel part of the community.'

The 'welcome' that Brianna found at this church was the kind of hospitality that welcomed her not just in words, but in body, too. *Come in – we've been expecting you,* the church told Brianna, when she was physically included in the life of a congregation. *There's room here for people like you.* She was not pushed out of sight. Brianna *fit,* as she sat in spaces that had been prepared for her, among the congregation, in the presence of others like her. Zoe, a part-time wheelchair user, found it just as powerful when she worshipped in churches that had made room for her to sit in the midst of the Body of Christ. Good physical access was so spiritually significant to Zoe that she described it as the gospel:

> The experience of just being a worshipper there is so profoundly different … When you can just join in like everyone else. When I can stay in my chair and be in the Body, it's so powerful. And I just keep telling everybody, 'Go and look at that, and you need to tell people that [access] is there.' Because it is the gospel.

At these churches, choices made about the use of the church building were transformative, rather than marginalising. What a difference it made for Zoe and Brianna, who have never forgotten these experiences of embodied welcome.

A theology of toilets

> **⁶[The accessible toilet] was their storage cupboard.⁹** Nicki

Imagine you are seeking a new church community. What is important to you? Denomination? Style of worship? Shared values and beliefs?

How much do you have to think about *toilets* when you're making this decision?

When it comes to choosing a church, some disabled people will travel many miles to find a community that worships in a physically accessible building. For some of us, accessible facilities are more important than a church's denomination, its style of worship, or even its theology. If disabled people cannot *come in* and *stay in,* we cannot participate in a church community. For many of the storytellers we spoke to, toilets were a make-or-break access feature that made it possible – or impossible – for them to stay in church for the whole of a service.

When Maria was looking for a new church, appropriate toilets were at the top of her list:

> Another thing I look for in a church – good toilet facilities! Not a building with just one toilet that opens directly into the foyer where everyone else is stood around, but more than one toilet, with cubicles that open out into a self-contained room, so you can be as slow as you need to be, without feeling like you are being timed, and with a subtle exit from the main part of the church, so you don't have to create a scene if you go out part way through the service. Important stuff!

For Maria, whose chronic illness means she needs extra time to use the toilet, a church with appropriate toilets not only affirmed her dignity, it enabled her access. The right toilets could open the church gates to Maria. That's why she prioritised accessible toilets in her search for a church, sometimes above teaching, worship style, and other elements of church life that she might have preferred to guide her search. Sadly, in follow-up emails after her interview, Maria told us that she had not yet found an embodied welcome in a church that offered the access she needed – including access to toilets.

Toilets are a vital requirement for storyteller Nicki's access to churches, too. She now attends a church about an hour's journey from her home, after a long search for a community that took her through two other churches, where a familiar mix of poor access and attitudes left her feeling as though she was neither valued or wanted there. Toilets featured in her stories of rejection or acceptance from these communities:

> I need to use the toilet at least three times in a Sunday morning service. [The accessible toilet] was their storage cupboard, so there was a massive roll of carpet offcuts in there, the changing trolley, the cleaning trolley. Every time I went to the toilet, they emptied it and immediately put everything back in again… Not only that, then the lock on the toilet door broke and nobody fixed it. Eventually, I said, 'Look, it has been broken for a few weeks. Is anybody going to fix it?' They said, 'It's okay – it's only ever used for changing babies' nappies and they don't really mind.' I was thinking, 'You haven't grasped that *I* use it and *I* mind. I don't want people walking in on me.' I don't know if they didn't care, or they didn't realise, but it told me all I needed to know about the fact that actually they didn't see me as a person at all, with needs or anything … I kind of got the feeling we were a bit of an inconvenience.

Why an inconvenience? Not just because of Nicki's access needs. Her church preached about physical healing – by which they meant *cure*. Nicki believed that the presence of her body was a challenge to church members' views about healing and disability, as we discuss in Chapter 6. The toilet was a symbol of Nicki's theological misfitting in this church, and so the community chose not to see Nicki's need for it. Inaccessibility kept out the disabled people they could not imagine as part of their community, and perhaps would rather not have in their church. They invalidated Nicki's needs, an experience that will be familiar to many disabled people.[155] As they did, the church sent her a clear message: she was not a valued member of this congregation. But Nicki's story had a hopeful ending. Even though finding a more accessible church meant a long weekly drive for her, she found her way to a community where members told her if the toilet was out of action before she set off. That was one of many ways she knew she was a valued part of the church. She was remembered, among people who could imagine her as part of their community, and who took practical steps to ensure that she could participate.

Toilets are theological. Disabled people cannot hear the gospel when we are stuck outside the church gates, all for want of accessible facilities that others take for granted. More than that, toilets are about *dignity*, which is central to our humanity. Kt remembered trying to get to faraway toilets on crutches at a Christian festival, and how people got in her way by praying for her healing, as though that was more important than her immediate need. Isabelle waited outside in the rain for the door to her church's accessible toilet to be unlocked. Through toilets, churches tell a story about disabled people's value in the Body of Christ. For some storytellers, when this important access feature was missing, or denied to them, it sent the message that they did not belong in a church or community. But accessible toilets meant that those storytellers could enter and stay in church – a vital first step to their participation in community.

Toilets are just one example of the practical, physical access that can make or break a disabled person's chances to participate and belong in a church. For the disabled storytellers we spoke to, other 'make or break' access features included accessible websites, clear information about buildings and service content, comfortable seating, safe accessible doors that could be opened independently, quiet spaces to take breaks in (especially for autistic and other neurodivergent people), service sheets in accessible formats (for visually impaired and blind people), and subtitled sermons and videos (for deaf people). We discuss these diverse access needs in the next chapter, when we look at the need for churches to create *cultures of access* for all disabled people, if we are ever to participate in Christian community life.

Communion on the edge

> **'Because the stewards don't go and talk to [disabled people] about the possibilities, they just don't take communion... They're not invited to have communion.'** Brianna

Among the stories we heard about disabled people being pushed to the edge of churches, perhaps the most shocking were those involving communion. As an encounter between God and God's people, communion is the central liturgical moment of many church services. As one of the central 'body practices' of the Church, participation in communion is a vital sign of our belonging in a congregation.[156] When storytellers faced barriers that kept them from receiving communion, they were set apart, through practices that showed them how little their bodies were valued in the Body of Christ.

Storyteller Miranda uses a wheelchair. It was important to her to receive the Eucharist together with the rest of her congregation, at the altar, so that she could feel like an equal part of her community. But in a church with a raised altar, Miranda's access to communion was dependent on the whims of church leadership. She was often left waiting to receive, right till the end:

> They use the main altar rail, which has got two steps in front of it. I sit back [from the altar ... So we have a complicated system, depending on which verger's on duty. If it's the main verger, he leaves the communion rail open ... and then I will go up and he'll call me up, and I know I'll go first. And they come down and they'll give it to me ... We have another verger, a part-time verger who makes me wait. And he's not going to open those barriers. And I sit there like a spare dinner in the middle, until everybody else has had their communion. And then I'm at the end.

'Power-laden choices' about access need not be malicious. Sometimes they are simply convenient, for those with power and privilege in

60

communities. Rather than leaving the gate in the altar rail open for Miranda, some vergers made choices that made it easier for them to serve the non-disabled majority in the congregation. But their decisions excluded one person from this central ritual of membership, this embodied encounter with God. There were other ways to centre Miranda's access, but for the most part, the building shaped this church's imagination about what communion should look like. As the community failed to imagine Miranda as a vital part of the church, they gave her the message that she did not fully belong. Despondent, Miranda eventually left the church. 'I'm a minority. Who really cares?' she reflected. Brianna told a similar story of exclusion from the Eucharist, at a cathedral where the high altar was used at the services that were most important to her. Brianna sometimes felt she had no choice but to walk up steps, in pain, to receive at the altar. She watched as other disabled people in the congregation did not take communion at all. Rather than thinking about how they could dismantle the barriers they were creating to the Eucharist, cathedral staff left disabled people on the edge. When Brianna spoke about feeling 'invisible and violated' by her experiences of inaccessibility at her church, communion was foremost in her mind.

Communion is an embodied encounter with the risen Christ, who rose in a disabled body.[157] Disabled people's inclusion in the Eucharist 'is a matter of bodily mediation of justice and an incorporation of hope,' Eiesland tell us.[158] Yet, in reality, for disabled people communion is more often 'a dreaded and humiliating remembrance that in the church we are trespassers in an able-bodied dominion.'[159] For our storytellers, when it was clear that liturgy mattered more than whether or not they received communion, it was a powerful symbol of their distance from God in the eyes of the Church. Their disabled bodies were not honoured as the imago Dei. Yet through Christ's body, broken for us, communion gives us grace to affirm all bodies as important in the Body of Christ.[160] As we come to the communion table that represents equality for all members of the Body, it is vital that disabled people are accepted as we are. God has been expecting us at the table, even when our church communities have not.

A Seat of Honour at the Banquet Table? Theologies of Access

Access tells us whether the Banquet table[161] is designed for disabled people, or designed to exclude us. In church buildings that are not designed for our bodies and minds, disabled people often know that we do not belong. We know it in our bodies, when we do not fit in the pews or at the altar. We know it in our experience, when we ask for access and are not taken seriously.[162] Churches are spaces of power, where disabled people are 'out of place' when our bodies and minds are pushed to the edge of the holiest spaces.[163] We are physically marginalised, not just by non-disabled architects who cannot imagine us among a congregation, but by majority non-disabled church communities and their everyday decisions about how to use the spaces where worship and church life happens. This is usually down to thoughtlessness, rather than intentional discrimination. But disabled people experience the same exclusion regardless. When we quietly leave, churches may stay ignorant of the barriers they have created, never knowing why we left. Disabled people are left carrying the pain of being shut out of community, wondering why the House of God has no room for us.

Access is theological. But, drawn in by the ableist values of the world, many churches do not yet understand the theological importance of access and justice for disabled people. Reflecting on the moment when Jesus gives Peter the keys to the Kingdom, Lamar Hardwick argues that the Church was established to give access to God's Kingdom, for *all* of humanity.[164] And, he says, Jesus had a few things to say about giving the seat of honour – the best access – to those the world values least, as he observed how the Pharisees treated a disabled man they had invited to dinner. *Give your place of honour to another,* Jesus advised them, *so that you will be honoured when the Host comes.*[165] These are the values of the Reign of God, which lives out justice with and for disabled people, honouring those left on the scrap-heap of society. Yet churches have rarely been the accessible communities that Jesus intended them to be. Speaking as a church leader, Hardwick confesses:

We have underestimated value. On the rare occasion when people with disabilities are present at the table, they have been excluded from the seats of honor. We have focused on selecting the right seats, and we have neglected to sip from the right cup.[166]

As we have been relegated to the edges of church buildings, so that we do not spoil the experience of worship for the majority, disabled people have been placed far from the valued heart of church communities.

Ableist churches cannot honour disabled people. Not while they share the values of the world, esteeming most those whom society considers beautiful, acceptable and powerful, and making this clear in where they devote their money and resources. Churches' budgets reveal their priorities. When churches argue that their resources to improve access are limited, they are working from within a capitalist *scarcity paradigm,*[167] rather than trusting in God's grace to support more diverse communities. We recognise that some congregations are custodians of structures built in the Victorian or even the medieval era, inaccessible by nature and design. Working within these architectural constraints, changes to layouts may take time and involve cost. However, in communities that offered genuine hospitality, many of our storytellers were willing to work around barriers with their churches, forgiving less-than-perfect access. As Nancy Mairs reflects, 'In asking that the entrance to a building be ramped, that the numbers on an elevator panel be brailed, that emergency services be equipped to communicate with people who cannot hear or speak clearly, no one expects all impediments to be miraculously whisked away. In insisting that others view our lives as ample and precious, we are not demanding that they be made perfect.'[168] Open doors are not a finite resource, and neither is love.

Practical disability access is far from a finished project in churches. Access to buildings is only the beginning of disability justice in churches, as we discuss in the next chapter. But in many of the stories we heard, churches were not yet offering the bare minimum of access, leaving disabled people knocking on the church gates. Without basic physical access, many disabled people still cannot *enter* a church, *stay* for the length of a service, or *participate,* as active, valued members of a community. And the more that disabled people get the message that churches are not places where we receive an equal, embodied welcome, the less likely we are to be found in the pews. Without just, equitable access that tears down ableist strongholds, the institutional church will become increasingly irrelevant to disabled people.

But accessing church need not be a disempowering experience for disabled people – not when decisions about access are made together with us, in consciously interdependent communities that value us, with all our gifts, limits and challenges to ableism. Access is the gospel, as Zoe reminded us. When our disabled storytellers could sit and fit among the people of God, they knew that they were valued, just as they are. Enabling access begins with listening and learning from the experts – disabled people – about the barriers that keep the gates closed to each of us, and how congregations can dismantle those barriers *with*, not just for, disabled people.[169] Churches willing to be transformed into 'communities of belonging and misfitting'[170] will create space where disabled people are honoured, just as we are. They will value our disruption and difference, as a prophetic call for justice. They will not hide us away in a side chapel. They will not ask us to leave disability at the church door. When they do, everyday ableism will be transformed into everyday justice.

So what would it mean, in practice, for a church to offer a seat of honour to disabled people? What does it mean for a church to be radically accessible in every aspect of their worship and community life – their church culture? To understand that, we need to listen to a wider group of disabled people about the barriers they have faced to participation, in churches where inaccessible cultures make no space for them. We will listen, too, to those who have found communities where they can participate, serve and lead, as together they open the gates to all.

CHAPTER 3

A Transformed Table: Accessible Church Cultures

'I just didn't fit into the way that they did church. I just didn't fit into the way that Christians did things when they got together.' Andrew

'Imagine, for a moment, what it would be like to live in a culture of accessibility. Where accessibility is muscle memory.'[17] This is how disabled writer Taylor Katzel thinks about *accessible cultures*. He imagines leaders and members of communities, disabled and non-disabled, working together to weave access into everything they do. In an accessible culture, disabling barriers are dismantled before they can become the norm – whether those barriers are systemic, physical or attitudinal. Churches installing new video screens can ask how they will make sure blind people know what's being shown on the screen; they can commit to using subtitles for deaf people and those with auditory processing issues; they can plan to reserve a few seats where people with energy-limiting conditions can see the screen while seated. Churches that give out a service sheet can include a guide to the service, explaining potentially mystifying moments and clarifying unspoken rules. That would help not just neurodivergent people, but those who are new to churches, too. A church with an accessible culture makes sure a diverse community can participate in everything they do. That's not a burden on a church – it's a cultural shift that benefits everyone.[172]

In 2021, a powerful story was shared among disabled Christians at the annual Living Edge conference on disability and church, a disabled-led event that centres disabled people's voices. Delegate Sarah told us about her experiences as an 'involuntary hermit' who can rarely leave her bed. The conference, she said, is the one Christian community where she does not have to leave part of herself at the door, 'like a pair of dirty boots.'[173] Sarah's words resonated with many of our storytellers' experiences of churches. They were often asked to leave disability at the church door. When they could not – when they needed subtitles, comfortable seating, a welcome for their adaptive technology, or information about the church they wanted to attend – the church gates were closed to them. These were churches with inaccessible cultures. Other storytellers had glimpsed justice, in communities that were beginning to place access at the heart of their church life. Through cultures of access, these churches aspired to enable disabled people to participate.

The Way We Do Church

> ❛ The main thing has been getting some [leaders and church members] to stop using the 'But we've always done it like this' mantra. ❜ Jane

Every church has a culture, which we could simply define as the way we 'do church,' as Andrew described it.[174] A church's culture lives out its values, embodied in all the ways its members think, act, and serve each other. Disabled people meet with justice – or exclusion – as communities make choices about how they 'do church'. Storytellers told us about communities that 'did church' in normative ways, creating barriers that left disabled people on the edge. And while some cultural values in churches exist for spiritual reasons, some ableism is about simple resistance to change. Those with non-disabled privilege in church communities may be reluctant to change how they 'do church' for one disabled person, as we'll see in some of the stories in this chapter. Often, when storytellers asked for changes to make church cultures more accessible to them, they were told, 'In this church, we've always done it this way'. Ableist church cultures can be rooted in pastoral power, when non-disabled leaders expect to make all the decisions in churches, and do not welcome disabled people's knowledge about access or calls for justice. These were churches that *invited* our storytellers, and even had good intentions to *include* them,[175] but which were not always willing to *transform* to welcome disabled people. But in churches that set out to weave access into every part of church life, as a community practice of justice rather than an afterthought, disabled storytellers were enabled to participate, serve and lead.

Hearing the word and seeing the truth

'The Church is very much hearing-dominated, in the way it's structured.' Andrew

Norms of *seeing* and *hearing* have power in churches. Gospel stories of the healing of blind and deaf people are read in churches almost every Sunday. Blind and deaf theologians have written about church *audiocentricity* (which centres those with hearing privilege) and *visiocentricity* (which centres those with sighted privilege).[176] For blind theologian John Hull, the words of hymns and prayers, and even the metaphors of the Bible itself, can privilege a sighted perspective.[177] It can reinforce our ableist thinking when, threaded through church cultures, our holy and liturgical texts associate blindness with ignorance or sin:

> When we refer to these qualities as being *spiritual blindness*
> we reinforce the prejudice, and collaborate in the continued
> marginalization of disabled people.[178]

We heard from several storytellers about churches that had not yet made the journey towards challenging the ways they privileged sighted and hearing people, and how blind and deaf congregants were marginalised in these inaccessible cultures.

Married storytellers Hazel and Victor, both blind, were long-term members of a Baptist church with an informal, charismatic culture. Sighted perspectives were privileged in this community's ways of 'doing church'. In worship, the assumption was that everyone could read the song lyrics, though they knew Hazel and Victor could not. As Hazel told us:

> If we learn new songs, frankly you have to listen. Because what they do is put [the lyrics] on an overhead projector. A few years ago the band used to teach them to you. But of course they don't do that now.

Making a simple request for their access needs to be met, Hazel and Victor asked worship leaders to tell them in advance what songs would be sung on the following Sunday, so that they could learn the words. As Victor explained, that rarely happened, and they were usually left unable to sing with their congregation:

> They could email the songs. They could pick up the phone and speak to us ... But at no time do they.

Congregational singing was not the only part of church life that raised structural barriers for Hazel and Victor. Video and other visual materials were also inaccessible to the couple:

> Hazel: They always read the Scriptures. However, if they show a video they say, 'We're just going to show you a video.' And it might have some speech on it and it might not but they don't tell you what it's about ...
> Victor: I just don't think they think enough about when they do something visual.

As Victor pointed out, this was thoughtlessness, more than intentional discrimination. Without an accessible culture, structural barriers were inevitable. The church's worship culture further entrenched those barriers. The worship group's preference was to choose songs on the day, by the leading of the Holy Spirit, but their sighted biases shaped how they expected the Holy Spirit to work. It is all too easy for churches' ways of 'doing worship' to become an idol, valued for itself, rather than as a means for all to encounter God. In a church that did not prioritise disability justice, the community prioritised the worship they were comfortable with over access for Hazel and Victor. Sighted privilege shaped a sighted church culture.

And yet, sometimes, transforming inaccessible cultures takes only a simple awareness of disabled members' access needs, together with a willingness to remove small barriers. Jemma, who is also blind, told us how well this had worked at her independent evangelical church:

> Simple solutions that are often of no cost to the church can make a huge difference, e.g. I have approximately four seats I can sit in and be able to read the words for worship, so my church always reserves one of these seats for me, and removes the seat next to it so my guide dog has some space ... In a previous venue my church used a second screen so I could sit further back and still see the words. They had a spare monitor and a cable, so again this simple adaptation cost nothing.

Jemma and her church worked together to come up with solutions to barriers, making sure that the sighted privilege of the majority did not eclipse Jemma's participation in worship, no matter how spontaneous. All it took was listening, learning, and remembering Jemma's access needs. Not all access solutions will be this simple and inexpensive, but many are. When churches allow disabled people to challenge power and interrupt their ableist thinking, grace makes space. The best solutions often come from disabled people ourselves.

Churches are also led by those with hearing privilege, as Deaf storyteller Andrew observed. Their strong cultural bias in favour of hearing and listening can marginalise deaf people.[179] As Deaf liberation theologian Hannah Lewis points out, biblical metaphors and intepretation are often at the root of our churches' audiocentricity:

> The concept of Jesus as the Word of God has been experienced

69

as something that does not relate to Deaf people, which creates and perpetuates the damaging myth that speech is superior to sign. In fact, as the Gospel begins 'In the beginning was the Word', we might view it as meaning 'In the beginning was speech'.[180]

Andrew became more aware of his free evangelical church's audiocentric, hearing-dominated culture over several years. As his hearing impairment progressed to the point where hearing aids were no longer useful, he began to find it more and more difficult to follow sermons. Andrew approached church leadership, hoping they would help him find ways to access the church's teaching. He first asked if they could subtitle the sermon, but they said they could not afford it 'for one person'. Graciously, Andrew tried to help them find more inexpensive solutions:

> Well, I did ask about copy [of the notes], but a lot of the preachers at my church… they often just have bullet points. They like to preach more informal, making it up as they go along. So you might have the OHP having three points … So I know what the three points are but I wouldn't know what the actual detail was of that.

Even communal prayer was inaccessible to Andrew. His fellow congregants prayed spontaneously from their seats, far from microphones and hearing aid loops, with their heads bowed so that he could not lipread. These cultural barriers had theological roots, making them particularly difficult for Andrew to challenge. 'That's what the New Testament Church did,' he reflected. 'But as a Deaf person … it wasn't accessible to me at all.' Increasingly, Andrew had no way to participate in a church that privileged hearing, and he left the church altogether. Andrew went on to embrace his Deaf identity as a gift from God, which included learning BSL, but he never returned to church. He was the 'one person' for whom his church would not transform. He was the one sheep who was not pursued.

Andrew was sure the church did not mean to exclude him, but the outcome was the same, even if this was not conscious discrimination:

> I always found the church to be very accepting of me. It was only when I got so deaf that I couldn't follow, that I found suddenly

— It wasn't that they didn't want me. It was like, I just didn't fit into the way that they did church. I just didn't fit into the way that Christians did things when they got together.

Just as so much ableism is, Andrew's exclusion was a by-product of the church's culture.[181] The church had not yet examined the hearing privilege at the heart of their ways of 'doing church'. If they had, they would have seen that their culture created attitudinal and structural barriers that left deaf members on the outside. Improvised sermons and informal prayer were central to church culture; Andrew's access was less important to the community. Their spiritual norms became Andrew's spiritual exclusion. Like Hazel and Victor, Andrew was ambivalent about whether this community could ever undergo the cultural change it would take to make their ways of 'doing church' accessible to him. In churches where ableism is deeply entrenched in inaccessible spiritual cultures, transformation must begin with repentance for injustice, and a reimagining of more just, equitable ways of 'doing church,' before there will be room for disabled people.

In churches that value the spoken word above other ways of communicating and teaching, many more disabled people are excluded. A one-way sermon preached from the front also privileges a particular kind of intellectual ability, creating barriers for neurodivergent people, people with learning disabilities, and those with dementia, among others. Storyteller Leah, who is autistic and dyslexic, could rarely follow the long spoken sermon that was the focus of services at her Baptist church:[182]

I often haven't got a clue what they talked about in the sermon because I just can't keep track. And some people will do, you know, the summary on the slides … through bullet points. But ten minutes later I've probably forgotten them anyway.

The culture of Leah's church was designed around an assumption that listeners could engage with a long sermon. But Leah processes information differently from neurotypical people, and found it difficult to concentrate, remember and follow through the sermon. 'If I don't understand it, then, well, I just never understand it,' she reflected. And yet Leah knew that this was not the only way of 'doing church,' after experiencing services where the talk was delivered more interactively, opening up her access to Christian teaching:

> One thing we had recently was we changed the evening service. We stopped having one sermon and we started having two five-to-ten-minute talks and one ten-minute discussion. And I think I found that much better ... You'd have a couple of different speakers and then there'd be a, 'Turn around and discuss these three questions with the people nearby.' And that, broken up with a summary after each bit, was helpful, because I had a chance of understanding what was going on when there's only five minutes to remember.

Sadly, this shift to a more accessible, interactive sermon structure did not continue at Leah's church. Even home groups moved too quickly for Leah to participate, and she was intimidated by the social interaction they were based around. Leah was a theological thinker, who shared thoughtful disability theology with us, and yet these cultural barriers left her believing that she could not understand the Bible or grow in her faith. She was longing to participate in accessible discipleship, designed to include neurodivergent ways of engaging.

Hearing, sighted and speaking privilege are still embedded in the cultures of many churches. Many have not yet examined their negative representations of blindness and deafness, nor the cultural barriers these create for deaf and blind Christians. And yet God is experienced through all our senses, not just hearing or sight. Disabled theologians, like our storytellers, are leading the Church to new ways of understanding God, for everyone, deaf or hearing, blind or sighted. In a powerful talk at the 2014 Living Edge conference, Hull rewrote the lyrics of the hymn 'Amazing Grace'. Instead of 'I once was lost, but now am found, *was blind but now I see*,' the lyrics became, '... *was bound but now I'm free.*' With one stroke of a blind man's hymn-rewriting pen, the song's language became inclusive of a group of people it has marginalised for 250 years.[183] Lewis shows how Deaf culture reclaims church culture from audiocentric, ableist ways of doing church. For Deaf people, who use British Sign Language, Jesus Christ is the *SIGN-OF-GOD*, rather than the (spoken) Word of God.[184] Deaf people are showing us that hearing is far from the only way to encounter God. Almost a decade after Hull's talk, it is long past time that we challenge the privileging of abled perspectives in church cultures that marginalise blind, deaf and other disabled Christians. Re-centring deaf and blind perspectives can be the start of a journey of transformation, as churches challenge their hearing and sighted privilege, and work towards creating accessible cultures together with disabled people.

Information in advance

> **'None of the [access] information was available.'** Tim

Church communities tend to assume that everyone knows how to find, enter and participate in their church. Yet disabled people can never take it for granted that we will be able to get into a church building or understand a service, when so many churches are inaccessible to us. In churches that create cultures of accessible information, communities tell disabled people, *We've been expecting you. Here's how you join us.* From maps and directions to content warnings about sermon topics, information in advance of a service could make or break some storytellers' access and participation in churches.

Tim, a pioneer minister in the Church of England, has a chronic pain condition and often uses a mobility scooter. He was all too used to attending church meetings and conferences where he had to work hard to find out whether a venue would be accessible to him:

> So I had to do the phone call of, 'How do I get there? ... How far have I got to walk from my car if I'm not going to use my scooter? What's the distance to the loo?' And all those questions ...They had a cracking website, and none of the [access] information was available and I was going, 'Well, you don't have the excuse that you've built on the structure that was already there. You still haven't done it.'

Zoe had a similar experience; she regularly struggled to find out whether churches and Christian events would be accessible to her. Disabled

73

people must do constant *labour* in advance of church services or meetings, spending precious energy on phoning or emailing to ask questions about access, to which non-disabled organisers may not have answers, if they have never considered accessibility before.[185] Access information in advance could make all the difference to Tim and Zoe, but they could not often find it on churches' websites. Because disabled people like them were not expected at church, it was rare that communities prepared for their arrival.

Failure to share information in advance can be more than just an inconvenience for disabled people. For Jemma, who has post-traumatic stress disorder (PTSD), it harmed her mental health:

> I have faced major issues with people understanding my mental health and being inclusive – things like not using content warnings, exposing me to PTSD triggers with no warning.[186]

Ignored when she asked for advance information about service content and structure, Jemma found it more and more difficult to stay and participate in church activities. It was traumatising for storytellers to be left in the dark about what happens in churches, especially for those who are neurodivergent or experience mental and emotional distress, whose access needs sometimes went unnoticed because of a lack of awareness. For other storytellers, a void of access information made going to church a physically painful experience. Still others gave up trying to get through the church gates at all. All for the want of some simple information, in advance, about access to church buildings and the content of services.

The alternative is to work towards a church culture that shares information in advance. This works in other contexts: it is increasingly easy to check access to cultural institutions, from theatres to museums, or to look up a restaurant's menu to check dietary requirements. So why not churches? Sarah, who is autistic, longed to see churches meeting the information standards of some secular institutions, helping disabled visitors and new members to avoid trauma, pain and wasted journeys:

> I would love churches to put up information on their websites, showing photos inside, showing the layout, showing really detailed

stuff. The best example I've ever seen was Windsor Castle. They have an autistic guide ... And it's got photos and explains where the lights are coming from ... And it's not about thinking, 'What does this disability need?' I think it is purely, 'What information do we have?' All that information needs to be available ... So if I walk into [a] church, I would know that there's this type of door, that there is a covered bit before we get to the door, there's a step here. That the books were this size print... And if you use the [hearing aid] loop, this is the person you speak to. It would be fabulous.

Sharing access information in advance does not take much disability expertise, Sarah reflected. It simply takes an expectation that disabled people will be coming through the door, and a willingness to share what communities already know about their churches. For neurodivergent people, who cannot always infer the meaning of symbolic gestures and shared social norms, a church culture of accessible information can demystify a service, as Lucy told us: she was always pleased to see service guides explaining the service, making it clear when to go up for communion and how to opt out of hand-shaking during the Peace. When instructions about what happens in the service are left implicit, autistic people may not have equal access. Lucy said:

> The fact that if you have got a service sheet and there are bits in bold, that normally means that everyone says them together at the same pace. Things like that are not often explained in a plain and clear way.

Lucy also suggested churches share sensory information, to keep neurodivergent people with sensory sensitivities informed, and others who might be reactive to noise, lighting or smells:

> Sometimes knowing how much incense might be around before you go into a service could be quite helpful. Because incense, I quite like in small quantities, but some of the services I have been to I can't breathe, there is that much.

Leah had even more ideas for ways churches could share accessible information. As an autistic, dyspraxic person, she found it difficult to recognise faces and find her way around. She was longing for photo-assisted directions to her church from local stations and bus stops, and a church membership list with photos matched to names. These simple access features could enable not just neurodivergent people to feel part of a church community, but those with dementia and learning disabilities, too. In fact, the potential benefit of storytellers' ideas for information accessibility goes beyond disabled people. Clear information about where to go and what to do in church can make for a less overwhelming experience for those who are new to churches, whether or not they are disabled. Through accessible cultures, churches that value outreach can live out and share the gospel with many more people in their communities.

Church: The place where we should feel most comfortable

‘Church should be a place where everybody feels comfortable. Actually, it's the place where most people feel least comfortable.’ Nicki

Disabled people want to *come as we are* to church.[187] We long to feel comfortable as the people we were created to be, in worship and community. And yet powerful norms govern how we should appear and behave in church. There is often an unspoken expectation that we will worship God through our bodies, by standing at key moments of the service.[188] Disabled storytellers told us about their sense of falling short, as they struggled to stand for songs or the Gospel, or when they could not kneel to pray, or could not keep their eyes open during sermons. The *stigma* of disability often brings with it a sense of shame and internalised ableism, in a world where disabled people's differences are often judged negatively by others. As Betcher puts it, ‘I am on public display; always seen, always overlooked.’[189] Churches that prioritise disability justice can help to reduce that stigma, encouraging disabled people to come to church as we are, and giving us permission to be comfortable there.

In the face of worship norms, some storytellers felt a pressure to *pass* as non-disabled, as far as they could. Church services became times of self-consciousness or fear for them. Storyteller Susanna, who has ME/ chronic fatigue syndrome, struggled to sit comfortably through the long talks at her church:

> In a church service, it's probably one of the few contexts where I'm having to sit and listen for half an hour, forty minutes or whatever for the sermon, and it's hard … I'm putting all my energy into keeping my head upright and not closing my eyes because I don't want the person speaking to think that I think they're boring, or something. At the same time, I'm really struggling to keep my eyes open.

To be seen as listening during a sermon is an accepted norm in church. Keen not to draw attention to her differences in church, Susanna put her body through stress and even pain, all so she would look like she was listening in the 'right' way. And if appearing to be listening in church is a compelling norm, sitting and standing may be an even more important one. Faith told us about the shame she felt in church, when chronic illness made it difficult for her to stand to sing:

> When I was newly diagnosed there was the pressure in worship to stand and sing. And I knew physically I wasn't able to do that … It's just nice to be given the option if you want to stand, stand. And if not, just remain seated. But not all churches give that option.

Storytellers were worried that, if they stayed seated, their behaviour would be seen as disrespectful to God or the church community. This was especially – but not only – true for those with invisible impairments.[190] Rigid liturgy left them feeling that they had to force themselves to stand, harming and devaluing their God-given bodies in the process.

Yet, in some churches, *inclusive language* about sitting and standing gave storytellers permission to worship as they are, without fear of stigma or judgement. Susanna told us:

> The church that I go to at the minute ... the minister would generally say, 'Stand if you're able or sit if you prefer.' That just makes such a difference. It really does ... It just takes that whole mental analysis over what I should be doing out of the equation.'

Clare told a similar story of the difference it can make when churches say, in an announcement or in a service sheet, that people are welcome to stay seated. One little inclusive phrase made space for Faith, Susanna and Clare to be more comfortable in church, without having to force their bodies to conform to normative expectations. On the opposite end of the scale, when storytellers' churches did not think about how they phrased their invitation to stand, disabled people began to feel not just invisible and unwelcome, but unworthy to worship God. In a Christian tradition where disability has been seen as deficit, 'uprightness' has become a moral imperative, Betcher tells us.[191] But we worship in spirit in truth,[192] not in posture. Justice is *interactional* – lived out in every interaction between disabled people and church communities.[193] Through disability-positive interactions and statements, churches can shape cultures that do not stigmatise those whose different bodies and minds mean we must worship differently.

The question of inclusive language can lead to animated debates. When Naomi once raised the issue of 'please stand' on Twitter, some frustrated ministers said that having to worry about such inconsequential phrasing was a step too far. But this phrasing was far from inconsequential to our storytellers; it was transformative. When church leaders said 'Please stand if you are able or comfortable to do so,' or did not ask congregants to stand at all, churches powerfully signalled to disabled people that their different ways of worshipping, their disabled ways of being, were valuable to the church community and accepted by God. *Liturgical responses are not more important than your inclusion*, these churches told disabled people. In communities of justice, everyone is welcome to worship just as they are.

For some disabled people, coming to church *just as we are* may mean we cannot arrive on time, or cannot make it to services held at challenging times of day. Disabled people feel time in our bones, as Kafer puts it.[194] Trying to fit ourselves around normative schedules, like early church start times, can be physically painful for some of us. For Susanna, the early timing of morning services was a barrier, when her fatigue was at its worst. For a long time, feeling the pressure to be present at the main church service, Susanna kept on struggling to attend on Sunday mornings. Eventually, she came to realise that it honoured neither God or her community when she forced herself to attend services at times that harmed her health:

> I've come to the conclusion that I'm not going to try and keep pushing myself to do Sunday mornings anymore. They're not designed for people with ME, so I think I've come to a point where I keep trying to fit myself in this space and, actually, I don't think God minds if I go in the evening instead of the morning.

Susanna's comment that morning services were *not designed for people like her to fit* was telling. She had the support of her community in finding her own ways to attend church, but the church culture still valued one normative way to 'do church' – weekly attendance at the Sunday morning service – over all others. And for Jane, who attends both Methodist and Anglican churches, the inflexible timing of services was a barrier that kept her from worshipping at the services she preferred:

> The main trouble now is that it takes me so long to get moving in the morning that I don't make it to morning services, and the Methodist church here only has morning services ... And when I said I would like a Book of Common Prayer service now and again, [the parish church's] response was, 'Well you can get that at 8 am', which of course was even more difficult for me to get moving for.

Once again, a disabled person was left having to prioritise access over everything else she was looking for in a church or service. Other storytellers struggled to make it to services on time because of barriers in their lives beyond church – when they could not find an accessible parking space, when they were refused access on the bus, or when their personal assistants did not arrive in time for them to get to a service. If disabled people are not on time to the service, we may be left waiting at the gates.

79

Maria was another storyteller who longed for afternoon services. As a stop-gap measure, she was finding her own ways to worship on the edge:

> I have been piecing together fellowship and teaching from attending Tuesday evening Care Group, and I have three Christian friends from the church I see regularly, so we can talk about God and Bible stuff and pray together. And I watch sermons on TBN Christian telly.

At a table that was not designed for her, Maria could only access a seat at the edge. And yet, rather than trying to fit service times that caused them suffering, storytellers like Maria found many ways to bend church time to fit their needs, from worshipping at online services to forming groups with other disabled Christians. Disabled people often live – and worship – on *crip time*, as we build 'imaginative life schedules' around the needs of our bodies and minds, which we can never take for granted.[195] Together with us, church communities can move beyond the attitude that there is only one way to worship as a church and it can only happen at 10 am sharp on a Sunday. As churches come to value many different ways of doing church, they may begin to broaden their imagination of the Church – not just with the disabled people who are too tired to attend morning services, but with parents running late because of childcare issues, with people living in poverty who have to work on a Sunday, and with many others who come to the church gates too late and find them closed.

One more way some storytellers made themselves more comfortable in church was through assistive technology, as they hacked their way past barriers. Assistive technology has been revolutionary for disabled people. Phone apps read text aloud to visually impaired people; Augmentative and Alternative Communication (AAC) allows nonspeaking people to communicate.[196] And yet disabled people's accessible technology is easily stigmatised as a symbol of difference.[197] Negative attitudes to technology laid bare yet more norms about what, and who, is acceptable in worship settings. When blind and visually impaired storytellers used their tablet computers to magnify hymns, or when neurodivergent storytellers used phones to manage their distraction, it was sometimes seen as one more sign of disrespect. Storyteller Rhona called her smartphone a 'blessing'; it allowed her to transform inaccessible hymn words and Bible readings into large print:

> [My church is] getting more used to me now, but when I first had my iPhone 6, years ago, because you could make [hymns] large font, it was great – but the tsking and the tutting that went on. 'What are you doing with mobiles?'

Rhona's use of her mobile phone was a visible, stigmatised symbol of the way she misfit in church culture. Subtle disablism from fellow churchgoers arose from their ignorance about the ways blind people use technology to access printed materials.[198] These *microaggressions* left Rhona nervous to use her phone in church in future. But Rhona remembered visiting a church with a more accessible culture, where they enabled her use of technology:

> The minister says, 'Hymn number whatever.' So I'm getting the hymn up [on my phone]. And this guy taps me on the shoulder. I thought, *Oh no, for goodness sake, here we go again.* He said, 'Are you using your mobile phone to find the hymns?' And I thought: *Don't start, just don't start* ... Anyway, he comes back two minutes later with a huge iPad saying, 'Oh we're collecting iPads year after year, adding them. On a Sunday morning we download onto the iPad all the hymns. And all you have to do is scroll.' And I thought: *Can I invite you to my church?* It was fantastic, just being accepted, you know?

Rhona was delighted by the embodied welcome she found at this church, where her needs as a visually impaired person were not only accepted, they had been anticipated in advance. As members of this church gave Rhona an iPad, they told her, *We've been expecting you.* Sadly, Rhona had not always experienced this level of access in her own church. 'A prophet is not welcome in their own home,' she wryly told us. Rhona was hopeful that attitudes to disabled people's personal uses of accessible technology could still change in churches, as more non-disabled people begin to use phones and tablets to take notes or read the Bible in church. But that would be *accidental access.* We can't wait for non-disabled people to find out what disabled people have known all along – that we can meet God through technology. A church with an accessible culture would welcome all the ways that disabled people use technology and equipment to participate. That transformation could help others to hack the parts of church that they find alienating or difficult, too. Imagine churches that encouraged new Christians to find a Bible text at the touch of a smartphone button. Accessible cultures help everyone to fit.

With an imagination expanded by their disabled experience, storytellers imagined churches that would signal to us that we are welcome to come as we are. People with chronic pain envisioned beanbags and comfortable seats in place of hard plastic chairs; autistic people dreamed of safe sensory environments that would not harm them. They were longing for communities that would offer a practical welcome to everyone who cannot find a place for their bodies and minds in one-size-fits-all churches. Churches with accessible cultures would embrace disability culture and disabled ways of being, rather than asking us to fit majority ways of doing church. As storyteller Esther put it:

> When we go to church and pretend that we're something we're not, it's almost like it nullifies all of the worship and all of the ministry, because we're not being real.

But in communities where disabled people are safe to be the people we were created to be, when – in Esther's words – we 'get real' with God and others, the whole Church may discover more about God than we could ever have imagined. Church is rarely a place where we are comfortable to be ourselves, as Nicki said, but in transformed churches, we could be. The Kingdom of God is a table transformed by and for all of us, with room for all the diversity of God's creation, including disabled people. Just as we are.

Social church

❝I think … when people think of friendship, they think perhaps of what their idea of friendship is.❞ Anthony

From informal after-church coffee to home groups, church life is unavoidably social. Attendance at social groups and events is an expectation in most church communities. And yet for some disabled people, church social life can be inaccessible or intimidating. When church social culture is not designed for you, it can be difficult to find a place to belong.

Church coffee culture was not designed for Rhona, as a visually impaired person:

> I have to rely on somebody asking me if they would like to go for a coffee for me. And most days I can't bring myself to ask them ... And if I go out and try and do [coffee] I either have to be first so that there's no queue, so I get there and then I just have to stand absolutely still. Or I have to be last. And then no doubt the nice tea and coffee lady will say, 'We did finish ten minutes ago. You're a bit late ...' And I would have said most times I don't get a drink.

If Rhona wanted to enjoy coffee with others at her church, she either had to hope for unreliable pastoral support from others, or she had to try and adapt herself to coffee organised around sighted people's needs. She ended up feeling like she was the problem, when her community's routines were the real barrier. Rhona was not alone in finding church social life physically and culturally challenging to access. At Victor and Hazel's church, social events were organised through a website that was inaccessible to them, as blind users. Instead of removing the digital barriers, leaders told them to ask someone else to book for them – every time they wanted to join in with a gathering. The couple suggested alternative ways to sign up for events, but nothing changed. This was a church that had not challenged its own pastoral power, where Hazel and Victor were expected to rely on help from leaders forever. Their need for dignified, independent access was not understood. 'How many times do you ask [for help]?' Victor said. 'I feel like I'm sort of bashing my head, so why should I bother?' When they did manage to attend, they found that meals and gatherings were designed for sighted people. At one church dinner, everyone moved tables between courses – a challenge for Hazel and Victor. No one thought of honouring their presence through a more accessible meal. The banquet, literally, was not designed for them.

Then there were the storytellers who found church social life stressful to navigate, like Mims, who experiences long-term mental distress. Through her confirmation group at her large church, she met others with mental health diagnoses, and they began to support each other informally. For Mims, it was an accessible 'way in' to community life. But as members of the group moved away, Mims began to struggle to meet people. Large home groups were a source of anxiety. 'If you don't actually join one of the groups, it's kind of like, at what point do you actually feel a part of the community?' Mims insightfully asked. The social pressure of after-church coffee hour threw up yet more barriers for her:

> When I am depressed I can't do it. When I am manic I can't do it … It is one of the main reasons I very rarely go to the Sunday morning service now. It has got too big. Even just the noise level in the coffee room – you can hardly hear yourself think. You have to shout to have a proper conversation.

Mims tried to do after-church socialising differently, inviting members of the church out for coffee at local cafes instead, but that only worked if people were willing to join her, and not everyone understood how stressful Mims found social events. 'I am yearning for a smaller church where everybody knows each other now,' she told us. As much as Mims loved her church, when she was unable to fit in the social culture there, she found herself on the edge. Leah, who is autistic, had a similar story of intimidating after-church coffee and home groups, with their unstructured small talk, where she felt pressured to participate. The social culture of church paradoxically kept them on the edge of community life. These were storytellers whose 'bodies and neurology are at the centre of a political struggle',[199] who had to fight constantly against structures that excluded them. They could not participate – not just as they are.

In some churches, regular attendance at groups is seen as a sign of commitment. Being involved in home groups, meetings and service several times a week was almost a requirement at Leah's church. That level of social involvement was far from comfortable for her, as an autistic person:

> I missed a couple of services and someone emailed and said, 'Where are you?' I get this expectation that everyone should be really involved and should be going to so many things and should have a good circle of friends, and some things I don't have, and others that I don't want.

Leah often needed short breaks from church and its overwhelming social culture, but that was not how her community 'did church'. She was marginalised by norms of participation. In the same way, when Maria became too unwell to attend multiple church meetings and services each week, her commitment to her church was questioned. Concerned about her absence, Maria's church leaders invited her to meetings to discuss her attendance:

> I did explain that [I was ill], but they weren't sympathetic because they were annoyed with me. This meeting was a telling off and I was supposed to say, 'I'm very sorry and I will start attending.' So pulling out the ill health card and saying, 'Actually I can't, I'm [going] downhill and it's just too much now.'

There was rigid pastoral power at work at Maria's church, where leaders defined how members should attend. Despite Maria's discussions with church leaders about the disabling barriers and challenges she faced at church, they did little to enable Maria to attend. While she was recovering from an operation, leaders were a little more understanding:

> [I told them that] another reason I was reluctant to go to church – any church – was because I'm so used to being taught that belonging to a church means you attend regularly, and that you commit your time and talents to your church, but I don't want to commit to doing anything at the moment. [They] said they didn't expect me to do anything at church during this 'season', and that if I needed to piece together some fellowship and teaching from different sources for now, that was okay.

But this was only conditional acceptance of Maria's situation, just for a 'season'. Leaders expected Maria to return eventually to active involvement in church. They failed to understand that, in contrast with the short-term illnesses that non-disabled people experience, Maria was not going to recover.[200] The barriers she faced to attending church were permanent. Because the church community could not imagine people like Maria as members, their culture of regular attendance was unlikely to change. Not for her, and not for other disabled members.

Church cultures are shaped by models of group membership and 'joining in' that do not work for all disabled and neurodivergent people. Certainly not for Anthony, who is autistic. He attended Anglican churches as a young man; at one point he was discerning a call to ordination. But Anthony found himself alienated from the social culture at his church, where the requirement to join in was a challenge. He spoke of what he called an ' "everyone must have fun" brigade' in churches, where he was encouraged to be social in ways that were not comfortable for him:

> You come across people with Asperger's, who often don't particularly enjoy joining in, [with church members] sometimes putting pressure on them to join in ... thinking they're doing the right thing. It's actually completely counter-productive, because it seems like they're refusing to take no for an answer.

In church, Anthony experienced the ableist assumption that discipleship must be social, and that 'there is something wrong with you', in his words, if you do not want to join in with home groups or discussions. In his experience, there was only one normative way of being social in church – through established groups, with their own social culture and rituals that Anthony could not easily participate in. Instead, Anthony told us that neurotypical people in churches need to learn about neurodivergent and disabled people's own ways of 'doing' friendship:

> Friendship in the church is absolutely a good thing, but ultimately if someone was a true friend, they wouldn't try and force you to do something you didn't want to do ... I think like anything else, when people think of friendship, they think perhaps of what *their*

idea of friendship is. And if they are a non-disabled person, who is active in the church and has a lot of friends who are likewise, as far as they're concerned that's what friendship is … But it's sort of a question of them having to learn about us, and us having to learn about them.

Anthony's insights share the responsibility for change with churches, asking them to rethink their ways of being community together *with* us. Too often, disabled people are asked to do all the work of adapting to inaccessible environments and situations. Anthony was hinting at the 'double empathy problem,' the theory that suggests that when people with very different perceptions of the world meet, they do not find it easy to empathise with each other. Neurotypical people often misunderstand autistic people's different ways of thinking, being social, and being human.[201] But Anthony was sure that God created disabled and neurodivergent people with all our differences, and there is nothing 'wrong' with us. He had once longed for church communities that would honour his different ways of being. But it was too late; he had left churches many years ago, alienated by neurotypical social cultures where he did not fit.

When churches dismantle the barriers that close the gates to church life for disabled people, communities will be enriched by our presence. But for now, there is an expectation, deeply embedded in church cultures, that the 'ideal' church member will be present every Sunday, active in church, and able to join in socially.[202] Many disabled people cannot live up to these normative expectations. We heard many other stories of barriers to church social life, ranging from Andrew, who found informal social groups inaccessible as a Deaf person, to Sheila, who was unable to join a home group because they all met in houses with steps up to the entrance. When large churches prioritised growth over relationships with members, it could leave disabled people on the edge, longing for communities that could get to know them and their access needs, as well as their gifts.[203] And when storytellers could not be present or social, their commitment to churches often came under the spotlight, while barriers went unacknowledged.[204] For a few storytellers, supportive church communities encouraged and enabled them to belong to churches in their own ways, but disabling barriers kept many others from playing a full part in church life, sometimes deepening their alienation from Christian community. They found other ways to grow in faith and connect with other Christians, but local church community stayed out of reach. In ableist churches, disabled people cannot belong.

The harm ableism does

❛I asked multiple people multiple times if we could have more light at prayer meetings. Nothing happened.❜ Jemma

When church communities do not challenge the ableist ways they 'do church', the result, for disabled people, can be trauma and harm. Disablism can fester in ableist churches where pastoral power is at work. We may deal with microaggressions, shaming, and painful negotiations for access with gatekeepers. At its worst, discrimination and disablism may leave disabled people feeling ashamed of the people we were created to be. After one too many traumatic experiences in ableist churches, some of our storytellers never returned to church.

We told Fern's story of her stressful attempt to access a church building in Chapter 2. She went to a church that advertised itself as wheelchair accessible, and found herself being pushed up two wooden planks. As she made her way up the unsafe ramp, onlookers added to the pain of access barriers by staring and making comments about Fern and her wheelchair:

> A crowd gathered to watch ... while giving the usual comments that wheelchair users will be very familiar with (along the lines of *learner drivers, licenses, too young looking [for a wheelchair], can I get one of those ...*).

Many disabled people are used to these kinds of awkward comments – as non-disabled people deal with their discomfort with disability – but that makes them no less traumatic. For Fern, the staring and comments were 'othering', compounding the physical barriers that closed the church gates to her. Disability theorists would call this an example of *psycho-emotional disablism,* when structural ableism becomes personal, through disempowering encounters. Psycho-emotional disablism can leave disabled people feeling helpless and unsafe, giving us the sense that we do not belong.[205]

Psycho-emotional disablism was a weekly feature of Brianna's churchgoing experience. She told us how carefully she had to negotiate for access with staff and volunteers, in a church where pastoral power left all the decisions in the hands of gatekeepers. She was reliant on their support to get around the inaccessible cathedral building, and yet they regularly watched Brianna struggle to get around without offering help:

> You have to keep [the vergers] on your side because sometimes I need support in order to get to the high altar, or whatever.

One Sunday, she was humiliated – in her own words – when vergers publicly asked her husband whether Brianna would need the toilet during a service:

> I did a very deliberate: '[Verger], thank you so much for telling [my husband] about the toilets.' I think I said in some sort of convoluted way, 'You've asked my husband instead of me …' It's so, so frustrating.

Intimidating negotiations with those in power made Brianna vulnerable. She was sure her future access to services and communion depended on her being seen as 'nice'. That meant doing careful *emotion work* with staff and leaders every Sunday.[206] When disabled people are justifiably angry at exclusion, it is not uncommon for us to have to stay polite and grateful, lest the access we are asking for be denied to us. Exhausted by the *emotional dissonance*[207] of having to keep vergers and clergy on her 'side', Brianna became increasingly worn out by the way she was treated at her church. She thought about leaving, but she stayed in the hope that she could help transform the cathedral. Even though her activism for better access to the cathedral was often treated as personal complaining, she remained faithfully committed to her advocacy for all the disabled people who worshipped there:

> I have this fight ... I try very hard to do it through education, through talking, through creating a cause ... But I have cried bucketloads over it, because I do feel completely invisible and violated by it.

Brianna's anger and shame was born from her disempowerment in the midst of injustice. We heard many similar stories of churches where disabled people had to negotiate with gatekeepers, who held the 'keys' to their access. Unless storytellers managed these negotiations carefully, their situation could deteriorate into profound exclusion. It can be risky business for disabled people to ask for the access we desperately need. In churches where disabled people are expected to receive, but not to contribute, asking for access can be seen as a defiant challenge to power. And yet, in spite of these traumatising experiences, Brianna kept knocking on the church gates, not just for herself, but on behalf of many other disabled congregants.

Jemma is visually impaired and has post-traumatic stress disorder. She shared another painful story of access requests denied by gatekeepers at church. Because Jemma is night blind, she becomes anxious if she has to sit in the dark. Yet her church insisted on holding prayer meetings in low lighting, to 'set the mood'. Jemma takes up the story from here:

> I asked multiple people multiple times if we could have more light at prayer meetings. Nothing happened until at one very busy, very dark prayer meeting, someone was moved by the Spirit and started to cry out. That was the final straw for my brain, that was already struggling to cope with the triggers of [feeling] trapped, the noise, the cries.

Jemma then had a flashback to a past experience of medical trauma. She became very distressed:

> Anxiety was now through the roof ... I couldn't get out of the room and I had no way of leaving and getting home. I was now psychologically totally unable to pray ... One of the leaders came over to me and I burst into tears very publicly and told him how much I hated myself because now my PTSD was even stopping

90

me praying, how I hated my brain and I just wanted to be normal. I completely broke down.

This access fail was not just a minor inconvenience to Jemma. The experience affected her health and her self-esteem. It pushed her to the edge of church, preventing her from joining her community for future prayer meetings. Left with flashbacks and distress, Jemma had to work through the experience with her mental health team. She began to feel unsafe in church at night, afraid that darkness would trigger a further episode of PTSD. 'I could not attend prayer meetings anymore,' she says. Only later did Jemma realise that *she* was not the problem; the issue was her church leadership's resistance to dealing with cultural barriers. Jemma and her church eventually worked out a simple solution. Today, in prayer meetings, half the room is lit and half is in darkness. It cost the church nothing, except the cost of listening and being willing to change, but a more prompt response could have prevented Jemma's trauma altogether. Jemma shared a sobering reflection about the ways disabled people can be damaged in unequal access negotiations, when a gatekeeper has power over us in church:

> What gets me is this whole situation and a whole lot of really difficult mental distress could have been avoided – the leaders knew the dark was a trigger for me. I had spoken to them about it multiple times, but it took me having a very public PTSD crisis for them to take the situation seriously.

Keen to prevent psycho-emotional disablism from happening to other disabled Christians, Jemma had some simple advice for churches:

> The single most important thing is if someone with PTSD tells you their triggers, respect this and don't push their triggers on them. It can be hard to make yourself vulnerable and talk about triggers.

It is rarely easy for disabled people to ask for our access needs to be met. It can mean making ourselves vulnerable with those who hold the keys, sharing personal details of stigmatised conditions or embarrassing impairment effects. When we take this kind of risk, it is because we are dealing with real, urgent barriers, and we need those in positions of power to listen. Speaking powerfully about the consequences of being abandoned in such an unsafe situation in church, Jemma said, 'This damaged me.' Disabled people cannot belong in unsafe churches. In Jemma's church, the maxim *But we've always done it like this* left her in a vulnerable position.

Other disabled people echoed these painful stories of the damage that can be done by psycho-emotional disablism in churches. Clare was asked, by a pastor, whether her ME/chronic fatigue syndrome was real, a common stereotype about the condition. Sarah talked about the ways some churches 'shame' disabled and chronically ill people into attendance. Storytellers had their experience of disability denied and their access needs ignored. This is *epistemic invalidation* – the denial of our reality as disabled people by those in power, who, without lived experience, either cannot recognise ableism or will not take it seriously.[208] The trauma of invalidation can stay with disabled people for a long time, colouring our future responses to churches. So many of these disabled people's painful experiences of disablism were rooted in pastoral power, in churches that could see disabled people only as being in church to receive care, and could not hear storytellers' cries for equal access and justice. Other storytellers were harmed by a failure of imagination, in churches that only knew one, non-disabled way to 'do church'. Until church communities value disabled people enough to transform the ableist ways they 'do church', many of us will continue to find church a traumatising and marginalising place to be.

Theologies of Radical Hospitality: A Table Designed for All

'Access is not a synonym for justice', disability theorist Tanya Titchkosky argues.[209] Thinking about access is only a first step towards honestly examining the ways that power works on disabled bodies and minds in ableist communities and spaces, and then dismantling ableism. And yet many of the storytellers in this book could not even get past the first hurdle of access into communities' ways of doing church. In an indictment of most churches' inaccessible cultures, many of our storytellers had found that they could not cope in standard Sunday services. Church was not designed for them. If disabled people cannot get through the church gates, what chance do we have to participate in a faith community? If we cannot fit into the ways church communities 'do church,' can we ever find justice in churches?

Our cultures grow out of the stories we tell. As churches tell stories – or stay silent – about access, participation and the sins of ableism, they tell disabled people whether or not we are imagined and wanted among their communities. When they told Andrew that subtitles were too expensive for 'one person,' his church told a story about how little they valued him. When Brianna's church dismissed her disability activism about access to communion as mere complaining, they told her that disabled people did not matter there. Whenever church communities say that disability access is too expensive or unnecessary, they tell disabled people that our bodies, minds, and ways of being are not loved in these churches. And when the Body of Christ devalues us, some of us may come to believe that *God* does not value us.

The Gospels tell us a different story.

For disability theologian Erin Raffety, the story of Jesus and Bartimaeus, the blind man,[210] is a model for a Church that takes disabled people's access seriously. Here is a man who boldly calls out to Jesus, in defiance of the non-disabled crowd who stand in his way. Jesus 'dignifies Bartimaeus' humanity by entering into dialogue with him', asking what Bartimaeus needs, rather than assuming.[211] Because we are used to seeing disabled people as bit-players in the story of redemption,[212] when we read this story, we tend to focus on Jesus's ministry to Bartimaeus. But Jesus only stops and pays attention to the man on the edge of the road when Bartimaeus calls him 'Son of David' – a subversive title used by those without privilege in the Gospels. He is reminding Jesus of his privilege. Before that, Jesus just keeps walking:

Bartimaeus' lament makes no apologies and presses in on the hearer, Jesus, even toward the form of rebuke. It's a far more challenging question to think not what do we do with a disabled person who is unruly, but what do we do with a Jesus who fails, at least at first, to listen? Where has the Church failed to listen, because we did not want to hear what was being said?[213]

When Jesus finally does listen, both he and Bartimaeus leave the encounter transformed by each other's mutual hospitality. Churches are called to listen to disabled people just as radically as Jesus listened to Bartimaeus' lament for justice,[214] as we guide them in creating cultures of access.

Whenever churches set out to create accessible cultures, they are practising hospitality. Hospitality is a foundational Christian virtue, with its roots in the Biblical tradition and the early Church.[215] Jesus puts mutual hospitality at the centre of his ministry. From allowing himself to be challenged by Bartimaeus, to celebrating his Last Supper in a borrowed room, and even perhaps in being offered another's tomb at the end of his life, Jesus blurs the line between host and guest. We see in the person of Jesus one who welcomes and is made welcome. But this radical notion of two-way hospitality has been somewhat lost in many churches, as hospitality has become a watered-down notion of politeness, of niceties, of offering tea and biscuits, rather than modelling Jesus' dynamic example as host and guest.[216] Influenced by their history as care providers, many churches remain places of pastoral power, where church leaders and communities define the conditions under which disabled people may participate. For disabled people, a one-sided model of hospitality can involve a *conditional welcome* that leaves us as permanent guests in churches.[217]

Stephanie Spellers writes about three kinds of churches, each with different models for reaching those outside the church gates: *inviting* churches, *inclusive* churches and *radically welcoming* churches.[218] *Inviting* church communities are often intentional about welcoming new people, but their unwritten invitation reads: *Come as you are, as long as you learn to do things the way that we do them.*[219] Disabled people cannot come to these churches just as we are.[220] Other churches make a commitment to *inclusion*, consciously setting out to welcome the marginalised. But when calls for inclusion in churches come from the centre, without input from those on the edge, inclusive congregations may end up offering us a place only on their own terms. Inclusion may help us to make it through the doors, but it does not always enable us to participate in community. Shaped by a paternalistic pastoral model, a vision of inclusion may imagine disabled people as 'the objects of service but not the subjects with whom [churches] engage in genuine partnership and embrace'.[221] In these churches, leaders may have some awareness that disabled people are missing from the pews, but rarely do they ask us *why*. Inclusion does not transform the pastoral power dynamics in churches; power still flows from host to guest.[222] Those who are a threat to that power are less likely to find a true place of belonging, however sincere the invitation from churches may be. As we have seen in this chapter, disabled people are praying for far more than an invitation to join in with churches' old, inaccessible ways of doing things. Unless the underpinning structures of power in churches are firmly addressed, a vision of inclusion will not result in communities transformed into places of justice for disabled people. Just as in the Gospels, Jesus alternated between guest and host, so disabled people must not be left as permanent guests in another's space, forever in the role of the 'welcomed'. We will only find what Spellers calls a *radical welcome* in communities that are rooted in their identity in Jesus, and his example of mutual hospitality and justice.

If churches cannot transform to become places of radical access and mutual hospitality, they fail in their mission.[223] Like Jesus responding to Bartimaeus, churches must show that they are ready to be challenged on inaccessibility, ableism and injustice. Storytellers asked churches to create cultures of openness to disability, where mutual listening is welcomed:

> 'I think it's worth churches, when somebody starts to attend, or if there is somebody who becomes disabled whilst they're a member … to actually talk to them about it. It might not be comfortable to say, 'Look, can I talk to you about your disability and how it affects you?', but ultimately that's the best way to find out about how somebody's disability affects them.' (Nicki)

> 'If you've got a regular attendee, ask them what they would like to do. Don't assume – don't ever assume. Don't assume about the able-bods, any more than the dis-bods.' (Miranda)

Storytellers did not want churches to pretend disability does not exist, or that we are all the same. That only erases our experiences of difference and marginalisation. Instead, they were longing for disability-affirming churches that celebrate difference and condemn ableism. This may mean change at all levels of church culture: rooting out ableist cultural practices, such as lyrics of hymns that use disability as a negative spiritual metaphor; being honest about how Christian discourses may alienate disabled people; consciously working to create disability-affirming liturgy and community life.[224] For those with power and privilege in churches, hearing that their churches are institutionally ableist is likely to be challenging, especially when that prophetic truth is told from the edge. Like Bartimaeus, our storytellers were used to being told to keep quiet about their experiences of dis/ableism. Disabled people have long lived in a world where 'experts' have decided how we should live; the same pastoral power is at work in many churches. But when disabled people resist Christian ableism, it is ministry to our churches. We are showing them how to transform into Kingdom communities of justice.

What would a transformed table look like for disabled Christians? Disability theorist Robert McRuer says that 'a place at the table' usually means 'integration into society *as it is*'.[225] The powerful do not ask what happens at the table, or for whose benefit. Disabled people may be invited to the Banquet, but has the table been designed for us? Are there bean bag chairs and wheelchair spaces at the table? Is anyone thinking about what time the Banquet will be held, or whether the language spoken around the table is British Sign Language? Instead of inviting us to a table we cannot access and a Banquet we cannot participate in, transformation would build a new table, a table built around justice, as churches reimagine all their physical, social and cultural ways of 'doing church,' shaping new communities which are no longer shaped solely around the needs of non-disabled people.

A few storytellers found their way to churches like this, where communities were building conscious cultures of access and justice. They were imagined and expected there. Shona remembered radical hospitality in an Anglo-Catholic church when she was on a pilgrimage:

> My sister (who is also deaf) and I decided to sit near the front
> to get a better view of things, and the woman who was signing

realised we were deaf and asked if we needed an interpreter.
We explained that we didn't sign and ... she asked if we'd like
a lip speaker for the Mass. I was expecting someone to maybe
convey the important bits of the Mass to us, but this absolutely
wonderful man (who was a priest) not only lip-spoke the entire
Mass for us, but also the entire sermon, which was extremely
long! I was just so moved that he had done this ... it was
wonderful to feel so included and part of things.

This was a rare moment of inclusion for Shona, who was more used to
having her access needs and leadership potential overlooked through
poor deaf awareness. But, just as traumatic experiences of disablism in
churches can stay with disabled people for a long time, so can experiences
of justice. Shona never forgot the way this community was challenging
and transforming their audiocentric culture through their ministry of
radical access, even to a one-time visitor. One sheep; one church that
went looking for her.

Other churches were working to create cultures of radical access
and justice, not just *for* disabled storytellers, but *with* them. When Susanna
realised that she needed to give up on Sunday morning services, it was
through her home group that she discovered a different way to 'do church':

[The house group is] so much easier for me to cope with than
a larger service with lots of people, noise and everything. It is
just so much easier to sit in a living room with people you feel
comfortable with ... People from the house group are the ones
that have been there for me. They're the ones who have been
calling and checking, took me to hospital and picked me up from
hospital, bought me shopping and done things. The fact that I
haven't physically been there: they're not calling me and harassing
me to come, and they're not ignoring me until such time as I
reappear, which I think is very special. I don't think that that is
something that enough Christians have experienced from church.

The group 'became church for me', Susanna reflected. They created a place
of access for Susanna, enabling her to belong, with no expectation that

she would belong in the same ways as non-disabled members. Through disabled people's ministry of presence, churches like Susanna's were transforming together with their disabled members, who led the way.

Storyteller Rhona told us a Gospel story of another religious institution transformed, where disabled people found radical access where they had once only found exclusion:

> He overturned the tables of the money changers and the benches of those selling doves. 'It is written,' he said to them, "My house will be called a house of prayer", but you are making it "a den of robbers".'
> The blind and the lame came to him at the temple, and he healed them.[226]

Rhona found hope for a transformed Church in this story of Jesus, angry at injustice in holy spaces. Who tears down the powerful religious strongholds that dishonour God and God's people as they push disposable bodies to the edge. Who forms a new community, together with the disabled people who once waited outside the Temple gates. As Rhona concluded:

> Jesus cleared out the Temple so the disabled could come in. I liked that a lot!

If the ways Christians 'do church' are disempowering and harmful for disabled people, it is time we changed those ways.[227] As disabled people share in the ministry of hospitality, challenging power and playing a full part in the life of the Church, the 'us/them' divide collapses. Storytellers called for churches where they could come and worship as they are, becoming part of the 'us'.[228] In radically accessible churches, disabled people will no longer just be invited to the table. We will shape a new table together with the rest of the Church. This is incarnational hospitality. This is justice. This is *metanoia* – repentance that leads to change, 'for the sake of the just, whole, loving reign of God'.[229]

That's when disabled people will no longer be expected to leave any part of ourselves at the church door.

CHAPTER 4

Distinctive Gifts: Disabled People's Service and Ministry

> ❛The hardest thing was being seen as someone to be looked after. I work full-time. I'm a wife and mum. I don't need to be wrapped in cotton wool, and I certainly don't want to "pew fill" until God takes me home!❜ Nicki

Go to any church conference or event on disability inclusion – especially those led by non-disabled people – and you are likely to hear a lament from the church leaders present. 'Including disabled people is so expensive,' some say. 'Our small church just doesn't have the resources.' Or, 'We don't have the experts we need to include disabled people. Where will we find experienced Sunday school teachers, BSL signers or access consultants?' Or, perhaps most frustrating of all, 'What is the least we have to do, to comply with the Equality Act?'

As disabled people who are often present at these events, we find it painful to hear ourselves represented as nothing but a *problem* – especially by church communities who are called to value the gifts of all in the Body of Christ, and to recognise as indispensable those parts of the Body that 'seem to be weaker'.[230] This is what the benevolent, charitable concept of *inclusion* is often reduced to, when it is shaped by those in the centre, not by those on the edge. Disabled people become a problem to be solved, rather than a source of gifts and blessing. In many churches today, disabled people are seen as those who are in the pews to be served, rather than as those who can serve others.

Throughout Church history, churches have reached out to those on the edge of society. Remembering Jesus' regard for the poor and marginalised, churches set up schools for those whom society would not educate, hospitals for those whom society would not treat, and soup kitchens for those whom society had left destitute.[231] They shared the gospel through words and hospitality alike. But there is a dark side to this history. What began as benevolent mission became paternalism and colonialism. When the powerful reach out to those on the margins, it is easy for them to believe that they have everything to offer, while the objects of their charity only have need. Christian pastoral care and mission have marginalised and disempowered disabled people, while Christians imagine they are saving the 'wretched of the earth'.[232] We have been used as motivation for charity, which frequently centres the giver, more than the receiver. This 'performance of giving' is all too common in churches, Sharon V. Betcher tells us.[233] For those in power, it can feel rewarding to do good for the 'needy' – and much less challenging than asking questions about *why* they are in need.[234] This is the *pastoral model,* which gives churches the power to define what disabled people need and to provide it through charity.[235] Seen in churches as objects of charity, mission and pastoral care, disabled people are less likely to be imagined there as ministers, leaders, or those with our own calling. And if disabled people are in church only to receive from others' ministry, we cannot share our gifts.

Instead, disabled Christians are seeking to *participate* in church life, as full, active members and leaders. In Fiona MacMillan's words, participation 'means joining in, as well as getting in'.[236] When disabled people can share our distinctive gifts and ministry, we will no longer be reduced to targets of churches' care and outreach. Our participation will bless churches, shaping them into communities that reflect the diverse Kingdom of God.

In this chapter, we share stories of disabled people who wanted to participate meaningfully in churches, as far more than just an opportunity for the ministry of others. In Nicki's words, they wanted to do more than fill the pews. These were disabled people who longed to serve others, but whose churches often placed unjust barriers in the way of their service and leadership. Disabled clergy and ministers had to fight against discrimination, stereotypes and structural barriers, simply to fulfil their vocations. And yet a few churches recognised gifts in their disabled members, in communities where storytellers were called to share distinctive perspectives and skills, shaped by their lived experience of disability. Here, as disabled people ministered to others, church communities were blessed – not burdened – by their presence.

Disabled People's Service in the Congregation

One way to think about Christian ministry is to divide it into three parts: the *Word* (preaching and teaching); the *Sacrament* (liturgy, leading services, and presiding over or supporting with communion); and *Service*.[237] Service honours our mutual ministry to each other and the community, from making tea and coffee to volunteering in a church's night shelter. We are not all called to be priests, but we are all Church; Jesus commanded each of us to be 'the servant of all'.[238] So we start this chapter by sharing the stories of disabled laypeople's volunteer service in churches, in churches that wanted to serve disabled people, but did not always want to be served by them.

Disabled people's gifts unrecognised

     ❛ The Church isn't complete until disabled people can actively contribute and take part, not just as objects of pity and charity, but as active participants whose experiences are seen as important too. ❜ Fern

As a former church planter with a heart for those on the edge, Nicki longed to serve the church communities she attended. In some churches, she found herself marginalised by the perception that she was there to be looked after, not to serve:

> The people there saw me as somebody to be carefully looked after, that I couldn't do anything for myself. I told them that I worked full-time and that I did normal things, but it was like they didn't hear it. It was so against what they assumed about me that they couldn't take it on ... It was almost like they felt like they had to be a good Christian and take care of me.

It was a classic example of Betcher's 'performance of giving'.[239] This was a church shaped by pastoral power. In the community's view, Nicki was in church so that they could demonstrate God's love for a disabled person – but they could not imagine how God could minister through Nicki *to* them. She had no chance to lead or serve in a culture of dependency like this. But Nicki knew she was a valued, participating member of churches where she could serve others:

> I knew that [I was included] because at that church I was serving ... I helped run the youth group on a Friday night ... They had some young people who had some life challenges. One in particular, a boy who, he'd lost his mum and just had so many issues just opening up to somebody and talking to them, but he liked playing table tennis. We used to play table tennis for hours. We'd talk while he played ... I actually felt like God was using me there, as more than just somebody to be a number.

Nicki eventually found a church that fell somewhere between these two extremes. The leadership was open to Nicki's ministry, but the inaccessible design of the building kept her at the back, preventing her from being active among the congregation. She shared with us a simple, powerful cry to participate in her community through service:

> When we get our new building, the first thing I want to do is join in and do normal – just basic, normal stuff in the service. I want to share communion. I want to take the offering. I want to just go and

ask someone if it's okay to pray with them or share something with somebody, just so that people realise that I'm not different.

It's not a great leap from *expecting* disabled people to be cared for, to only *allowing* us to be cared for. Nicki challenged this pastoral model view, believing that she was just as capable of service and leadership as non-disabled people. She knew that churches could enable her service, not just through accessible buildings that did not disable her, but through attitudes that did not underestimate her gifts as a disabled person.

Other storytellers found their gifts overlooked in churches that could not imagine disabled people serving others. Unable to leave her bed as a result of ME/chronic fatigue syndrome, Deirdre has never been able to attend her church in person. While Deirdre could not speak more highly of her community's pastoral support, she found it painful to be seen only as the target of ministry and pastoral care, rather than recognised in her full personhood:

> It is one thing not seeing people but quite another to have them come into your house (albeit to help you) and still hardly see them, as I was confined to bed at the time and they were, of course, in the kitchen for the most part. I did try to remedy this. There were often weeks when I didn't actually need any food done, so I would invite the person involved round for coffee instead. Their immediate response was always something along the lines of 'I'm sorry, I haven't got time'. In other words, they would have had two hours to cook for me but didn't have thirty minutes to be with me ... While I totally applaud church involvement in social action, we become so busy doing things *for* people that we have no time to be *with* people.

And Deirdre was easily forgotten when she tried to take a more active role in her church. She longed to share the unusual time and opportunity she had to pray, from her singular position as someone as someone who was permanently at home because of long-term illness:

> A few years ago now they were asking for people to sign up to pray for the children's work ... I think it specifically said it was a

good way for the housebound to get involved. I immediately got
someone to sign me up but I've never heard a thing from anyone
in spite of several reminders ... My attempts to be on the church
prayer chain have met a similar fate.

Because Deirdre's church community saw her primarily as someone
who receives care, they found it difficult to imagine her as someone who
could serve others. Deirdre wondered if a church disability advocate
could remind churches to work together with those who cannot always
be present in the building, whose gifts are valuable to their communities
even at a distance, but whose ministry easily goes unrecognised by a
pastoral model that can only see disabled people's needs.

Faith was equally blessed with time to pray. In lives lived on *crip
time,* disabled people may be gifted with time in ways that non-disabled
people are not, especially those of us whose world has shrunk down to a
single house or room. But Faith had tried, and failed, to share her unique
calling and opportunity to pray with churches. In her online prayer group
of disabled people who could not leave their homes, many shared her
experience:

The group that I'm in contact with, because we're housebound we
tend to pray a lot. And I think the Church doesn't recognise that as
a gift.

Faith and Deirdre's churches could not easily see the value of their prayer;
a gift discovered through disability. Churches are used to positioning
people either as recipients of pastoral ministry or those who offer
pastoral care; the truth, as Jesus reminds us, is that we are all servants of
all, and we are all served. In non-disabled majority churches, stereotypes
about ministry, and about who ministers, can keep communities from
seeing disabled people's time and calling to pray as a gift, lived out in
unexpected corners of the Church.

Victor felt called to lead an Alpha group. Proposing the idea to
church leaders, he met not with encouragement in his service, but with
worries about how a blind man would serve dinner during the Alpha
course:

The person who was running Alpha … came up with all the
negatives. You know, like, 'Think of all the things that could be
difficult and wrong …' It wasn't like, 'How could you get around
this?' So I just, you know, once the barrier was up I just said no …
It's [the Alpha leader's] job to pose questions and start a debate.
And I can definitely do that. They were thinking more of the dinner
times, serving tea.

When Victor's church leaders could only see disability as limitation, their
attitudes became an obstacle, keeping them from recognising leadership
potential in a disabled person. Disability, not gifts and leadership potential,
was the focus of decisions around whether Victor could serve. The
church might instead have found ways to overcome the disabling barriers
they were creating, perhaps by reimagining Alpha as an interdependent
team activity where Victor led the Bible study and others served food.
But that was not how the church 'did Alpha'. Victor's comment 'once
the barrier was up, I just said no' was telling. In a church where his
leadership potential was not recognised, Victor was discouraged from
trying to share his gifts again.

   Then there was Talitha, who has cerebral palsy and uses a wheelchair.
She was generally happy at her church, but she got the sense that she
was not seen as someone who could serve and lead there:

I do quite a bit [with the] hospitality team … The easiest thing for
me to do is welcome on the first floor on the way into church.
Some people wonder why I'm sat there looking lost. I have to work
hard to display my team badge and say, 'No, I'm here to welcome
…' Not everyone accepts that we [disabled people] can actually do
things like that.

Talitha met with little encouragement when she tried to offer other
forms of service and leadership. Longing to help confront disempowering
attitudes at her church, Talitha asked to lead a Bible study on the Gospel
story of the paralysed man lowered through the roof, with a disability
theology focus. She was disappointed when her study received only
criticism. 'There was no encouragement in the topic,' she said. 'That did

hurt a bit.' Talitha had a sense that the criticisms of her Bible study were not just about her skills as a leader, but also about the topic. The pastoral model positions disability as a niche, marginal ministry of the Church, rather than seeing the potential of disabled people's own ministry to transform the whole Church.[240] At Talitha's church, that perspective may have been keeping them from recognising and developing Talitha's gifts and calling. When churches do not value disabled people, they will not value the vital new perspectives we bring, gifts that grow out of our lived experience of disability and marginalisation.

Disabled people have distinctive ministry and service to offer in churches, often *because* we are disabled. The expertise that emerges from disability can be invaluable, in churches that do not know how to include those whom they have unwittingly but painfully excluded. But when storytellers tried to share their advocacy and expertise in disability access and justice, many met with resistance. When an inaccessible church website kept Hazel and Victor from joining social events at their church, Hazel asked whether she could redesign the website to meet accessibility standards for blind people. Her offer went ignored:

> One of the jobs that I do, employment that I do, is test websites. And I've actually told them. I said, 'You know, I test them. [The website] is not good ...' But no one is doing anything about it.

It was a sharp contrast with Hazel's secular life, where she is a professional whose access expertise is respected. Miranda, another experienced access consultant, was disappointed when clergy were uninterested in her offers of advice on improving step-free access, at a church where access was so difficult, it eventually factored into her decision to leave. These churches were sitting on a wealth of expertise that could help them become more accessible to all disabled people. Yet there was a clash between these churches' image of a disabled person as someone who passively receives from others' ministry, and the reality of the experienced disabled experts in their congregation. When pastoral power cannot recognise disabled people's wisdom, our distinctive gifts can be undervalued.

When disabled storytellers' service and expertise were not

recognised, they were often left vulnerable and dependent, their participation in church life curtailed. In an inaccessible church building, Isabelle was reliant on the support of other members of her community to get around. When her church was reordered, she jumped at the opportunity to advise on wheelchair access, as an expert by experience. But the church turned down Isabelle's offer of service:

> I kept saying, 'Can I be involved with the access?', etc. 'No. We're involving someone. It will be fine.' You know, 'We've brought in a company who knows what they're doing.' And then they make things that are really impractical ... Instead of a single door on the church, we ended up with double ones which weren't wide enough either side for a wheelchair by about an inch ... And changing the lock on the door so [I] can't get to the toilet. I know it's fine. Someone should go and do it for you. But there's something about having to ask. You shouldn't have to ask.

The pastoral model led Isabelle's church to believe that solutions come from 'experts' – who lacked the true expertise that comes from disabled people's lived experience. Mistakes that Isabelle could easily have spotted left her even more reliant on the help of others for basic access to church. For Isabelle, the indignity of constantly 'having to ask' for access was the fallout. Churches that only offer the bare minimum of access force disabled people to become dependent. Kt reflected on why *having to ask* can be so disempowering for us:

> Kt: There should be a good model of interdependency ... [A community] should model: 'Isn't it great we can help each other? But actually, it ends up being: And I'm going to have to ask for help again.

Non-disabled people may argue that, as a church community, we are already all interdependent on each other. But this pat answer overlooks the power differentials between disabled and non-disabled people. Few non-disabled people are regularly left waiting in the rain for someone else to open doors. Not only do we have to ask all the time, we may not always get the help we ask for. For disabled people, goodwill is a precarious thing; not every church member treats us with grace. In churches where they were forced to become dependent on others' care and support, the pastoral model reinforced the disempowering stereotype that disabled people have only limits and needs, keeping storytellers from serving. It was a vicious cycle, for many storytellers.

For some disabled people, when church pastoral care sees us as incapable, the dependency it creates can be actively harmful for us. For nearly a year, Mary worked in a position of leadership, in an internship in a Church of England congregation. When she declared her mental health diagnoses, church leaders were initially positive:

> Before I went there I told them I [about my condition], and they were like, 'That's fine, we still want you. We really like you. You'll be great.'

But the work environment at the church began contributing to Mary's worsening mental health. She left university; self-harm became more troubling for her. As her mental health worsened, the church began to focus on Mary's pastoral care. Leadership made it a requirement of Mary's internship to accept counselling from a fellow congregant with no qualifications. The counselling was not only ineffective, it contributed to Mary's distress. 'It all went out of my hands,' Mary said, lamenting the loss of her agency. Reflecting on what went wrong in her internship, Mary called for better education in churches about mental distress, and more awareness of the harm that uninformed, unwanted pastoral support can cause:

> I think people in churches are well-meaning but they don't really know what they're talking about. And it's really not the best thing to recommend that someone who has a mental illness talks to someone else who's not professional ... It's fine if you're just feeling a bit down. But once you started taking it out on yourself and you dropped out of uni and you're failing everything, then it's not really the best thing for them to have done.

Seeing their pastoral care as the answer to Mary's needs, rather than part of the problem, the church could not look humbly beyond their own pastoral care for the support that Mary needed, and refer her to professional support services.[241] The church community made harmful mistakes in an attempt to meet Mary's needs. With Mary receiving more appropriate support elsewhere, the community might have been able to focus on nurturing her gifts as a leader, even in the midst of her illness. But the church was not yet ready for Mary's service. Mary has continued to serve faithfully from the edge of churches, sharing share peer support and solidarity with other Christians experiencing distress:

> I'll do everything I can to help other people ... When I'm talking to young people, teenagers, I quite often tell them that what they're going through now is going to help someone else, because they'll overcome it and then they'll be able to help someone else ... I just talk about my mental health. I don't hide anything.

After her difficult experiences of professional-led pastoral care in churches, Mary came to believe that disabled people can better support each other, through shared experience.[242] This is not a form of pastoral service typically recognised in churches, where pastoral power still flows from leadership to disabled people. Yet Mary's distinctive service could have helped to transform these churches' pastoral care among disabled people, helping them to understand that disabled people can empower, lead and serve each other. It could only have happened in a church where they were able to see Mary's distinctive gifts, rather than allowing her pastoral care needs to eclipse them.

We heard other stories of similar painful pastoral care failures, in churches that saw themselves as the charitable answer to disabled people's problems, but where they were unprepared for the reality of disabled people's lives. Claire's pastor doubted whether her ME/CFS was real. Maria was told by ministers that Christians should not take antidepressant medication. Leah was told by a church leader that she could not possibly be autistic, invalidating her experience of neurodiversity. And Mims found some clergy unable to deal with her experiences of distress:

> I went [to church] quite manic one night and I was talking to one of the priests after an evening service ... She just sat there looking

at me completely blankly. I mean, what I was saying probably was quite mad, but there wasn't any response from her ... She just looked completely out of her depth and like she didn't know what to say.

Church communities tend to see themselves as the solution to needs that arise from illness,[243] as theologian Stephen Pattison argues:

It is indicative of a trend in Christianity to regard itself as perfect, omnipotent and all-sufficient in its own right. That means ministers and others may be very reluctant to acquire relevant knowledge and techniques from non-church sources such as psychotherapy and counselling. It also means they may be unwilling to acknowledge the limits and failures of belonging to a religious community and using 'religious' methods and techniques.[244]

When leaders and communities could only see disabled storytellers through a pastoral lens, churches elevated themselves to the *answer* to disability, rather than asking whether their pastoral care was part of the *problem*. As they saw disability as an individual issue, and often imagined their own charity as sufficient to 'fix' it, churches failed to see disabled people's need for justice – or their own role in injustice.

There is a gap between the pastoral rhetoric of welcome and the reality of inaccessibility and injustice in churches. Disabled people have gifts that can help to fill that gap, but only if churches can first listen to our critiques of pastoral power. To make the most of disabled people's gifts, churches must shift away from pastoral models of charity and care, and start seeing us as experts in our own needs, as Kt and Zoe told us:

Zoe: We become our own expert don't we? And that's the biggest message, isn't it, in terms of access? If I leave nothing else with the churches I'm working with, it's, 'How about asking people in your church how you can help them?' Quite simple but massive.
Kt: Yeah. I know me better than you do.

Disabled people are used to having our experience overlooked by a society that devalues everything about us. As disability scholars describe it, our lives and ways of being are rarely seen as having 'worthwhile existential status'.[245] Communities that can only imagine disabled people as bringing *needs*, will fail to see how God can bless churches through our experience, knowledge and service. When disabled people's gifts go unrecognised, we cannot participate in shaping a Kingdom vision of justice for all in our churches.

Ordained Ministry, Church Leadership and Disabled People

> 'Is there space for me to be a leader and participate in the church, completely as I am? Because sometimes I'm not sure. If I'm tired, or I need to sit down because I'm in pain, and I preach, will people see that weakness and question whether I'm competent?'
> ### Esther

'Even as a child, I had this real sense that I wanted to be a priest.' This is how Esther began her story — not with the years of discrimination she has faced through her long journey to ordination, but with a testimony of her calling. But Esther's journey to ordination has been a long struggle against injustice. It was a recurring theme among the disabled church leaders, ordinands and priests we spoke to. Regardless of the denomination in which they served, many of these ministers had institutional ableism in common.

As she grew up watching her church community respond to her mother's impairments, Esther was already internalising a sense of how disabled people with a calling to ministry are treated in churches:

> She had lots of mental health problems. Then, towards the end of her life, she was more and more disabled with MS. I don't think I realised it at the time, but I was watching the church's response

to her, and seeing a lot of mismatch. I didn't like what I saw ... I watched [her] gradually become an outsider and have to let go of her calling to ordained ministry.

By the time Esther went to Bible college, she was experiencing her own mental health problems. In one of several incidents there, she was barred from going on a placement she had organised for her cohort, as staff told Esther that her mental health problems could destroy the college's reputation. 'Clearly, I was mentally ill and I couldn't be trusted', is how Esther summed up the discrimination. It was to be the first of many sanist, disablist incidents that would bar Esther's way to ordination, over and over again. Bruised by her experiences at Bible college, and now diagnosed with fibromyalgia as well, Esther went through periods of self-doubt about whether God would call a disabled person like her to the priesthood. 'Clearly, there isn't space for people like me [in the ministry],' she thought. Yet, in the midst of her struggle, meeting ministers with experience of mental distress was a turning point for her. When Esther could see that God had called other disabled clergy and church leaders, Esther knew the same could still be true for her too.

With the support of her church leader, Esther entered the Church of England vocational process. It would be yet another painful battle against discriminatory attitudes, under the scrutiny of vocational committees, which are often made up of people who share society's prejudices towards disabled people. At her first Bishops' Advisory Panel (BAP) interview, Esther's interviewer focused on her working-class background and experiences of illness. For Esther, these are the challenges through which God has shaped her gifts, a potential source of blessing to churches. But for her interviewer, these social disadvantages were signs that Esther would be a problem to the Church of England:

This man sat there, from beginning to end, with an attitude that demonstrated very clearly to me that he'd already made up his mind about me ... He focused on all my weaknesses ... He looked on it as if, 'You're not reliable.' The first thing he said to me was, 'Why should the bishop spend all that money on you?'

This was another moment where Esther could easily have given up on her call to ordination, had an ally not intervened. Esther met with her bishop, who made the unorthodox decision to send her back to selection committee again the following year. The next year, she was approved to train for ordination.

But one more incident of discrimination would bring Esther to the brink of career-ending disaster before she was even ordained. She was offered a role as a curate, in a church where leadership were supportive of her disability access and health needs. But curacies can only be taken up on condition of a successful occupational medical assessment. Esther failed the medical, just two months before her ordination, despite reassurances that the medical was just a formality, to help make 'reasonable adjustments' to her role.[246] 'I'd already bought my robes,' Esther said. 'This was heart-breaking.' It looked as though one interview with a stranger was about to end her journey to ordination – again. Esther was devastated:

> I've had to prove myself in ways that so many other people don't.
> I meet one person, and my whole future could potentially hang in the balance.

One more time, an ally stepped up, one who believed in Esther and could see past institutional barriers. Esther's training college put her in touch with a senior officer in the diocese. 'She was one of the first people to acknowledge how hard this was,' Esther remembered. With the diocesan officer's help, Esther put together reports from psychiatrists, leaders at churches where she had worked, and staff at her college. It was extra labour that many non-disabled people will never have to do to prove themselves. To have any effect, the reports would need to downplay Esther's impairments, rather than showing how her disability could be a source of gifts. But finally, Esther was given medical approval to begin her curacy.

Reflecting on her experience, Esther was sure that the discriminatory attitudes she encountered did not arise out of nowhere. They were rooted in bad theology and institutionally ableist church structures. When disabled people's calling as ministers is underestimated, it begins with a limiting theology of disability that cannot imagine how disabled people can be priests. Disabled ministers are forced to prove they can 'overcome' disability, as though it is a deficit that must be hidden from view. Instead, for Esther, disability is one of the ways God has shaped her gifts, and is a vital part of her.

> I was sponsored to be tried for the calling of stipendiary ministry. That's with everything that I bring. You can't separate those things out, because actually the most powerful thing that I have to give in ministry is what I have learned through my journey. I wouldn't have that depth if I hadn't been through and continue to go through what I go through. [But] people want to put aside the uncomfortable bits.

Esther was clear that the institutional church must dismantle ableism in its theology and culture. A lethal combination of bad theology and ableist church structures left Esther struggling against Christian ableism, working twice as hard as others to show how God is calling her *with* her experience of disability, not in spite of it.

'How are you going to do communion?' Barriers to disabled people's ministry

❝ One of [the priests] keeps saying, 'Well, how are you going to do communion?' Well, we'll just move. We'll just put the table out the front [of the raised altar]. ❞ Isabelle

In churches, a ministerial *ideal* defines the perfect church leader, who represents God. Our modern, fallible prejudices about perfection shape the Christian image of the ideal priest. Storytellers in church leadership had to negotiate their ministry around church buildings and cultures that privileged non-disabled bodies and minds. These inaccessible structures of place and culture often find their origins in church policy towards disabled ministers and clergy. In the 1980s, Nancy Eiesland criticised the American Lutheran Church for its ableist institutional policies that allowed the church to discriminate, based on an assumption that disabled people were unlikely to be suitable ordinands because they could cause 'distraction and congregational discomfort' and disruption to ritual.[247] Today's institutional churches vary in their policies about disabled clergy. Some have frameworks anticipating how they will make 'reasonable adjustments' for disabled and chronically ill ministers.[248] The Church of England, on the other hand, still has a canon law that reads:

> No person shall be admitted into holy orders who is suffering, or who has suffered from any physical or mental infirmity which in the opinion of the bishop will prevent him from ministering the word and sacraments of or from performing the other duties of the minister's office.[249]

We have already seen this policy made manifest in Esther's experiences of barriers to ordination. As disabled minister Tim Rourke has pointed out, this canon law individualises disability, making the ableist assumption that impairment itself can 'prevent' people from serving as minister.[250] As it asks disabled people to prove they are not *too* disabled to join the non-disabled church hierarchy, it treats disability as a deficit that falls short of priestly perfection, rather than addressing the stumbling-blocks churches place in the way of disabled ministers. Impairment is not a barrier to church leadership — institutional ableism is. There has been very little research on disabled clergy, and we do not know how widespread their experiences of institutional ableism are.[251] But in the stories in this book, we see disabled people facing barriers at every level of leadership, from processes of ordination or selection for ministry, to the day-to-day work of pastoring churches. Many of these barriers are rooted in a pastoral model that expects disabled people to be served in churches, but cannot imagine us in leadership.

Church architecture reinforces the idea that disabled people are passive objects of ministry, while non-disabled people lead.[252] Storytellers in ministry were expected to preach from raised pulpits, stand for the

Gospel, and offer communion from altars with steps. As a mobility-impaired priest in the Church of England, Kt noticed how much of the traditional role of a minister is based on a 'physically able way' of leading, shaped by church architecture:

> It was that kind of construct that says things can only happen if you do it in an able-bodied way. Like prayer ministry, having to stand up. And to preach you should be in the pulpit really, because that's what we do in our church. No, I can preach from the floor, thanks.

Ableist leadership practices are shaped by inaccessible church environments – and vice versa. Zoe is a priest with a chronic pain condition, who remembered serving as a visiting minister in an Anglo-Catholic church in her deanery. Clergy were unhappy when Zoe asked to sit to assist with communion:

> And when it came to being there for a month and assisting with the Eucharist. 'But you can stand to do that can't you?' 'No.' 'But you can stand to do this can't you?' 'No.' 'Well, how will you read the Gospel if you're not going to stand?' And then we got to [lifting] the chalice and it was: 'Well, don't bother.' And I had to sit there and say, 'It's really difficult I know, but that is what I've been ordained for.' [The priest] was saying that parishioners were going to find it difficult. And it really wasn't the parishioners. I ended up saying, 'Do you know what, I do this every week somewhere else in this deanery. Your church ain't that different.'

With a priestly culture shaped in part by their building, clergy at this church struggled to adapt around a disabled priest. Standing to read the Gospel or assist with communion was not inherent to Zoe's role, but these were part of the church's rigid ideal of what a priest does. Zoe had to negotiate carefully around her access needs, balancing respect for church practices with refusing to give up her right to minister in ways that were accessible to her.

It is not only the physical aspects of ministry that are barriers to disabled leaders' ministry. Cultural barriers can bar the way to leadership, especially when disabled people do not fit churches' ideal of the non-disabled priest or minister. Andrew, who is Deaf, was at one point being prepared for ministry by his non-denominational evangelical church. 'I felt my particular gift was in teaching,' Andrew said, 'whether preaching or in a small group.' Andrew's community was encouraging of his ministry. And yet everything Andrew was expected to do as a church leader was inaccessible to him. He could not lead small discussions in home groups, because he could not follow informal conversation or hear others' prayers with his eyes closed. Preaching became increasingly difficult when he could not follow the teaching at his church. His church community could have worked to dismantle these cultural and structural barriers, but they did little to enable his ministry as a Deaf person. When Andrew said, 'I didn't fit into the way they did church,' he was reflecting particularly on leadership. At his church, the ideal minister was hearing, not Deaf. Cultural barriers placed the same kinds of limits on Rhona's ministry as a local preacher in the Methodist Church. Church leaders found it difficult to imagine how they could adapt communion around a blind minister:

> I [assist with] a communion on a Wednesday morning sometimes which means going round with the individual little glasses ... on the tray. And somebody high up in our circuit said: 'Well, you can't do it.' 'Why?' 'Well, you can't see to walk round with it, can you?'

There was no reason why Rhona could not share communion differently, but rigid cultural expectations of how ministers should 'do communion' were a barrier to her leadership. It was another failure of imagination, where a non-disabled majority church could not see past their priestly ideal. Yet congregants could easily come to Rhona to receive, she pointed out. 'They can take the cup off me.' Rhona's disabled perspective led her to imagine communion – and leadership – differently.

For some storytellers, issues of physical access, church cultures and the ideal of the priest all collided, compounding the barriers to ministry. Emma had been a lay pioneer minister[253] in the Church of England for several years when she became chronically ill with a number of auto-immune conditions. Losing most of her eyesight and mobility in the space of just a few weeks, Emma suddenly found herself no longer able to read the words of hymns, find friends or navigate the church building. On top of these barriers to worship, Emma was suddenly faced with occupational barriers to her ministry that she could never have anticipated:

> My licence was up for renewal and somebody in Church House basically said, 'So now you're disabled, we won't be renewing [your ministry licence].' So I forwarded the email to my bishop. And he rang me up and he went, 'Yeah, leave it with me. What nonsense. God called you. God knew this was going to happen. God is calling you still.'

In an echo of Esther's story, it was only because an influential ally intervened that this apparently routine occupational disability discrimination was prevented. It would otherwise have forced Emma out of ministry, simply because she is disabled. The encouragement from the bishop was a turning point for Emma, renewing her sense of God's calling even in the midst of new experiences of disability. 'I needed to hear that,' she reflected. In a Church where disabled people are not expected to lead, serving as a disabled minister can be a confidence-shaking challenge. For Emma, the barriers have still not gone away:

> Over the last four years I've found that the least enabling and least accessible place is the church – not my parish church, but the organisation of the church. Every training or meeting requires a journey and often ends up in an inaccessible building. Every time, I have to ask for material to be emailed because I can't see anything printed or on screen – this is a huge challenge and causes issues almost every time.

Emma has found that the institutional church assumes that its ministers are non-disabled, expressed in the way the Church of England 'does leadership'. This assumption creates structural barriers, keeping Emma from ministering as effectively as non-disabled people. But this has been far from the end of Emma's story. Disability was a new beginning for Emma's ministry, as God called her into service with other disabled people who have been hurt by churches. Writing to us during the early days of the pandemic, Emma left us with sobering last words about ableism in the church where she serves:

> Who knows what the future months will bring or how the church will leap back into ableist thinking and leave us behind. But I'll keep shouting that it's not okay.

Navigating the often ableist power structures of churches is easier with support from allies and a community. Some storytellers in leadership were personally known and loved in church communities that came to see the gifts they had to offer. Isabelle had been known in her church for many years. When she first began discerning her vocation as a non-stipendiary minister, Isabelle expected negative reactions, after past experiences of ableism in Christian communities. She was delighted when her church supported her ministry:

> I thought people would think, 'Why can't we have someone healthy doing it?' But actually there hasn't been [that reaction]. And they were told that I'd been accepted [for ordination] on Easter Sunday, and the whole church erupted into clapping. It was really affirming.

In a similar story, Emma told us how, as she adapted to her new impairments, her congregation accepted her different ways of leading and offering pastoral care:

> The people within church and the people within community have just been fabulous. They've known me a long time. So they've seen me change and [given me] so much positivity and support, no negativity … When I say to people, 'Look, I'm a wheelchair user. Would you mind coming to me? Because my house is totally accessible, because I can't get in yours.' They're like, 'Of course, that would be wonderful.'

The congregation's attitude was a complete contrast with people who did not know Emma, especially other clergy. Knowing Emma and Isabelle well, their church communities came to see that they were every bit as called and capable as non-disabled ministers. Of course, these churches were not perfect, but these congregations saw past limiting pastoral model beliefs about the role of disabled Christians. Disabled people's ministry of presence can transform churches. Yet disabled clergy should not be left dependent on finding an understanding community where they are accepted as individuals. Frustratingly, many storytellers were.

Isabelle and Emma were embraced by their churches in their ministries, but they were in the minority. Churches' ideas of perfection are more often based on ableist cultural values, many seeking this perfection in their leaders. When churches can only imagine a priest as non-disabled, disabled ministers must hide the truth of who they are, in what disability theory calls *compulsory non-disability*.[254] Disabled people had to adapt to the role of minister, but churches rarely adapted the role to them.[255] A few churches saw past limiting pastoral model expectations, seeing the potential for disabled people to serve and lead, just as they are. But most storytellers experienced *ministerial marginality*,[256] in churches that could not easily imagine disabled people as ministers or priests. In their experiences, we may even hear echoes of Levitical laws that kept stigmatised disabled people out of the holiest places in the Temple. Yet, as Jesus fulfilled the Old Covenant, he opened the Temple gates and welcomed disabled people in. Ancient laws about access to priesthood should have no more power in our churches.

The answer is not simply to decide to *invite* more disabled people to minister in ableist churches. Not without first dismantling the institutional, cultural and architectural barriers that make it difficult or impossible for disabled people to serve and lead. Denominational cultures that see disability as deficit are backed up by church policy, manifested through vocational committees and other gatekeepers that may know little about disability. For those disabled people who are accepted into ordination or leadership, the role of the minister remains fraught with occupational barriers, not least because of an unspoken expectation that ministers should be super-human, working punishing hours with little flexibility – an unhelpful standard for any minister, disabled or not. All these barriers can have a chilling effect on disabled people exploring a call to ordination or leadership, leaving some discouraged from discerning their vocation before they even begin, as Esther told us:

Unless the whole culture changes, unless everybody gets on board with it, you are still going to get disabled people either too afraid [to explore their calling], or they have stood up and said, 'I want to explore my vocation', and they've been told, 'No'.

Unless churches address their institutional ableism, the non-disabled ideal of the priest will never change, and disabled people will remain marginalised in ministry.

The Transformative Service of Disabled Christians

⁶I see [that] as what my ministry is, to make it all right for people to be limited.⁹ Zoe

In churches that are ready to value disabled people, we may find good soil, where the ground has been prepared to nurture our gifts. In the face of priestly ideals and institutional ableism, faithful disabled storytellers modelled a different way to minister, showing the Church that it is possible for the same person to be served and to serve others. This should not be revolutionary; the Church should have learned this from Jesus' ministry of mutual hospitality. When more disabled people are enabled to lead, perhaps we will all come to understand that people from every background can be called into God's service.

Jemma knew that disabled people can only serve when we are enabled to serve. 'I am growing in my church and I am able to take on responsibility to serve and lead,' she said. Her church was working to recognise her gifts and make service accessible to her, within a growing disability-positive culture where she could flourish. Alongside her general gifts of leadership, the church began to recognise Jemma's distinctive disability ministry, as she reached out to others on the edge. In the midst of the COVID pandemic, Jemma began to run one of the church's social media accounts, using her digital gifts – developed as a disabled person who accesses the world through technology – to help her church expand their online ministry:

> Through serving I am able to grow in the gifts that God has given me and help others ... During lockdown I am leading a Zoom prayer meeting for anyone that wants to join at my church. This has been a big step for me ... but all the feedback I have had has been encouraging.

Encouraging Jemma to work in an internship at her church, the church worked to make the role accessible to her. Her path to leadership was gradually being made into level ground by a community that recognised her gifts and enabled her ministry.[257] It was interdependence in action; the church was just as blessed by Jemma's ministry as she was blessed by the accessible church culture that enabled her service.

Like Jemma, Susanna had gifts that arose from her lived experience as a disabled person. Susanna's house group recognised her gifts of prayer as a distinctive form of service to her church:

> The prayer ministry is something that is really important to me because one of the few things that I can do as part of a Sunday service is I can pray. Our house group was thinking and praying about this, and we developed a prayer ministry for Sunday mornings.

The reasons that some disabled people have the gift of time may not be pleasant, especially when we find ourselves unable to work or function to a degree that may leave us poor, isolated and made vulnerable. And yet God can use all these circumstances, in churches that are willing and able to see our distinctive gifts. The new prayer ministry drew in not just Susanna, but others in the congregation. As Susanna's community began to see her as someone who could serve others, they were blessed not just by her prayer ministry, but by others she drew into service with her.

For a few storytellers, the simple fact of their existence as disabled people in ministry and service profoundly changed their churches for other disabled congregants in their churches. It was a ministry of presence.[258] At Emma's church, Herman was a lifelong congregant. In his last year of life, as his mobility declined, Herman used a wheelchair to get to church. That was when Emma began to realise how her ministry empowered others:

People would push him up in the wheelchair and it was wonderful. And I said to him, one day, 'I'm so pleased you still come.' [In our church] there's me and one other, we're both wheelchair users. And Herman said, 'If you two didn't come to church in wheelchairs, I never would have felt I could.'

Herman was in church on the last Sunday of his life. Emma's visible presence as a disabled leader had a profound impact on Herman's sense that he could be welcome in church. In activist parlance, Emma was modelling the maxim *You can't be what you can't see.*[259] In churches where disabled people have a visible role in leadership and service,[260] we have a vital role in opening the gates to other disabled people, who might otherwise never come to church at all.

Seeking this level of transformation in their churches, some storytellers worked hard to shift their churches' thinking on disability. Slowly, some churches came with them on a journey beyond a limiting pastoral model of disability, to an understanding of the potential of disabled people's service. Mims faithfully advocated for her church to include mental health in their disability ministry:

The priest that was in charge couldn't – wouldn't – see mental health as a disability ... I actually had to go to a meeting and literally go through the history of the mental health movement ... But it was actually quite a convincing argument. We went in one meeting from them not really believing that mental health was a disability, to a week later me being asked to talk at the next meeting and it mainly being about mental health.

Calling for disability justice in churches almost always involves a fight for recognition, at first, as Mims found. This is prophetic work, in churches that may have an inadequate understanding of people with mental distress, especially as a justice issue.[261] Mims' expertise was a gift to her church. As they came to see Mims as an expert, not just in her own needs but in her disability advocacy for her community, the whole church benefitted. As churches and Christian communities begin to centre disabled people's experience, there will be disabled prophets in congregations who are willing to draw on painful experiences of access failures, to help transform churches into places of justice for disabled people.[262] At Mims' church, an increasingly diverse disability ministry is part of her legacy there.

Disabled people's ministry of presence may be challenging to the churches where we are calling for transformation. The disruption that comes with our leadership may be a source of fear to communities that prefer the status quo, as Kt told us. In one church where she served as priest, Kt sat to offer communion, and parishioners came to her to receive it. Some preferred to receive from a standing priest, who offered communion from person to person, in a way Kt could not. Kt actively confronted her community with their ableist attitudes, asking them to choose whether they wanted to receive from the (seated) priest, or to receive from lay servers:

> If the important thing is that the priest gives it to you, then I will sit in the middle on a stool and you can come to me. But, I said, you have to choose. Because it will change from what you're used to, and it is a practical change. It's not a theological one. We're not doing anything bad with the bread and the wine. God is still here. I just say the words and he does the rest, which is very handy. So in the same way that my gender doesn't affect what God does to the bread and wine, neither does my disability ... But of course, for a lot of people, they struggle with that.

Kt asked people to think about what was theologically important in the role of a priest or leader, and what was only expected of priests because of tradition, appearances and ableism. If taking communion 'properly' was so important to the congregation, Kt knew that most of them would eventually come to accept it from a disabled priest. Disabled people's bodies and minds can be disruptive, never fading quietly into the background in the way the godly bodies of priests are supposed to.[263] As disabled ministers disrupt the expectation that priests must be powerful and self-sufficient in order to represent God, they challenge power and privilege in church hierarchies. Zoe remembered how her presence as a visiting minister in one church challenged their pastoral model ideas about who ministers, and who is in church to be ministered to. 'It was absolutely about that power dynamic,' she reflected. Yet, in the long run, Zoe's presence helped to transform the church: 'It went very well, the month there, and it's changed things,' she said. Through a faithful ministry of presence, disabled clergy and leaders can help churches to accept our disruption not as unholy but as prophetic, as we help communities to rethink their limiting beliefs about who offers ministry and service, and who is in church to be ministered to.

At first, that may mean a slow, painful struggle against ableist values in churches. Yet this is vital work. Despite the ableism disabled leaders may face, their leadership is prophetic, bringing transformation to churches. Disabled people's service can challenge churches' theology of weakness, strength and power, leading the Church back to a biblical model of interdependence. Sometimes, disabled people's limits are at the heart of our ministry, as Zoe powerfully described:

> For most of us, the gifts are our limits ... I see [that] as what my ministry is, to make it all right for people to be limited. Because then if you start by saying 'I could really do with a hand with this. Do you mind getting that for me? Oh, and let me know if there's anything I can do for you,' it's incredibly empowering. But in a really different way to society.

As a disabled person, Zoe's awareness of her body was a gospel ministry, echoing the undignified humility of a God who limited Godself for us all. In society and churches alike, some limits and needs are acceptable, and some are stigmatised.[264] Disabled people's limits have always been judged; we have been seen as monstrous, inhuman, inherently vulnerable, unworthy of society's resources, and too impure to enter the Temple.[265] We can be uncomfortable reminders of the fragility and mortality of all bodies. We transform these ableist attitudes when we show how living with impairment or illness 'creates different *ways of being* that gives disabled people valuable perspectives on life and the world'.[266] In the face of underestimation, discrimination, dismissal of our gifts, and institutional barriers, disabled people's faithful leadership can show churches a more authentic practice of genuine mutual support, among all who share in community life. In Desmond Tutu's words, 'God has created us for interdependence as God has created us in His image – the image of a divine fellowship of the holy and blessed Trinity ... God has created us to be different in order that we can realize our need of one another.'[267] If churches can come to see the value of disabled people's different and distinctive ministries, they may learn to see beyond a pastoral model that limits our participation in Christian community life. Then will the Body of Christ see how God calls people with every kind of body and mind to leadership and service.

'If You Can't Go, Then I Don't Want to Go': Theologies of Participation

For most of Christian history, churches have focused on *care* for disabled people, rather than enabling our *participation*, as disciples and leaders. This is not to say that pastoral care in churches is unimportant; disabled people may seek pastoral support in all kinds of life struggles, whether related to disability or not. But when disabled people's role in churches is *only* to receive paternalistic care and charity from the non-disabled majority, we are held back from playing a full role in the community life of the Church. And when it is not paired with an examination of injustice, pastoral care can fail to recognise disability oppression.[268]

Disabled people have given the world alternative models of care, models that value our participation. Feminist disability scholar Margaret Price believes that, if communities truly care about disabled people, they will ensure that everyone can play a full part in the life of that community.[269] In the words of disability activist Mia Mingus, this vision of care says, 'If you can't go, then I don't want to go.'[270] So a congregation might decide not to use an inaccessible space for a service, because if a disabled person can't come to the Banquet, no one in the community will want to be there. *Where you go, I will go.*[271] *Where you cannot go, I will not go either.* Inspired by this collective vision of care, some disabled people are caring for and enabling each other, in the midst of an ableist world where

Our care had been something it wasn't safe for us to say we needed, because there was no care out there ... as disabled people, if we wanted to have any kind of independence, we had to deny that we needed any help at all.[272]

As they challenge disempowering care systems through their own consciously interdependent communities, the disabled-led care communities of the Disability Justice movement are weaving together 'a collective commitment and way of being',[273] where they 'dream care for each other into being'.[274] They are showing us that interdependence is about justice. It means becoming alert to ableism, to the ways we make some people more dependent than others, even as we hide our own dependency. This is care that ensures that disabled people can participate, knowing that the community is incomplete without us. This is care that empowers us all to serve and be served. This is care that shares power, between those who have traditionally offered service and those who have traditionally received it.

In the Epistles, Paul gives us a Christian model of interdependent caring communities that chimes with these disabled people's vision of care. Reflecting on spiritual gifts, Paul tells us that every part of the Body is unique and irreplaceable, and that the most unexpected members of churches have gifts to share in service to their communities:

The eye cannot say to the hand, 'I don't need you!' And the head cannot say to the feet, 'I don't need you!' On the contrary, those parts of the body that seem to be weaker are indispensable ... But God has put the body together, giving greater honour to the parts that lacked it, so that there should be no division in the body, but that its parts should have equal concern for each other.[275]

Do not overlook the gifts of those who 'seem to be weaker,' Paul advises the church in Corinth. The diversity of the Body of Christ is its strength. For our storytellers, this diversity looks like active participation and leadership, as disabled people — 'to be able to participate as I am', as storyteller Esther put it. In churches where we all share power, we will

127

all move between roles, sometimes caring for others, and sometimes allowing ourselves to be cared for.

Disability theologian Doreen Freeman believes disabled people need more than pastoral care from churches.[276] Disabled people have deeper insights about disability to share with churches, she says. We bring these insights from the disability culture that celebrates our lives, the theologies through which God liberates us, and the sociology that examines ableism and oppression.[277] Disabled people will only be seen as more than opportunities for others' ministry when churches come to see us as co-creators in Kingdom communities: not just as objects of care, but as blessings to the Church.[278] Because, in the words of disability theologian Heather Renée Morgan, 'the Body of Christ cannot be the full Body without the inclusion, participation, belonging, encouragement and active engagement of the spiritual gifts of all our bodies and minds, disabled and abled alike'.[279] Together with disabled people, the whole Church can be enriched by a new vision of *ministry with* each other.

PART TWO
Opening the Gates:
Disabled Prophets Speak

CHAPTER 5

Theology at the Gates: Disabled People Telling Our Own Stories

In 2016, disabled Christians and allies gathered for a conference titled 'Prophets and Seers: Calling from the Edge'. That year, the annual Living Edge conference was inspired by the work of blind theologian John Hull, as we remembered his call for the church to listen to the prophetic ministry of disabled Christians. Addressing the conference via a streamed talk from his home, disabled Methodist minister Donald Eadie told us:

> Theology must not be left to the fit and strong. Theology must also be wrestled for through pain and disability; these are the raw materials of our encounters with a mysterious, silent, hidden and powerless God … It is our experience that the church finds it difficult to receive the gifts of God through those who live with impairments. We are an uncomfortable presence.[280]

Disabled people speak not from the centre but from the edge; not from a place of power, but from the midst of marginalisation, rejection and weakness. As we do, we offer our experiences as gifts to the Church. Eadie told us – experiences of darkness, waiting, pain, and of our bodies as the dwelling-place of God.

But the Church has not always received the gifts we share. The Church too often speaks about disabled people, without us.[281] Just as we have been for centuries, disabled people are still the objects of non-disabled people's thinking, as they try to make sense of a world where disability is part of the mystery of human reality. Fiona MacMillan and Samuel Wells reflect on why this is a problem:

> So much of the time the voices heard on disability – particularly in the church – are non-disabled people who speak from study or research or observation or living alongside someone. Theirs is good and important work, but somehow it has become the dominating voice ... There are insights to be gained and huge amounts to be understood, but it is from the centre looking out, rather than from the edge ... If it is the only voice, it can do damage. There is a power that comes with being listened to, being heard. But that can only ever happen when we are willing to speak, and if we have the opportunity, the tools, and resources.[282]

To be constantly spoken about without the opportunity to speak about oneself is silencing.[283] When only non-disabled voices are heard in the Church, the result is a gospel for non-disabled people.[284] Others impacted by disability may have important experience to share, as carers and family members. But disabled people have our own stories to tell the Church, rooted in our lived experience of difference, oppression, and another *way of being*.

Disabled people are beginning to speak back, however, in stories *by* us and *for* us, and by allies who centre our stories. This is theology from the gates.[285] As disability theologian Shane Clifton tells us, *crip theology* is reimagining disability, not as a mistake or a problem to be fixed, but as part of God's good creation. This is 'a way of thinking about what it means to be a human soul, a bodymind, in relation to God, others, and the natural world'.[286] Disabled Christians are speaking about ourselves from the margins, on social media, in rare disabled-led conferences and video series, and in poetry, memoir and storytelling.[287] We could call these stories *lived theology*, but that would make them sound less important than books by elite theologians.[288] In fact, storytellers' prophetic stories, rooted in their lives as disabled people, can renew the Church from the edge.

In this chapter, storytellers share their distinctive disability theologies of God, faith, and humanity. They tell stories of *God with us,* as they reflect on what the incarnation means for people living with impairments, and what their experiences can teach the whole Church about our common humanity. They share stories of *God like us* – a disabled Christ, resurrected with his scars, who affirms disabled people as we are. And they tell stories of *God for us,* a God of the margins, who calls the Church to live out Kingdom justice. But first, they tell us about the difficulties of telling their own stories and finding theology that speaks to their experiences. A Church that wants to be different from the world must seek to listen to stories like these. Transformation of ableist theologies will only come when we open the conversation to new voices.

Theology About Us, Without Us

‘It's hard to find material about disability and theology that is actually written by disabled people.’ Jemma

As storytellers told us, the barriers that kept them from contributing to the Christian conversation about them were substantial. To speak, lead and be listened to in the Church takes money, education, expertise, energy, and accessible resources.[289] Many disabled people do not have these privileges. Because of these and other structural barriers, we are under-represented in paid academic positions, in the universities and seminaries where theology of disability is written.[290] When academia has a long history of researching disability without disabled people's input,[291] it is hardly surprising that theology of disability is also dominated by non-disabled scholars. This is what philosopher Miranda Fricker calls *epistemic injustice*[292] – our lived experience is not part of accepted knowledge about us.

The first hurdle for our storytellers was finding any disability theology that centred disabled people's own experiences of disability, written *by* and *for* disabled Christians. They rarely knew where find teaching that reflected their lived experience of disability and faith, as Jemma told us:

It's hard to find material about disability and theology that is actually written by disabled people. Many, many books are written about disabled people and the Church, but our own voices are not heard.

Even ministers did not always know where to find the stories of the disabled people of God. Esther was an ordinand attending a college with liberation theology programmes, but she had not been able to find disability theology with relevance to her life and faith:

> Officially, no, I haven't discovered any disability theology. I don't know where I would find it. I'm keen to.

When storytellers did find some theology of disability, it was dominated by non-disabled people. Jane could only find non-disabled voices leading the discussion about disability and faith. She did not know where to find more authentic reflections of her disabled experience in Christian teaching:

> I used to belong to a listserv [about disability and Christianity]. It seemed to me to concentrate (as a good many books do) on abled people theorising on the spiritual aspects of how [learning disabled] people could be enabled to understand Christianity, rather than on the lived experience of disabled people, and I'm afraid I lost interest.

These stories *about* us, told by a chorus of non-disabled voices, can drown out our own stories. 'I have done a lot of thinking about [disability and faith] on my own', Jane told us, because she could find few books to help her reflect on her lived experience in the context of faith.

When disabled people's voices are missing from theology, it has practical implications for the ways we are treated in churches. Storytellers told us how Christian teaching on disability can lack insight into disabled people's real lives, because it rarely centres our own lived experience. Jemma had been hurt by uninformed teaching from leaders with little understanding of disability:

> I also think leaders don't know enough about the theology of disability to be able to effectively teach [about it]. There have

been times when I have shared theories or points of view with leaders who had never heard them before ... This means I can feel unsupported ... I often feel misunderstood or struggle to understand how teachings apply to me.

Other storytellers were just as unsatisfied with the Christian teaching they had heard about themselves and their lives. Mims was worried about the effects of uncritical theologies of mental health, which she felt could harm people experiencing mental distress in churches:

I feel really uncomfortable with all the demons – Jesus casting out the demons. I know that in biblical days that was the only framework that they had to talk about mental health. But I still suspect that within church circles, there are a lot of people that still, unconsciously, even, still feel there is an element of evil and demon possession [for people with mental distress] ... When you read the theology [of mental health] it is really lightweight. There is nothing like that in it. It is all about not being afraid of people and being their friends and being on a level with them. It is all very nice, but it is very twee.

As a more meaningful alternative to these 'lightweight' theologies of mental and emotional distress, Mims called for more 'open discussion' about the issues faced by people with mental health problems in churches, led by people with lived experience. She believed people's own stories of mental distress could help churches to understand how to do less harm. Anthony was equally frustrated by neurotypical theologies of autism, which too often assume that autistic people suffer, he said. He was looking for Christian teaching that honoured his experience of neurodivergence. When theology does not centre disabled people's voices and experiences, it can overlook our authentic experiences of disability. It can obscure disabled people's cries for justice, access and participation in churches.

Even when storytellers could find some disability theology, practical access barriers prevented them from reading it. Emma could find very little theology in formats that were accessible to her, as a blind person. It was a barrier to her work as a minister:

> The classic thing about most books is they're not actually very accessible if you're blind. It is mighty hard. Not very much is put into audio. I will tend to go straight to authors and publishers and say, 'I'm a minister, I'm interested in your book or I want to lead a small group ... Could I have an electronic PDF version?' Some publishers say yes, and some authors manage to convince their publishers, but it is hard to get [accessible] versions of books.

Deirdre was in a similar position, seeking accessible teaching in the midst of chronic illness. 'I can't read a book because of problems with posture, concentration, etc.,' she told us, 'but audiobooks are great.' But she could not find any Christian teaching on disability in audiobook form. Jemma, who was studying theology, was very frustrated to find that her course books were deeply inaccessible to her, as a blind person with multiple impairments. Physical, economic and social barriers all impeded Jemma's studies:

> In terms of study programs in theology these are really difficult to access and accessibility is often not even considered when they are created... There is also a huge issue with books on theology available in alternative formats that really hinders me and is cost prohibitive. I have a Kindle and use the software on my computer to make books accessible electronically, but this means I can't 'borrow' books, I have to buy them, and they are often really expensive. Many books are not available in large or giant print, audio or Braille and this is really prohibitive. Until Christians with print disabilities can access content on an equal footing we will never be equal.

Large and giant-print Bibles can be prohibitively expensive too, Jemma told us. Even resources for her own spiritual growth were inaccessible to her. As Jemma's perceptive final comment shows, these barriers gate-keep disabled people from the knowledge we need to be equal, in a Church where theology sets the agenda for the conversation about us.

When disabled people try to enter the conversation, we may even meet with hostility, from theologians and church leaders who see us as the *objects* of theology, not the *subject* of our own stories. Most stories about disabled Christians are still told within *pastoral theology*, which focuses on the pastoral care of disabled people.[293] This is theology *about* disabled people. The assumed reader is non-disabled; disabled people are the object of discussion.[294] Churches and theologians that do not allow disabled people the agency to tell our own stories are complicit in the social injustice that prevents us from speaking for ourselves. Some of our disabled storytellers met with hostility or apathy when they tried to speak for themselves. Rhona was hoping to attend a Methodist conference on mental health, but she could not afford the cost of attendance. She told the organisers that she receives benefits, and asked if she could pay for her ticket in instalments:

> [They said] 'No. Absolutely not. The tickets are £150 up front.' I said, 'Well, you realise mental [health] issues often go with low earning potential? Therefore you're going to penalise the very people – unless you want it all to be the professionals. The white middle class intelligent professionals.'

Listening to Rhona, Kt wondered how far her experience of exclusion was an echo of the pastoral model, and churches' low expectations of disabled Christians:

> Kt: Most of these conferences, whether they can articulate it or not, assume it is the able and fit who are going to come to minister to the people with mental health [problems]. 'Those poor lovely people who are struggling ...' There is a bias in all of these things that actually the people who are going to be able to come to these [conferences] because they can afford to, or are able to do it without too many hoops, are the fit, healthy, able, middle class, probably white men who can afford it and can get to it. And who can then go back and administer to these disabled people and mental health people. Rather than it being the very disabled people themselves turning up –
> Rhona: Who have got their own stories to tell, that would probably be more beneficial than any lecture.

When disabled people are always seen as objects of theology, that mindset can easily slide into making *instrumental use* of disability, for the benefit of non-disabled people. Ethnographer and theologian Erin Raffety reflects on how easy it would be to use her disabled daughter to tell her own story, and to silence her daughter in the process:

> It is far too easy for me to tell a story of my daughter that centralizes my own healing, growth, and learning. I get to be the protagonist rather than reckon with where my ableism has caused me to speak past her. But her silence, not unlike the apparent silence of God in the face of lament, should shake me to the core.[295]

Disabled people have rarely been well-received, at first, when we have told our own stories about God, faith and disability.[296] When Nancy Eiesland began to speak powerfully about a disabled God, many took offence at her image, wanting instead to see God only as powerful and transcendent.[297] As Rhona and Kt reflected, this silencing begins with disabled people's exclusion from the settings where theology is shaped – academia, seminaries, church conferences. Often, the first barriers that keep us out of these spaces are practical. It was poverty that prevented Rhona from attending her conference, a barrier that impacts many disabled people. 'You've got the double problem of poverty with disability,' Rhona reflected. Nonetheless, there is *theological invalidation* behind many of these barriers,[298] in churches that cannot imagine disabled people telling our own stories, so do not enable us to tell them. When disabled children of God are silenced, we cannot call a powerful Church to change. It is because of our *social location* as disabled people – our experiences of injustice – that churches need to hear our stories. When disabled people are left waiting at the gates of the places where theology happens, the Church will miss out on our vital perspective on the one thing we know more about than anyone else: disability.

Disabled People Speak Back

‘[Disabled Christians] have got their own stories to tell.’ Rhona

Because theology shapes disabled Christians' experiences in churches, our own theologies are vital. Despite our limited access to theology, disabled people are capable of telling our own stories about God, faith and disability. Storytellers shared renewed, vital images of God and humanity, rooted in their experience as disabled people. Here we share a few of their *resistant readings*, as they read the Bible in ways that challenge traditional, ableist interpretations.[299] Disabled people are reaching out to the Church in mission and ministry, sharing a transformative gospel from beyond the church gates.[300]

In a Church that has often used disability as little more than a plot device, storytellers were seeking more authentic biblical models for their disabled lives. Yet they were not always confident that they could (or should) interpret the Bible from the starting-point of their personal experience. Although this did not stop storytellers from forming their own thoughtful disability theologies, some were hesitant to express their different, distinctive stories. 'I've never read a book about theology and disability,' Miranda told us; many Christian books are 'too intense' and academic for her, she said. Miranda was nervous to tell her story, when she had never heard it reflected in Christian teaching:

> I just – the healing bit – I suppose I could get panicky over it when people – and I'm not good on the answers. I think even now, to this day, if somebody [asks me about healing], I'm almost surprised. Why have you got to expect me to be healed? I think it's only in the last month, certainly not two months, when somebody said to me, 'Are you going to get any better?' And my answer to that one is, 'This is the finished model.'

Miranda had a distinctive story of her own to tell, from her embodied experience, in which she was not focused on seeking a cure through healing prayer. But speaking back against mainstream theology of healing was difficult for her. Some other storytellers shared their stories just as tentatively, wanting to make it clear that these were 'only' their own views, rather than 'real' theology they had heard in sermons or read in academic books. 'I'm not a theologian,' Fern said, 'so my views on this could be very inaccurate.' In a similar way, when Leah could not access

Christian teaching because it was not accessible to her, she was left feeling that she did not understand enough to speak for herself:

> I'm firm with my beliefs, but I think it makes my faith really kind of, surface. It doesn't go as deep as other people seem to ... I'm always stuck at the 'new Christian' level of understanding.

In churches, more value is given to the stories about God told by those who have training – church leaders or academic theologians – than to the 'ordinary' theologies of laypeople and church members.[301] Leah keenly felt the effect of those value structures. She believed that church leaders' theology was more valid than her own. Despite their hesitancy, Miranda, Fern and Leah all shared powerful interpretations of the Bible, from their embodied perspectives, as we will discuss in a moment. Yet it was not easy for them to contribute to the theological conversation about themselves.

To grow our confidence in telling our own stories, disabled people need to hear the stories of others. Christians understand the Bible together, in community.[302] Many storytellers were seeking an interpretive community – a community of pride, celebration and lament, where they could interpret the Bible together with other disabled people.[303] Between Naomi's first interviews in 2015 and the later interviews in 2020, more storytellers were beginning to discover a slowly-growing pool of theology and resources written *for* disabled Christians *by* disabled Christians. Fern had encountered mainstream theologies in churches that made her feel 'less than human'. But when she read stories and thinking by disabled Christians, Fern took her first step on a journey to a more affirming understanding of her personhood, as a disabled person:

> [I have] discovered amazing resources that have helped me come to terms with disability and faith and reframe it all in a new light. Joni Eareckson Tada, 'Disability and Jesus' online, Kate Tupling et. al's book *Pilgrims in the Dark*[304] and taking time to think, listen, learn and reflect. It's been a journey from fear of it all, to anger at the Church, to now sadness but also hope too. I'm beginning to know I'm not alone in my experiences, and that has helped.

When disabled Christians cannot easily get hold of theologies that make sense of our experiences, networks are one way we can share and shape our stories of faith and disability together. Frustrated by a lack of disability theology that resonated with their experience, a few storytellers went as far as to develop their own communities with other disabled Christians, often online. We discuss some of these disabled-led communities in Chapter 7. As isolated storytellers began to realise that their lived experience was part of a wider shared experience, that revelation was the beginning of a new ways of thinking about disability, God and disability, brought to life in a growing disabled Christian movement, where disability theology is not languishing on inaccessible bookshelves, but impacting our lives, right where it is needed.

Sadly, though, not all storytellers had access to disabled Christians' networks, deepening their sense that they might be 'the only one'. Isabelle was one of several who had never had the opportunity to discuss disability and faith in Christian settings:

> It's very difficult because I tend to think by discussing things ...
> [Disability] is not a subject that you tend to discuss. So, you know,
> you don't really get the chance. So it's just your thoughts going
> round in your head.

This sense of isolation, of being alone on the edge, was common among the storytellers who had no contact with other disabled Christians. To redress the balance, many called for research, theology and Christian teaching that reaches disabled Christians and amplifies our stories, and which they can afford, access and understand. Like some disability theologians, they were calling for Christian theological traditions to centre disabled people and our stories, not as the cared-for objects of pastoral theology, but in a collaborative model of creating *theology with*, not *for*, disabled Christians.[305] Disabled people's full inclusion in Christian churches is impossible while theology is inaccessible to us, Eiesland tells us.[306] And until disabled people are enabled to tell our own stories about God, faith and disability, the Church is missing out on a vital part of the story of God.[307]

Reimagining the Bible

> ‘They didn't know anything about [tetraplegia], did they, when the Bible stories were written?’ Miranda

As storytellers looked boldly at the effects of biblical interpretation and ableism in their lives as disabled people, many found new imaginative and creative ways to relate to biblical texts that have been used to marginalise them.[308] When non-disabled people do all the interpreting, disabled people are always metaphors for non-disabled people, never the true subject of interpretation. To speak back against ableist interpretations of the Bible, storytellers imaginatively identified with disabled characters in the Bible, unearthing their untold stories, and giving them voice where they have been silenced.[309]

When Hazel read the healing narratives of blind characters from her perspective as a blind woman, her disabled experience kept her attentive to ableist interpretations that sighted listeners can easily miss:

> Well funnily enough, the end of the sermon this week was about Jesus healing a blind man.[310] And I had to laugh because [the minister] said, 'You've got to remember this man was blind, and what trust he had. He threw down his cloak. He was never going to find it [again]. The man was blind.' There's me and [my husband] sitting there, and I thought, 'I wonder what he's thinking.' I just sort of laughed, you know, and I said, 'Well, you'd be surprised.'

As a blind person who is able to function in the world, Hazel recognised readings of the Bible that centre sighted people's (faulty) stereotypes about blindness. As ableist readings limit Bartimaeus's agency and ministry, they underestimate Hazel in the process. Interpretations of the Bible that use disability as a plot device, a 'metaphor to think with,' to point non-disabled people to God, were irrelevant to Hazel's real experiences as a blind Christian.[311]

Resisting similar ableist readings of the Bible, both Victor and Miranda identified with the paralysed man lowered through the roof in Mark 2.

[312]Victor asked practical questions about how the man got up to the roof at all, from his own perspective as someone who struggles to access churches. Miranda imagined the roof removal as an access adjustment: 'Lowering through the roof – well, that was an access arrangement ... It worked!' Miranda read the story from her own social location, as a wheelchair user with tetraplegia herself. She asked whether churches could learn from the extreme access example of removing a roof, so that disabled people can meet Jesus. Would most churches ever go as far as this man's friends did? For Miranda and Victor, the paralysed man in the story was more than a plot device to make theological points. He was a real disabled person like them: the subject of their interpretation. These storytellers' anti-ableist interpretations opened up new questions that might never occur to non-disabled readers. Rooted in lived experience, disabled people's readings of the Bible can draw the whole Church into new ways to think about the Bible.

Stories of God with us

'*There is a real anguished voice in some of the Psalms that I find real comfort from.*' Mims

Many storytellers shared theology formed through long years of contemplation on the ways that disability shapes their relationship with God. They did not believe that they had to reject their bodies and minds in order to think about God – in fact, they knew that their bodies, minds and disabled experiences were ways to understand God and the Bible.[313] Disability led storytellers to think about God in three ways, as they told stories of a *God with us*, a *God for us, and* a *God like us.* These are stories that can transform a privileged Church, as it comes to understand the God that disabled people know, in the stories we bring from the edge.

Empowered by their relationship with an incarnate *God with us*, some storytellers told stories of lament in disability. Disabled people can lead the church into places of lament that our modern culture is lacking, places that disabled people may even struggle to find for ourselves. Storytellers' lament was shared in resistance, in a society and Church where, in the quest to be 'normal,' we can easily forget that our full humanity includes experiences of pain, sadness and struggle. Esther reflected:

> A lot of my thinking in theology has been evolving. Like I said, watching my mum and how she was treated in the Church, and having to really question this whole concept of, 'By his stripes we are healed.' Right, so you're entitled to healing? Then there's me going, 'But people die, so surely that's the ultimate failure, then, if that's what it's about.' I've had to wrestle with the theology for so many years ... The most important thing that I've learned from Job is what compassion really means. When his friends come along and they sit in silence with him for seven days. So before they open their mouths, which is when they get it wrong, they sit with him and they take on his suffering. They tear their clothes and they suffer with him, which is compassion... I've had no choice but to be real. I've had no choice but to face disability and poverty at times, and the effects that has.

Esther had learned that compassion is sometimes better than the endless quest for cure, and that the silence of solidarity is sometimes better than pat answers. Other storytellers echoed Esther's longing that other people would be Christ to them in their difficult experiences. Deirdre and Fern both wished that other Christians would simply sit with them in their lament, in pain or distress, rather than seeing them as targets of their service.[314] Esther's thinking about compassion was shaped by her suffering through illness and her struggle against marginalisation – all her lived experience as a disabled person.

Mims was another storyteller who drew strength from stories of lament in the Bible, in the midst of her mental distress:

> I also find Job really helpful, you know, what he has to go through and comes out with. Some of the Psalms as well ... there was clearly distress, anguish. There is a real anguished voice in some of the Psalms that I find real comfort from.

Mims was drawn to the deep experiences of lament she found in the Bible, and spoke of the incarnate God who meets her in her suffering. She found comfort in her imaginative identification with biblical characters who affirmed her in her pain, as much as she was also comforted by those who affirmed her joy in the person she was created to be. Like Esther, her theology of lament was experiential, emerging from her own story of disability. In Esther and Mims' discovery of the revelation of God in pain and oppression, they shared experiences in common with disabled minister Tony McClelland, who writes:

> Jesus on the Cross is not God's way of curing the sickness of the world, but rather God's way of staying with us in the brokenness ... to open up new possibilities for creativity there, just there where the pain and confusion are. And not just for the hours of the dying on the Cross, but for ever.[315]

In a world where it has rarely been safe for disabled people to lament, theologies of pain and suffering are a gift we can receive from each other, as well as a gift we can offer the Church. Disabled people may be reluctant to speak of pain among non-disabled people, who may interpret our lament as a sign that disability is nothing more than tragedy. 'Acknowledging the realities of pain opens up profound vulnerability,' Julia Watts Belser tells us. 'There are very few spaces where I can examine loss or suffering in spiritual safety, without fear that I will have offered it up to ableism's arsenal.'[316] This may be especially true in the Church, where theology tends to focus first on our suffering,[317] and where communities may seek to 'fix' us rather than sitting with us in compassion and solidarity. Through their disabled experience, storytellers were motivated to look for streams of Christian thought that make space for lament, which do not pretend to have all the answers to the mystery of disability.[318] Those who took the risk of sharing their stories of pain and lament, in the presence of an incarnate God who suffers with us, offered a prophetic alternative to modern society's obsession with toxic positivity, at the expense of our humanity. Their theology of lament is a gift to the Church. This is a story of God with us.

Stories of God like us

❛Jesus was disabled too, after the crucifixion. I can't quite believe I've never noticed that.❜ Fern

Our stories about God are metaphors, shaped by our own experience. 'Our idea of God tells us more about ourselves than about him', as theologian Thomas Merton puts it.[319] Theology has been excluding disabled people – and many others – for a long time, as our society has come to represent God as white, male, straight, cisgender, non-disabled and neurotypical.[320] There has always been a disabled God at the centre of Christianity, but the Church has been reluctant to look too closely at Christ's wounded and disfigured body, preferring an image of divine power.[321] Instead, the Church has imagined Jesus as a 'white, middle class, elite privilege, educated, healthy man,' as storyteller Kt reflected:

We've never had a different narrative, a shared narrative, moving away from that norm. It's the yardstick. Anything that isn't that is viewed as suspicious or somehow not true … Disabled bodies make embodiment uncomfortable as an idea, and certainly make incarnation untenable, because 'Jesus was a fit healthy Greek.'

If a powerful, privileged image of God is a true picture of the divine, then the Christian faith has little to say to any of us whose bodies do not reflect this image, including disabled people. But disabled people know that this 'God of the powerful' is far from the Bible's image of a *God like us*.[322] Eiesland tells the story of a disabled God, a story told by one disabled person, who had lost hope in the possibility of a *God like him*:

After a long silence, a young African-American man said, 'If God was in a sip-puff, maybe He would understand.' I was overwhelmed by this image: God in a sip-puff wheelchair, the kind used by many quadriplegics that enables them to maneuver the chair by blowing and sucking on a straw-like device. Not an omnipotent, self-sufficient

God, but neither a pitiable, suffering servant. This was an image of God as a survivor, as one of those whom society would label 'not feasible', 'unemployable', with 'questionable quality of life'.[323]

Inspired by her shared lived experience with this disabled man, Eiesland dared to imagine a *God like us,* who shares disabled people's first-hand knowledge of injustice and rejection. She is not alone in her radical claim that God is disabled – her story of a wounded God joins Anton Boisen's story of a Jesus who experiences psychosis,[324] and Serene Jones's story of a traumatised Christ on the cross.[325] The idea of a disabled God has resonated with many disabled Christians. Not because the image literally, physically represents each of us – most of us do not have wounds in our hands and side as extensive as those of Jesus – but because it calls us to see God differently from the alienating, 'perfect' divine image we have been mis-sold as a true and universal picture of God. The risen, wounded Jesus is the revelation of a God in whom we can recognise ourselves, who affirms us not as fallen or broken, but as a vital part of the *imago Dei.* A disabled God gives disabled people the permission and the courage to wonder if God might have a body like ours, a mind like ours, a *way of being* like ours.

The disabled God is a story that reflects many disabled people's authentic experiences of God, faith and disability. Even storytellers who had not read Eiesland's book were talking about the disabled God. Jane was one of many who had been inspired by the image of a Christ resurrected with wounds, without being sure where the idea came from:

> I wish I could also remember where I read that Christ was resurrected with the scars of the nails and the wound of the spear in his body and yet is still considered perfect. I must have discussed with others but it has slipped my mind.

And although Fern had never read any theology of the disabled God, she reached similar conclusions to Eiesland, after reflecting for herself on faith and disability:

> Jesus was disabled too, after the crucifixion. I can't quite believe I've never noticed that. Even though we're explicitly told about how

after the resurrection he had wounds, etc. But we don't discuss that side of it ever, which is weird as it's right there. Maybe [the story is] not just the nice fairy-tale version.

Whether storytellers identified with an incarnate *God like them* or a resurrected *God like them,* the image of a disabled God affirmed them in their different bodies and minds, rejected by society and the Church alike.

For some storytellers, an incarnate *God like them* is a God who can identify with them as disabled people, in their deepest experiences of illness and impairment. Mims shared the story of a crucified God who identifies with her in mental distress:

> I think with mental health, one of the very special things is that Jesus can't have been on the cross and not had a mental health problem. When he says, 'Father, Father, why have you forsaken me?' That is a bit of paranoia, that [God] is not there anymore, isn't it? That is a sentence of paranoia.

In Christ, the disabled experience enters into God, and we experience 'the Good News that God is with us and in it with us'.[326] Mims' insights echo emerging work in mad theology, where others have spoken about a God who meets them in their depression, paranoia and voice-hearing.[327] Mims' story resists the idea that the disabled God is only for physically disabled people – neurodivergent storytellers and those experiencing distress also found comfort and affirmation in a *God like them.*[328] So did co-author Emily, sharing her story when she was interviewed as a research participant. Through the complex experience of a body that regularly caused her pain, as well as joy, Emily identified with an incarnate Christ who had a human body like hers:

> Living in my body, it's really made me think deeper about incarnation and what that means. And what it means that God was formed in a body, especially when I have such a love/hate relationship with my body. If God had a body, that must mean that the body is important. It's ongoing. I sometimes really hate my body. And I'm like, 'Oh well, just remember incarnation.'

Emily was disappointed to find that her church's teaching had little to say about Christ's experience of a fragile human body, and how the incarnation can lead all of us to a deeper understanding of our own embodied humanity. Disabled people's experiences of bodies and minds are not always positive. Many people with chronic illnesses are very aware of our fragile bodies, through experiences of pain or fatigue; autistic people's sensory experiences are so different to those of neurotypical people that we can find it traumatising when our bodies encounter a sensory world not designed for us.[329] To be able to forget you have a body is a privilege, one that most disabled people do not enjoy.[330] A deeper understanding of the full range of human experience and embodiment, from joy to suffering, and of the God who enters into that full human experience, is a healing gift that disabled people can offer to a Church that often forgets the importance of embodiment. A *God like us* can expand our understanding of the incarnation to make space for all our authentic experience of bodies and minds, including those of disabled people, who are reflected in Christ's incarnation, just as we are.[331]

The image of a disabled God can be a place of identification for disabled people, whose rejected bodies have rarely been seen as the *imago Dei*. But, even more powerfully, many storytellers believed that a disabled God has the potential to transform the Church into a Kingdom of justice. As Fern reflected, if we could take a disabled Jesus seriously, it could show us all how we have devalued the disabled people of God:

> It makes you wonder if [a disabled Jesus] would find church completely accessible. Would we pray for healing for him – but in doing so, would that erase the whole crucifixion? Would we think it was his fault it had happened? Would it mean we wouldn't pay attention to what he said or who he was?

In all the ways the Church has marginalised disabled people, Fern wondered whether the Church has devalued a disabled Christ – and whether justice begins with when we finally come to see a disabled Christ as holy. Esther also believed that the concept of a disabled God could transform a Church and society that rejects not just disabled people, but anyone whose bodies and minds diverge from the norm. Esther challenged the Church to understand that God limited and disabled Godself through the incarnation, so as to become like humanity:

> If you're God and you become human, you've disabled yourself, haven't you? You have put yourself into a condition where there are limitations, where you're mortal.

From this theological starting point, Esther called churches to learn about a different kind of God, beginning with the experience of disabled people, who reveal a *God like us*:

> What disabled people can teach [the Church] is that it's okay to be who we are, to interact the way we do, and to see things differently and experience God differently ... Is there something about the disabled person who has had to learn to accept that they are different, to accept and discover ways of communicating their truth and their experiences of God? Is there something about disabled people understanding the depth and the cost of compassion? Is there something about disabled people understanding that healing is not about our physical state of being? The freedom that you can find, when you are alongside people that are just different, and they know God loves them ... the freedom that gives others to start accepting themselves, is just amazing.

For disabled people like Esther and Fern, a *God like us* does not reject our bodies, minds and ways of being. This God does not ask us to live up to harmful ideas of perfection. Esther's theology resonates with Julia Watts Belser's, who asks us to consider 'Not what does the tradition say about disability experience, but what does disability experience know that the tradition doesn't yet understand and needs to be tapped into?'[332] As we experience the Spirit's liberation, and begin to live authentically as the people we were created to be, disabled people show the Church how to do the same. Disabled people's experiences can point us all to a more complete picture of God and humanity than a non-disabled Church is usually willing to imagine – a fully incarnated God who became like us, and a resurrected God whose wounded body reveals a new reality for humanity.[333]

In a *God like them*, many storytellers saw *their* story, as disabled people, reflected. They challenged churches to come face-to-face with a Jesus who was wounded, marginalised and disempowered, yet still divine. As Zoe and Kt put it:

> Kt: He comes back with the wounds still on his body. He comes back as God.
> Zoe: And the revelation of God ... I think we forget, the book isn't a revelation. It was a person, and somebody with hideous wounds. It was a broken person, with the revelation of God.

Jesus' 'hideous' body honours those of us who are seen by society as *monstrous*.[334] Christ is resurrected in the kind of body that our society would look upon with horror, before they turned away. But the disciples do not turn away from Christ's resurrected body. They put their hands in the holes in Christ's hands and side, recognise him in his wounded, resurrected body, and declare, 'My Lord and my God.'[335] Jesus does not shrug off the wounds of sin and oppression inflicted on him – he bears them forever, reclaimed as signs of his divine identity.[336] This God shows the world that, however monstrous it considers our bodies and minds, we cannot be abhorrent. Not when a disabled God meets us where we are, shows us scars like ours, and says, 'Don't you recognise me?' A wounded God looks upon all bodies and minds that fall short of society's standards, and affirms that disabled people are part of God's good creation. In the resurrected Christ, disability is redeemed, not as a problem to be fixed, but as a vital reality of the divine image, and a new model of wholeness for humanity.[337] In a *God like us*.

Stories of God for us

‘Jesus came for the broken. Not for the rich and the able.’ Rhona

AT THE GATES

A disabled God is the beginning of the story, not the end. As storytellers identified with a God who is like them, they asked what difference that vision of God could make to the world and the Church. They told us how, as a disabled Christ embodies an entirely new vision of humanity, he turns all of society's values upside-down, throwing power and privilege into chaos. When a disabled Christ announces the Reign of God, the values of that kin-dom are the reverse of society's values. Zoe called it the 'upside-down Kingdom of God'.[338] Storytellers' prophetic cries for God's justice were born of their disabled experience, in a world where many disabled people are poor, disempowered, devalued, and rarely listened to. They challenged disability injustice as part of a broader social system of privilege and oppression. They knew that the God of the margins has a particular concern for poor and marginalised people. This is a *God for us*. In Zoe's words:

> The Kingdom of God is meant to look really different to a well-run organisation. Jesus, our King, rode on a ridiculous unbroken donkey. He looked like a fool. And therefore that's our model of power.

Zoe and Kt spoke about how they had more often experienced churches that focused on the power and transcendence of God, that 'skip[ped] straight to the Resurrection,' as Kt put it, rather than taking a 'journey' through the crucifixion and understanding why the disabled God matters. Yet disabled people often have deep insight into inequality, from the perspective of our disabled 'bodies of knowledge'.[339] Rhona reflected on what the experience of disability can teach the Church about the Kingdom's reversal of societal values:

> The best gift of being partially sighted, for me, is that I can understand the brokenness of the marginalised in the churches... And then you've got the James 2 passage [verses 1-4] that I just love because it's so real. Where James says, 'Who are you going to welcome into church?' Is it the guy dressed in the pearly suit that's the head of the synagogue, going to sit in the front row? Or is it the tramp with the smelly clothes that you're going to say, 'Just sit at the back please?'

> So disability, it's just part, for me, of the whole theology of
> the church. That Jesus came to turn values upside down, with the
> Beatitudes. The Church needs to be turning their theology upside
> down. Jesus came for the broken. Not for the rich and the able.

Disability is one way God chooses what is weak in the world to shame the strong,[340] storytellers suggested. They asked what churches can learn from the marginalised, as they begin to honour and be transformed by those on edge, turning their values upside-down.

The idea of an upside-down Reign of God led many storytellers to call churches to confront their own privilege and power. Inspired by Jesus' mission to the margins, and their own experiences of disability inequality, they called for Churches to become alert to social injustice. Andrew reflected on unexamined power in churches, from his perspective as a Deaf person:

> My observation is that quite often the Church follows what the
> privileged society wants ... I think if Jesus was here, I don't think he
> would be going along with what the privileged did. I think he would
> be interested in people who are on the margins of society.

Churches should be seeking to break down the barriers that privilege creates, Andrew reflected, when it divides those who have power from those who do not. Fern was just as frustrated by a Church that, she felt, often allows the world's standards to guide whether or not they value disabled people:

> I think sometimes the Church needs to stop and engage in a
> narrative about disability *with* disabled people, and not just take on
> the lens of a capitalist system that associates a person's worth with
> how much they can earn and produce in society.

In contrast with a society that gives most value to those who can be productive, Fern and Andrew spoke of a Jesus who offers a counter-cultural alternative. This Jesus challenges churches that are more interested in growth and prosperity than compassion and community, they said. This Jesus values us not for the money we can earn, but for the people we were created to be. A privileged Church cannot see the inequalities that disabled people experience, Andrew said, reminding us why disabled people's perspectives are vital for transformation.

Other storytellers imagined a compassionate Jesus of the margins, who would today be living alongside and supporting those experiencing poverty and oppression, including disabled people. They called the Church to be Jesus to the outcasts, in a Kingdom that honours those who are least valued in society. For Susanna, this is a ministry of solidarity, of being with those on the edge:[341]

> If Jesus was living here in this community in this age, he would be with the people that don't have anything to eat, with the people being sanctioned from benefits and are having to do without, with the people aren't able to work, with the people that aren't able to get a bank account, and with the people that are lonely and need somewhere to go. That's where Jesus would be, who he would be with and who he would be ministering to. So, as a church, those are the people that we should be honouring and the people that we should be ministering to. I think that's very biblical.

In the same way, Charlotte believed that Jesus cares about those at the sharp end of social oppression. She called churches to challenge the inequalities that lead to marginalisation, without romanticising the 'poor' or becoming caught up in the charity model.[342] Charlotte's commitment to marginalised people began with the biblical command to honour the least and the poorest in society, just as Rhona's did. Charlotte said:

> I really think that it's important to be alongside people where they are, and not to conform to society's norms. To be counter cultural, because that's what the Gospel is … I think if you look at the Gospels and what Christ is saying, Christ is there for the poor or the marginalised … Maybe God's prosperity is different. Maybe it's about love and compassion.

Here, Charlotte echoed liberation theology's claim that God is on the side of those who are poor and marginalised.[343] In a kin-dom of God that reverses the values of society, the voices of 'the least of these' will be heard,[344] storytellers said. Churches will stand up against societal ableism and the social conditions that disabled people are living in. They will make a commitment to valuing us, in the midst of a society that cannot see our inherent value.

The prophetic stories of those at the church gates have the power to transform a privileged Church, sharing gifts of renewal from the edge. These disabled storytellers could only speak back against injustice because they had experienced it deeply and first-hand. Because of their disabled experience – not in spite of it – they could imagine a depth to God's justice beyond what the Church often preaches. These disabled people's stories call the Church to live in the values of the upside-down Kingdom, embodied in a *God for us*.

Theology of the Disabled Liberators

Just as we cannot leave disability at the church gates, we cannot put it down when we pick up the Bible. We cannot think about God as anyone except ourselves. Because we cannot take our bodies and minds for granted, disabled people often understand our relationship with God *through* our lived experience, not in spite of it. Starting with our 'bodies of knowledge',[345] we tell stories about God that non-disabled people have not heard, and that they have much to learn from, as disability theologian Julia Watts Belser reflects:

> My disabled experience might actually tell me something extraordinary about the nature of God ... this disabled body knows something about God, not in spite of it but because of it ... What does disability experience know that the tradition doesn't yet understand and needs to be tapped into?[346]

This understanding, that God is revealed through our disabled bodies and minds, is a radical challenge to a Church that can imagine the divine image only as physical, mental and intellectual 'perfection'. When traditional images of God are ableist, disabled people can offer the Church a more expansive truth about God, 'which no longer views the able-bodied experience as the theological norm, but rather sees the *imago Dei* in the resurrected yet disabled Christ and in persons with disabilities'.[347] As we imagine a *God like us*, a *God with us* and a *God for us*, disabled people's theology liberates churches to become places of justice. Storyteller Esther found that, in a church that embraced what disabled people were teaching them about God, she could be the person she was created to be:

> There was just something [at that church] about being who you are. I think the whole point of church is that we realise who God is, and who we are in his image. That's what changes lives, I think.

In this transforming community, Esther she was encouraged to bring her whole self, as a disabled person – made in the image of God.[348] Beginning with what our disabled experience teaches us about God, disabled people are modelling new, anti-ableist ways to do and be Church. These storytellers' insights about God join those shared by Black theology, feminist theology, queer theology, and many other first-hand stories of rejected bodies and marginalised experience that are transforming the Church. To hear these and many other silenced stories from the edge, the Church needs to start by listening to those hesitant voices who begin their vital, experiential, transformative stories with, 'I'm not a theologian, so I might be wrong, but …'.

Churches that truly value disabled people will enter 'dignifying dialogue'[349] with us, as Jesus did, centring our perspectives and stories. They will listen to the disabled Christians crying out for justice from the edge, showing churches how to transform. They will see our disruption as ministry, pushing churches out of their comfort zones, helping them to transform into communities that look a little more like the diverse Kingdom of God. That's when they will learn that theology is deeply practical, for disabled people; the Church's theology shapes everything from the ableist words of hymns, to church design that keeps us from belonging. Injustice has told disabled people one story about God's relationship to us. We speak back with very different, redemptive stories: of bodies taken seriously and difference embraced, of lament and celebration, of liberation and justice, and of longing to be accepted just as we are, as we were created to be. We are all theologians, and God speaks to and through us all. A Church that took disabled people's disability theology seriously would be a truly counter-cultural challenge to society.

Through our own 'frontier theologies',[350] disabled and neurodivergent Christians are daring to imagine more and more images of a *God like us*, in a prism of fragmented Light, a rainbow as diverse and unique as we each are, from Bingo Allison's neurodivergent understanding of a Jesus who thinks as differently as autistic people do,[351] to Rachel Holdforth's print of the blind Christ leading a sighted disciple (see front cover). This is a God who is with us in all our experiences, from pain to paranoia, in the lives of people whose bodies, minds and experiences give us distinctive insights into compassion, lament and being human. This is a God who becomes one of the marginalised, and announces the upside-down Reign of God, in which we will all be liberated from the power of sin in the world.[352] These diverse images of a disabled God are powerful for disabled people, who need a God we can identify with, and who can identify with us. This disabled God could be powerful for non-disabled people too. A disabled God can speak to non-disabled people about (in)justice, diversity (or the lack of it) in the Church, and the urgency of valuing all bodies and minds in a world that does not. Non-disabled people need to gaze on a disabled Christ, and not turn away, asking what God's wounded, monstrous body means for their exclusion of disabled people, and for their relationship with their own fragile, human bodies. Disabled people's stories have the power to transform the Church, liberating us all from the sin of ableism.[353] Such transformation would have a powerful impact for all disabled people, whether or not they can read theology written down in books. This would be *epistemic justice*[354] – justice that centres our lived experience and knowledge – in a Church that values disabled people's ways of understanding God.

If the Church is ever to hear these transformative stories, those who are not disabled must be *reflexive* – honest and thoughtful – about their power in the conversation about disability, faith and the Church. They must ask how they are sharing their power to speak with disabled people. Al Barrett and Ruth Harley explore allyship through the response of the Roman centurion to the Resurrection. Rather than centring himself in the story of the Jesus movement, the centurion's role as an ally would have been

> to find creative ways of *stepping back*, of 'clearing' the space he has already occupied, to enable the agency of others. Here, 'solidarity' takes flesh as *amplifying* – to his fellow Romans – what he is hearing from his 'others,' as cheerleading from the side lines when others venture to speak and act, and as multiple acts of passing on.[355]

Theologians and church leaders who are committed to anti-ableist transformation of society and churches will invite and enable disabled people to *participate* in the conversation about us, passing on opportunities to speak, and working collaboratively with communities of disabled people.[356] We have power-sharing models to draw on here, from citizen participation to emancipatory disability research.[357] These are secular ways of thinking about participation, but when society is ahead of the Church, we may need to learn from the movement of the Holy Spirit in the world. Instead of speaking for us, non-disabled allies might then find instead that they are called to work with, not for,[358] those who do not share their privileges. Who are not silent, but silenced.[359]

We opened this chapter with Donald Eadie's reflections on disabled people's distinctive prophetic witness to the church. We close with his conclusion on the gifts disabled people are offering to the Church, if it can only listen:

> We bring our experience of our bodies, a source of wonder, pleasure and pain; the dwelling place of God, where we meet God in the here and now of our actual humanity ... We bring these gifts and many others, not as victims but as liberators.[360]

CHAPTER 6

Fearfully and Wonderfully Made: Disabled People's Stories of Healing

'If I was born in the image of God, and I was born with my eye condition, then I am perfect in God's eyes as I am.' Jemma

'I wouldn't be doing what I'm doing now if it wasn't for [disability] ... Yes, there are things that are painful and frustrating, but I don't necessarily need God to heal me from that. It's part of who I am.' Charlotte

Health, Healing and Cure

Disability theologian Kathy Black tells the story of Sig, who stopped taking his medication when his church told him he would be healed of his epilepsy if he only had enough faith. Sig died from a seizure that his medication could have prevented. 'The message he heard,' Black says, 'was certainly not *healing* for him.'[361]

Across many cultures and historical eras, different societies have imagined the concept of health in very different ways. In today's Global North, *wellness* is a modern obsession. Health has become a cultural value, a personal project that we are expected to work for.[362] Unsubstantiated claims encourage us to buy overpriced supplements and products, while we pay wellness gurus to lead us in the worship of our bodies – as long as our bodies meet normative standards of health. But the obsession with 'wellness' is really about privilege.[363] Health is social; injustice and inequality are at the root of much ill health.[364] Modern ideas about health and wellness are profoundly damaging to us all, but perhaps especially to disabled people, who are measured against ableist assumptions that our lives must be tragic and full of suffering.[365] As failed humans in a social project of perfection, disabled people can be uncomfortable reminders that everyone will one day succumb to frailty, illness and mortality.[366] And so disabled people have become a problem – in need of 'fixing'. A history of eugenics has pathologised disabled people's differences; the quest for the eradication of disability continues to this day, for example, in coercive 'treatments' that seek to normalise us.[367] Those of us who cannot be normalised are either pitied or vilified. In the UK, society has long represented disabled people as lazy, work-shy scroungers. When it does, it is building on ideas that have grown out of the Christian tradition, especially the pervasive link between illness and sin.[368]

For centuries, Christian interpretations of the Bible have associated disability with sin, the Fall, and God's punishment, in what Nancy Eiesland calls a 'sin-disability conflation': an enduring belief that disability and sickness are the result of an individual's sin, and that disabled people must be 'fixed' – made non-disabled – before we can be holy.[369] Today, even in churches that would never preach that sin is the cause of ill health, many Christians still believe that impairment and illness are a tragic result of the sin of Adam and Eve. But this story is hardly more positive for disabled people, when it imagines us as tragedies or mistakes.[370] In many churches, disability is seen as *deficit* – falling short. Today, far from the cultural world of the Gospels, we may imagine that stories of Jesus's healings are a template for 'perfect' health, based on ableist notions of normalcy. At first glance, it can seem as if disabled people exist in the Gospels solely to be healed, and then we disappear from the story.[371] But Jesus offered much more than physical cure to those he healed. His healing encounters were not about eradicating impairment. As Jesus transformed communities through compassionate encounters with marginalised people, and was transformed himself by the bold disabled people he met,[372] Jesus announced the Reign of God and its healing justice for all creation.[373]

Yet, in many churches today, overly simplistic theologies of healing have missed the holistic dimensions of Jesus's healing. The result can be a preoccupation with making disabled people like everyone else, as healing becomes understood as *cure*. That's when healing ministries can become one more way that the *imago Dei* is devalued in disabled people.[374] Disabled people's different bodies and minds can be a dangerous challenge to ableist theologies that imagine that all bodies must be cured, as a sign of God's glory, and so that we can be restored to God's image.[375] We may spend our whole lives with the uneasy feeling that we are only on earth to wait, until our bodies and minds are cured in heaven. Beliefs that God favours the righteous through health can victim-blame individual disabled people for our pain and struggles, alienating and shaming us, leaving us wondering why we have fallen short of God's blessing.[376] This is not just bad theology for disabled people. It can lead Christians to judge anyone experiencing pain and suffering. When it does, it distracts churches from looking at social inequalities and injustice, where structural sin is enacted *on us*. As Hannah Lewis puts it, this theology 'puts the whole focus on the transformation of the individual, like the medical model, and does not consider that the person's real "suffering" or need for healing may be caused by political considerations and unjust power structures rather than the impairment itself'.[377]

No doubt most Christians want to believe that healing ministries are inspired by love, in a reflection of the compassion of Jesus for those he healed. This is very likely the motivation of a great deal of healing prayer in churches. But, as we recentre the stories of disabled people's own experiences of healing ministry and theology, we must also look at what Shane Clifton calls 'the dark side of prayer for healing'.[378]

In this chapter, we share storytellers' experiences of harmful theologies of 'healing' that saw them as less than human, and their own Kingdom stories of full personhood as disabled people in Christ, created just as they are. Storytellers related encounters with harmful 'healing' practices that resonate with Sig's, where they were told that their impairments were the result of sin or a lack of faith, and that if they prayed harder, they would be cured. They shared painful experiences of being singled out for healing prayer in churches, simply because they were disabled. They shared the sense of constant pressure to seek a cure, which affected some storytellers' self-esteem, and made others afraid to go to church at all. Speaking back, some storytellers boldly shared that they were no longer seeking a cure. As others prayed for relief from painful conditions, they trusted in God's healing, which may not always look like society's expectations of health. As many spoke out against theologies that imagine them as falling short, they affirmed that they are 'fearfully and wonderfully made'[379] in the image of God – not in spite of their impairments, but *as* disabled people.

Compulsory non-disability and healing practices in churches

> **‘ I felt reduced to an object of pity, charity, and only worth something if I was seen as physically healed. ’** Fern

Many churches, in the past century or so, have gathered around healing miracles that seek to 'restore' ill and disabled people to an imagined state of perfection.[380] Disabled people are a diverse group, and our storytellers had different views on healing and cure. But many of them told us how there is an unhelpful preoccupation with healing – understood as cure – in churches of all denominations. This focus on cure often looks like *compulsory nondisability*: the ableist belief that disabled people must desire to be non-disabled, that we must constantly seek to be 'fixed'.[381] There is a difference between healing and cure, as disability theologians have argued.[382] But, as storytellers told us, in an ableist society, not everyone sees the need for this distinction.

Disabled people may find it discouraging to be prayed for, over and over, only to realise, slowly and painfully, that cure is not forthcoming. Deirdre could find countless audiobooks on miraculous healing, but very little teaching on living as a disabled Christian who has not experienced cure:

> I had stopped listening to any teaching about [healing] ... This is because most of the things I heard advocated 'building up your faith' by reading stories of healing ... The only thing that reading all these things did was stir up the question, 'Why them and not me?' and if anything, it diminished my faith. Add to that the guilt of feeling like that when everyone is saying you should be feeling something different, and it is not a very healthy combination, which added to my stress when I was supposed to be staying relaxed. So I stopped listening. The other thing I found was that they all seemed to be totally preoccupied with healing, rather than living in the here and now with illness in the meantime, and what God can do in our lives through that time. Even those written by people who hadn't been healed seemed totally preoccupied with healing at the expense of everything else.

Andrew described the focus on healing he had found in his evangelical and Anglican churches:

> They're obsessed with healing, praying for healing ... You get fed up with people wanting to pray for you. You're like a guinea pig. And sometimes you think they're using it as a way of fobbing you off.

Andrew was not alone in being the target of an 'obsession' with healing – or cure – for disabled people. For some, there was no way out of this expectation. When Victor told a leader in his church that he was only feeling worse after healing prayer, he was told, 'Don't be silly, and I'm going to pray for you now.' A Christian preoccupation with healing-as-cure was not healing for Deirdre, Andrew or Victor. Their stories are not uncommon. Shane Clifton writes that the disabled people he has interviewed about healing 'describe feelings of disappointment, frustration, confusion, anger, and guilt' in response to healing ministries which should be motivated by compassion and love. 'The trouble is that the message of healing is inevitably alienating to the 'unhealed,'' Clifton adds.[383] Just as Deirdre found in the books she read that emphasised doing personal spiritual work for a cure, this is healing theology that reflects modern secular ideas of personal responsibility for health. It can be just as harmful for disabled people.

None of this is to say that storytellers did not believe in God's miraculous cure through healing prayer. Many did. But lived experience still led many to question how healing prayer imagines disabled people. Nicki came from a Pentecostal church background, where healing ministries are often central to worship. In Chapter 2, Nicki shared her story about a church that ignored her need for an accessible toilet. At the same church, Nicki felt that the community's focus on cure made her an object of God's healing power. The church was unable to understand that Nicki had a different perspective on health and healing:

> I think they were hoping that, when they spoke about healing, I would come out for prayer and God would miraculously heal me. I would walk out and leave my wheelchair at the front of the church so that it could be there forever as a testimony. They have crutches and things from previous healings in their main church. I know that that's not how it's going to be, and I'm at peace with that. I'm happy that I know that God isn't going to heal me.

In some churches, healing practices can be flashy spectacles of cure, objectifying disabled people as they seek to demonstrate the glory of God through changes in individual bodies. Nicki was seeking a deeper healing than this, as she came to believe that God was working through her experience of disability. Nicki had even learned to be content with her understanding that God was unlikely to cure her, a feeling she shared with other storytellers, as we'll discuss later. Churches that treat empty wheelchairs and unused hearing aids as icons of God's power through miracles, instead of the tools of freedom and extensions of disabled people's bodies that they are, are objectifying disabled people.[384] The message is that impairment is deficit, and that disabled people can only glorify God if our impairments are eradicated. It is assumed that everyone wants a cure from all illness and impairment, and that we *should* all want a cure. When, like Nicki, disabled people instead believe that God works through us just as we are, we can be troubling to a prosperity gospel that preaches that God will end all illness and impairment.

While some healing ministries are objectifying of disabled people, others can be abusive or violent.[385] They can harm disabled people who, like Sig, stop taking their medication or come to devalue themselves. They can even cause immediate physical pain and damage.[386] Fern experienced physically intimidating and distressing forms of prayer, on more than one occasion:

> Within moments of arriving before finding a place to sit for the
> service someone from the front of the Church walked to where
> I was at the back, gathered several other people, and said they
> were going to pray for me. I had never met this person before. I
> didn't know them and they didn't know me. It was quite a horrible
> situation to be in, that again drew a lot of attention, when I just
> wanted to be normal … It seemed like I was being used as a model
> for show and for other people's gain, to be able to be publicly seen
> praying for me. They didn't know what was 'wrong with me' but
> did stop halfway through the praying to ask … By not stopping to
> find any of this out [they] removed my personhood, autonomy and
> voice. I felt reduced to an object of pity, charity, and only worth
> something if I was seen as physically healed.

These experiences of 'healing' were traumatic for Fern, as pray-ers objectified her to demonstrate their faith. Such non-consensual prayer is far from Jesus's model of holistic healing. At Fern's church, spectacular miraculous cure was expected, without ever asking if it was *wanted*. Fern's body became a *site for healing* for her church: an object and symbol of God's healing power, according to limited, ableist ideals of health.[387] The desire for miraculous cure may be about the anxieties of non-disabled Christians, who are seeking healing miracles as a sign that God is in control. But God's mysterious power over creation may look nothing like our ableist expectations.

Deliverance ministry was one particularly painful healing practice encountered by storytellers. For a time, it left some with a sense that disability is evil. Deliverance ministry represents illness and impairment

as spiritual in cause, the outworking of a demonic spirit, and it is often –
but not only – found in charismatic churches.[388] We might traditionally
associate deliverance ministries with mental distress, through a narrow
reading of Gospel stories, but storytellers with physical impairments had
experienced deliverance prayer too. Andrew described the long-term,
damaging effects of prayer to cast out a 'spirit of Deafness':

> I've been prayed for that the evil is taken out of me … In my early
> Christian [years] I remember thinking I was cursed, a period of
> feeling I was cursed by God … Firstly, it's not being very positive.
> It wasn't positive. 'It's a spirit …' And now that I know the Bible,
> theologically, I say they're wrong.

Andrew, who believed in the power of prayer for healing, contrasted
the psycho-emotional harm he had experienced through deliverance
prayer with more compassionate healing ministries that centred his
wellbeing. A theology of deliverance goes even further than a deficit
model of disability, associating impairment with evil, demons and the
work of the devil. This theology clashed painfully with Andrew's Deaf
cultural model, through which he celebrated his Deaf identity as part
of God's good, diverse creation. The two beliefs cannot comfortably
exist together.[389] Isabelle, who had experienced deliverance prayer for
MS, reflected on how intimidating these healing practices can be for
wheelchair users:

> It was a bit scary. The way it was said to me, 'Oh, I think that there's
> a spirit of MS.' That's how they started the conversation … I don't
> think people realise what that's like. If you're sat down, and they're
> standing over you, a lot of them, it's actually quite intimidating
> physically as well. It's not a position you want to put yourself in.

Like Andrew, Isabelle contrasted her experience of deliverance prayer
with compassionate ministries that honour a disabled person's own
experiences of healing. For disabled people, who are already in a
vulnerable position as a result of the way we are treated in society,
unexamined healing practices can be intimidating, invalidating and even

violent. For Isabelle and Andrew, deliverance ministry was a traumatising experience.

When healing prayer is performative and showy, it can overlook those disabled people whose needs are unseen, who have no crutches or wheelchairs to discard. Susanna's ME/CFS is invisible, and she was frustrated when pray-ers were only interested in praying for people with impairments that they could see. They overlooked Susanna's unseen need:

> When [the minister] got down off the stage, he went straight for someone in a wheelchair, and that just told me everything I needed to know, because it was like it was just looking at the outside. He's got no clue ... why that person was using a wheelchair, whether or not they would welcome prayer, or whether or not they needed prayer. He was just assuming. 'Someone is in a wheelchair. The wheelchair is therefore something to be healed from.' I just felt that was very negative, and there I was sat with an illness that I would have loved healing for, but I didn't look ill.

This healing service was not entirely about those who wanted to receive healing prayer, Susanna reflected. The agenda was set by the pray-ers, who were hoping for a dramatic spectacle of God's power. Our society's stereotypes of disability focus on physical and visible difference; disabled people who are invisibly impaired are often forgotten. Church healing practices can easily share that ableist bias. Spectacular healing ministry may even be a reminder of the history of the freak show, as non-disabled people treat our differences as something abnormal, which can only be resolved through a show of the supernatural.[390] Such healing ministry is 'othering' for disabled people. It may have little room for disabled people who are asking for gentle prayer that honours their own, nuanced experiences of God's healing.[391]

That was not the only way that healing ministries overlooked storytellers' real needs. A church obsession with healing-as-cure can distract from disabled people's cries for access and justice, when those in ministry do not listen when disabled people share our priorities. 'Christ often asks, "What would you like me to do for you?"', Charlotte reflected, during a discussion on healing ministry. 'Does the Church ask us what we'd like the Church to do? Not so much.' When church members prayed for cure for Andrew, he felt that the church was 'fobbing me off,' rather than accepting him as he is:

> I think what Jesus wants is that we have to learn compassion and care for each other. And we have to care for people where they're at, not where we want them to be ... But it's like, when you're ill you can't go to church. Well, faith healing, if you're healed you can come to church every week. That's what they want, they want to solve your problem.

It was easier for Andrew's church to seek to change his body than to dismantle the barriers and social inequalities that kept Andrew from participating, as a Deaf congregant. At times, Kt had found the same preoccupation with healing prayer equally ridiculous and irrelevant, when she had much more pressing needs:

> So you get up on your crutches. You start to walk to the toilet, and all the prayer ministry people are going, 'Oh, we can pray for her for healing, hurrah.' And they all come swamping you. And you're like, 'No, the biggest need I have right now is the toilet. You can pray for one to come to me ...' Naturally, if you have an obvious disability, you're the one that needs the prayer right there.

When non-disabled people imagine that we need a cure more than a toilet, they centre their own priorities, rather than asking us what we need. Andrew exposed the heart of much healing ministry: it seeks to remake disabled people in the image of non-disabled people, rather than recognising the image of God in a diverse creation. But Jesus's model of healing is for all of the Body of Christ; he transforms communities.[392] When church healing ministries ask disabled people to measure up to ableist norms of health, they distract from the reality that it is often church communities that are in need of healing – from sins of ableism that close the gates to disabled people. There is no need for churches to change when all disability has been cured, as Andrew wryly remarked.

Storytellers called churches to be critical of the theology that lurks beneath healing practices, and to ask whether their ministries are influenced by ableist values of compulsory non-disability. When disabled people's own experiences of healing are not listened to, churches will only be able to tell one story – that we need cure through healing prayer. Disabled people do not want the focus of all our churchgoing to be a sense of failure, a perception that our bodies and minds fall short of an ideal. We hear this message enough from secular society. Storytellers spoke instead of a holistic Kingdom healing that celebrates all the diversity in God's creation. Our flourishing as disabled people can co-exist with healing ministry that neither diminishes nor objectifies us, Fern said:

> Disability should not be assumed as only worth something if it is eradicated. For some people healing may well be right, that can't be disputed, but that should not be the only story a church can tell. There needs to be a more holistic approach and the disabled person needs to be active in that.

While theology comes to the logical conclusion that disability should be eliminated, the Church will fail to see the *imago Dei* in disabled people. Instead, Fern was praying for churches led by counter-cultural gospel values, which can recognise God reflected in all of us, just as we are.

Faith, sin and healing

❝ I went to one healing group and they said, 'You need to own your healing.' And I said 'Well, I don't heal myself. Jesus heals me.'❞ Faith

When disability is seen as a lesser state of being, the sin-disability conflation is often at work. Disabled theologians have written about the ever-present idea that disabled people's bodies and minds are a reflection of our sinful souls. John Hull tells us of a taxi driver who asked him what he had done to deserve blindness.[393] Today, some theologians and ministers still 'equate 'wholeness' with 'holiness',[394] seeing those with impairments as less than whole and less than holy. In modern churches, the 'disability as punishment' trope may come in a more subtle but no less harmful form, when disabled people are told that we lack the faith we need to strive for cure. Stephen Arterburn writes: 'I have worked with many people through the years who could have experienced healing but refused it ... They chose to ... wallow in the pool of self-pity and wade through their shame rather than to get up and walk the path of healing.'[395] The ancient idea that disability is a punishment or consequence of sin or faithlessness persisted in some storytellers' churches, in the form of a health and prosperity gospel that tells Christians that God will bless them with material wealth and physical health.[396] Some storytellers had run the gamut of victim blaming after healing prayer – they were told that their impairments were the result of their sin, a curse, and/ or a lack of faith. In a society where disabled people are held personally responsible for our state of health, this is a story we are already familiar with. For storytellers, hearing the same message from churches could be traumatic.

Jemma suffered when, as a new Christian, she was told her multiple illnesses and impairments were due to a lack of faith, 'something which totally destroyed me at the time', she said. Today, after exploring the Bible and disability theology for herself, Jemma believes that God's healing is about far more than simple cure. But the idea that her impairments were a sign she lacked faith was a source of harm and internalised ableism for Jemma, at a time when she was vulnerable to bad theology. In much the same way, Mims told us how a belief that faith leads to cure made her feel a 'pressure not to be depressed,' even in a church with a strong disability theology. On one occasion, after Mims gave a talk at her church on her experiences of mental distress, she was challenged about whether her distress was a sign of faithlessness:

> This guy came up to me afterwards ... He was saying, 'Don't you find faith in God means that mental health [problems] doesn't happen to you as much?' It is kind of like, I just get the feeling ... that people do, underneath it all, believe that if your faith is strong enough you won't get depressed.

Laura told us how a similar insistence on praying constantly for cure for her chronic illness became discouraging when, after many years, complete cure began to seem less and less likely. The impact on Laura's faith and self-esteem was difficult to bear:

> I spoke to friends from church and church leaders, some of whom
> prayed with me and for me, but nothing happened physically and
> the subliminal message I kept getting over and over again was
> that my lack of faith/prayer, or something I had done wrong, was
> stopping me from being healed. I started to wonder if this might be
> true, even wondering if somehow deep down, I wanted to not be
> healed, despite the pain and suffering I was enduring every day.

The constant pressure to build up their faith and seek a cure left many storytellers with endless deferred hope and self-blame, and with little guidance on living with disability in the here and now. Jemma, Mims and Laura were just a few of the storytellers who encountered a belief in faith(lessness) that locates all the problems that need 'fixing' in disabled people. That can do damage to our faith, rather than building it up, when we may come to see ourselves as unworthy of cure because we have not worked hard enough for it.

After years of difficult experiences of healing ministry, some storytellers had begun to challenge the assumptions and biblical interpretations behind victim-blaming healing theologies. After finding herself condemned as a 'failure' when she was not cured of her chronic illness, Fern reflected on the damage done to disabled people who are told our impairments are a sign we do not have enough faith:

> When I became unwell and disabled, lots of people said it must
> be a curse. People in the church told me and my family that it was
> due to sin, due to lack of faith, due to spiritual battles etc. ... Lots
> of people said that I needed to be healed quickly [as] a good news
> story of God. To be disabled therefore was a personal failure,
> and a bad news story, not something a church wants to highlight. I
> don't think it was perceived by many that there could be anything
> remotely positive associated with disability.

AT THE GATES

Fern saw deep into the heart of theology that associated healing with faith, devaluing and dehumanising her, and seeing disability only as deficit. She was left on the outside of her church community, feeling shame and internalised ableism.[397] Fern longed for 'someone to sit with me and be there and listen', and to ask God to bring whatever form of healing was right for her, but she could not find this more compassionate form of healing ministry. Eventually Fern left her church, seeking a community where she was valued, just as she is. 'I think there really, really needs to be a shift away from attitudes of condemning to attitudes of blessing', she said.

Through their lived experiences of healing as more than cure, storytellers spoke back against damaging theology that links faith(lessness) with disability. Jemma reflected on how seeking easy theological answers may be easier for non-disabled people than sitting with the mystery of disability:

> Sometimes when a person is not healed people try and look for reasons why this is, when really it's only God that can know. These reasons are often not theologically sound and place the blame on the individual in a way that is really unhealthy and unhelpful.

Susanna was coming to similar conclusions about the harm that a constant emphasis on healing-as-cure was wreaking in her life. She wondered whether, if God created her as she is, she needed to have faith in God's work in her life as a disabled person, and not wait for the empty promise of a cure:

> I'd been ill [for] well over 10 years at that point. I was like, 'Well, it's not going away … So am I being faithful by accepting that this is what my body is doing?'

As she grew in her disabled identity, Susanna began to wonder, radically, if seeking a cure might equate with doubting God. It was a theology that turned ableist assumptions of faith in healing upside down. In the same way, Faith boldly challenged an uncritical theology that focused on her own faith in healing:

> I went to one healing group and they said, 'You need to own your healing.' And I said, 'Well, I don't heal myself. Jesus heals me.' Certain things people can say can mess with your mind a bit. And if you're mentally not well, it can do more harm than good.

This is not the gospel; we do not earn God's grace, forgiveness and healing. In Faith's powerful understanding that she does not heal herself, and that Jesus is the only healer, she questioned a prosperity gospel that emphasises personal responsibility for health. The phrase 'own your healing' echoes ideas from the secular wellness movement, pushing us all to treat health as something to strive for, often at the expense of holistic, Kingdom experiences of healing in the midst of disability. But Faith knew that true healing points us to God.

To tell disabled Christians that we lack faith is an insult to our trust in God, in and through disability. It can take great faith and resilience to live with some experiences that come with disability. In spite of the messages they had heard about their own faithlessness, storytellers' faith was a response to God's grace in the midst of disability, as Miranda told us:

> I'm a fortunate person – my faith rarely wavered. Even when I became disabled, it was not a question of 'Why me?' or 'This isn't right.' It's just something that happened… But [faith is] just a blessing, isn't it? I don't think my life's bad. I think being disabled has given me so much.

When healing theology focuses on faith(lessness) in disability, the Church asks disabled people for a simplistic, performative faith that we must earn for ourselves. Instead, we may need space to question and doubt, through illnesses or impairments that can complicate our lives. Or, like Miranda, our faith may not waver, when we find that disability is far from the tragedy that society believes it to be. Miranda saw disability as part of the diversity of God's created world, after a random car accident that might have happened to anyone; she knew it was not a punishment from God. Unlike those around her, Miranda did not find it useful to worry about the reasons for her impairment.[398] Instead, she had faith that disability was an experience in which she could serve God.

She challenged those who believe, in Hannah Lewis's words, that 'the Kingdom of God cannot be coming in the here and now for people with disabilities'.[399]

When disability is associated with faithlessness or sin, a flawed concept of punishment imagines a heartless God refusing to help those who are longing and praying for healing.[400] It is theology that sees disabled people only as the result of a Fallen world. For Mary Elise Lowe, these broken concepts of sin obscure the reality that everyone is a sinner. They also obscure the social sins that are perpetrated against disabled people:

> The doctrine of sin must be critiqued and reframed in ways that both help persons with disabilities to understand the sins that are committed against them, and also encourage all persons to recognize their complicity in unjust structures, confess their personal sins, and create a space where forgiveness and reconciliation can be experienced by all.[401]

But storytellers' experiences suggest we may still be far from this more nuanced theology of social sin, oppression and reconciliation. In Sarah Anne Long's research into Christian attitudes towards disabled people's quality of life, she found that some ministers assumed disabled people's lives were 'difficult' and 'worthless', inhibiting their full spiritual potential,' leading some to believe even that disabled people are better off dead.[402] In many of our storytellers' experiences of 'healing' ministries and theologies, we see similar ableist and even implicitly eugenicist assumptions.[403] Influenced by a theology of health and prosperity, these healing practices reassure non-disabled Christians that as long as they are faithful and sinless, God will not strike them down with illness or impairment. But, as storyteller Jane reminded us, Jesus told his disciples that:

> 'Neither did this man sin, nor did his parents.' What *really* riles me is the concept of disability as punishment for sin.[404]

When disabled people are seen as worth less until we are cured, the inevitable conclusion is that we must have failed God. In truth, we have only failed the non-disabled people around us, who, anxious in their precarious privilege, are seeking a sign that their bodies will forever meet modern standards of health. But in disabled people's honest, accepting relationships with our bodies, we share another way to understand the human experience. The challenge from disabled people to the Church is to live with the mystery and temporality of all our bodies, knowing that we are each a humble part of God's unpredictable, diverse creation.[405] All human beings suffer, just as we all experience joy and peace. We *all* need God's healing in our lives, not just those of us whose bodies and minds diverge from society's norms. This is healing that values disabled people's flourishing above our cure.

Healing the wounds of ableism

> ❝God made me like this, and therefore there is nothing wrong with me.❞ Jane

Among disabled Christians, a growing cultural model of disability is helping many of us to celebrate our differences as a vital part of who we are. In theological terms, many disabled Christians are declaring that we are fearfully and wonderfully made, and remembering that we are full expressions of the *imago Dei*. In the details, disabled people may have different *teleologies* of disability – different ways of understanding why we are disabled, if we worry about this at all. Nonetheless, many of us know that God uses us, with our impairments, not in spite of them. God's image is not marred in disabled people, many storytellers told us; they knew that they not broken, and that they were loved, just as they are. What, then, does holistic healing and wholeness look like in the midst of these disabled people's diversity and lived experiences? Storytellers had a vision of God's Kingdom healing to share with the Church here, a vision that goes further than mere physical cure.

Disabled identity led many storytellers to question ableist assumptions in the Church's understanding of healing. If we are made in the image of God, some asked, why do we need to be 'fixed'? As a disabled person, Jane had come to see a difference between healing and cure:

Healing is being made whole, with the disability/condition – coming to health, coming to see yourself as whole. Curing, to me, implies removal of the disability/condition to make the person better … God made me and God makes nothing wrong, therefore there's nothing wrong with being disabled. Granted, pain and disability are often unpleasant, but what makes them *so* difficult is the lack of support and understanding.

Cure-focused healing ministries diminished Jane in her God-given disabled identity. She told us how she longed, instead, for Christian healing ministries that seek to heal the wounds of ableism:

[Healing] ministries and attitudes run counter to my own sense of personhood as a disabled person. It argues that there is something wrong that needs correcting. I think abled people who run healing ministries are more often after curing than healing. If healing at all, it ought to be connected with healing the wounds that these perceptions inflict – living with the disability, rather than wishing to be without it … What needs curing is other people's attitudes.

Only from a place of experience as a disabled person could Jane develop a renewed theology of healing that turns the concept upside down, allowing her to see how disabled people are harmed by the social sins of ableism, from which we, society and churches all need healing. Storyteller Charlotte had come to see a distinction between cure and healing, too emerging from her embodied perspective as a disabled person. 'I think people sometimes confuse cure with wholeness', she said, adding that disabled people do not need cure to become the people God wants them to be. But Jane had not been able to access much teaching on this radical, social model-influenced theology of healing. Some of her church leaders had been reluctant to discuss the issues that healing ministries present for disabled people. Jane had reached her own conclusions, as a disabled person in a world that devalues her ways of being. She knew she did not need to become non-disabled to be loved and used by God, just as she is.

Disabled people are calling for a more holistic, Kingdom understanding of healing in churches. But this does not mean that some of us are *not* also praying for cure, especially when illness and impairment are not always positive experiences. Laura's complex experiences of chronic illness have shaped her nuanced beliefs about healing and cure. When Laura, who comes from a Baptist church background, first developed a chronic illness, she firmly believed that God would cure her:

> At this point, I was of the understanding that because I was a good person and my illness was causing me daily pain and suffering, that God would eventually heal me ... My faith was the strongest it had ever been but I wasn't getting better, I was getting worse. This was the start of the re-shaping of my healing and suffering theology.

It was discouraging for Laura, at first, when she was not healed in the way she hoped, but it was the beginning of her journey towards a more expansive vision of healing. After her church organised a healing service, at which Laura was anointed with oil, Laura had an experience of partial healing that was a blessing for her. These lived experiences have together shaped her trust in the mystery of God's healing, which may be greater than cure:

> I am still trying to work out my own understanding of my chronic illness journey and God in that, as well as the bigger picture with regards to healing and suffering, but the most important thing I have learnt is that my lack of physical healing is not my fault and that God has not abandoned me/does not love me less because of [it], nor does it mean I cannot do what I am called to – it just looks different to the way I thought it would do.

As she trusted God to work in and through her chronic illness, Laura did not need to find all the answers to her experiences of disability. She was able to continue to trust in God for healing and blessing, without an expectation that healing would always come in the form she might expect.

Deirdre shared a similar story of continuing to pray for healing while letting go of the expectation of cure. During her 18 years of ME/chronic fatigue syndrome, Deirdre had been through some very difficult times; isolation and loneliness were often a feature of a life lived entirely from her bed. And yet, God had brought Deirdre peace and healing *through* her illness, even if not *from* it:

> God has transformed me through it. I am far happier and 'whole' now than I ever was before the illness. In a funny way, I wouldn't have been without the experience but would have liked it to be somewhat shorter!

Deirdre's qualified, mixed response to illness was not unusual among storytellers, who nonetheless believed that God had given them healing through experiences of disability. Some were still praying for a cure from pain, illness or distress, but that did not negate God's power at work in and through their lives as disabled people. Deirdre and Laura's theologies of their personhood and wholeness, loved just as they are, helped them to make sense of healing within all their multifaceted experiences of suffering and joy in disability.

With the knowledge that some disabled people are seeking a deeper healing than cure, how should churches pray for our healing? Storytellers told us that healing disabled people need may not be the healing that non-disabled people *think* we need. When non-disabled Christians asked, 'How can we pray for you?' without assuming the answer, it could transform disabled people's experiences of healing prayer. Charlotte attended a retreat, where, at one session, she spoke to other retreatants about her chronic illness. The next mealtime, she found herself being prayed for without her consent:

> One of the ladies came up to me and put her hand on my shoulder. Which is not always a good thing to do because I have odd pain sensation anyway. It might just send me up the wall with the pain. And [she] started praying for my healing. So when she stopped I turned round to her and I said, 'What healing are you praying for?' She said, 'Your disability.' I said, 'Well, I've had my disability all my life and I wouldn't be doing what I'm doing now if it wasn't for that. It's part of me. Yes, there are things that are painful and frustrating, but

I don't necessarily need God to heal me from that. It's part of who I am. There are other things in my life that have happened that have been quite traumatic that I do need healing for ... I think you should ask before you start praying for me. And find out whether people want that.'

Storytellers sought healing prayer for all the same painful life situations anyone else might, from bereavement to difficult relationships. Healing ministries only became oppressive when pray-ers assumed that disabled people's first need was cure from impairment or illness. Through her perceptive question, 'What healing are you praying for?' Charlotte called on churches to *ask,* as Jesus asked, and to listen. To value our disabled experience, and welcome our theologies of healing, even if these are challenge to preconceptions. It is a simple cry to re-centre the stories of disabled people in the healing theologies and practices that have been so painful for us. Many of us are still longing to receive healing prayer in Christian communities that have not yet understood what healing means for us.

Jemma had reached similar conclusions. As someone with multiple impairments, she found people assuming that she was seeking healing prayer for her blindness, without asking first:

It is critical in healing ministry to ask the individual why they are responding for or asking for prayer. So many times people assume I am responding for my eyes when I want prayer for a sore back or PTSD. I've been in situations where I have had to stop people praying because they just assumed it was my vision, because I had a guide dog ... Pouncing on people because they have an obvious disability is not helpful.

Several storytellers who have both visible and invisible impairments shared Jemma's concern that 'the disability you can see' is always the first target of healing ministry, as non-disabled people seek to 'fix' that which is obviously different. Jemma offered churches a practice of meaningful healing, instead. Like Jesus, she said, those offering healing prayer need to ask, 'What do you want me to do for you?'[406] and not assume the answer. Caring, counter-cultural ministries of holistic healing can accept the paradoxes of the disabled experience, praying for those who are seeking healing from bodily pain or from the wounds of ableism, while still valuing the wonderfully made bodies and minds of disabled people.

As storytellers revisited the Bible with the wisdom of lived experience, many began to see God's model for a deeper healing in the pages of the Gospels. Their resistant readings of the Bible gave them the confidence to explore a disability-affirming theology of healing, as the radical wholeness Jesus offered, that went far beyond cure. While training to be a spiritual director, Charlotte explored healing with a sympathetic group:

> We had a led meditation on Scripture, which was on the healing by the pool [of Bethesda]. In my imagination, I was there as one of the disabled people. And Christ healed the guy. And at the end, [the meditation leader] said, 'Come back, leave the place.' But I didn't leave the place, because I was one of the disabled people. But I didn't feel that I needed to be healed. I felt I was healed ... And I felt that I could look into Christ's eyes and that Christ accepted me as I was.

In Charlotte's interpretation of John 5:1-9, she centred the perspective of the disabled people in the story who were not cured by Jesus. They were Charlotte's model for wholeness in community, where some disabled and ill people may seek and find cure as part of their healing, and others may remain 'by the pool,' loved and valued *as* disabled people. In a safe, disability-affirming space, Charlotte was led towards a more expansive understanding of her own wholeness in Christ. Understanding that Christ loves her just as she is, Charlotte experienced healing in the midst of disability. Nicki came to similar conclusions. 'I'm happy that I know that God isn't going to heal me,' she said. Constantly praying for cure was not on Nicki's agenda; serving God just as she is, and recognising God's blessings in her life as a disabled person, was more important to her.

It was through eco-theology that Susanna came to an understanding of disability and mortality as part of God's created world, rather than a consequence of the Fall:

I think [disability is] just part of the natural world. Things grow up. Then they die, decay, go back to the soil and then stuff comes out, and I think we're just part of that process, really. That's the way that I relate to it. I don't see me as different because my body is tired all the time.

In a creation that reflects an awesome God, Susanna's lived experience gave her a different kind of hope, one that did not require biomedical cure before she could believe in God's glory revealed in all of creation – and in her. There is biblical precedent for this theology of disability as part of God's vast, diverse creation, 'transformed from a problem into a mystery'.[407] Susanna and Charlotte's theologies offered a profound challenge to the deficit model of disability that storytellers encountered in some Christian healing practices.

Disabled people know there is grace to be found in uncertainty, pain, and celebration of our differences. Our stories challenge a Church that has often conflated ableist, modern cultural values of 'health' and wellness with the Kingdom healing that Jesus announced for all creation.[408] In a modern world where medicine has whispered the lie that we can live forever, we may find comfort in hoping, with Augustine, that we will have new, 'perfect' bodies in Heaven. But when we do not stop to question our ideas of 'perfection,' each of us can easily begin to devalue our wonderfully made bodies, just as we have devalued all of God's creation. Through experience of disability, storytellers were offering the Church more holistic ways of honouring all our bodies and minds. Rather than focusing on cure, Fern called the Church to welcome distinctive wisdom from disabled people, forged through all our experiences of disability, both positive and negative:

There is more to disability and disabled people than suffering. In the Bible it talks about 'strength in weakness'. Many of us live with that day to day, minute by minute. We know what that means on a personal level. When it talks about not being prideful, we learn that every moment we cannot physically access somewhere and can feel shamed by people's perceptions of disability … I think I look at things in a different light now.

Here, Fern echoed the reflections of disability theologian Mike Walker, that 'illness can be a creative matrix that allows people of varied abilities to embody wholeness'.[409] Fern's wisdom did not come through being made less disabled. Quite the opposite. It was through her experience of disability that God showed her new ways of understanding healing, faith and the Bible. As theologian Donna Thompson affirms, 'healing in Christ is always cruciform'.[410] Through her experiences of cancer, Thompson came to see that Christ's healing does not always come through our prayers for the cup of suffering to be taken from us. Healing comes at the foot of the Cross. These storytellers shared the same theology of Kingdom healing in the midst of illness and disability, in ways that were far more profound than simple cure.

Disability and disabled identity in Heaven

> ' When I get to heaven, I shall still be in my wheelchair. Why would it be any different? ' Miranda

As much as physical and miraculous healing was not necessary to many storytellers in this world, neither could some of them imagine any need for this kind of 'healing' in Heaven. Leah, who is autistic, wondered whether it was neurotypical people who would need healing from the wounds of ableism in Heaven:

> I have thought about [healing in Heaven] actually. I didn't work out what the answer was. But I think I came to a middle where I thought that there'd either be healing or it wouldn't be a problem. So, you know, other people's attitudes or whatever it is that gets in the way … I don't think all disabilities are necessarily a problem. So if they're not a problem, why would they be fixed? If other people's imperfections get in the way, then it might be those that are changed.

Leah located imperfection not in her autistic self, but in the attitudes and actions of those whose sins of ableism create barriers for her. Leah's theology grew out of a cultural model of neurodiversity.[411] In defiance of society's fixation with cure for neurodivergent people, Leah's Christian faith led her to believe that autistic people are part of the diversity of God's creation. It was a view she shared with other neurodivergent storytellers. Anthony reflected, 'If somebody's definition of healing is stopping people from having Asperger's sydrome so they are just, in inverted commas, "normal", that's quite dangerous, I think.' Although Anthony believed that no one can know exactly what Heaven will be like, he felt that he would still be himself there, because neurodiversity is integral to his personality. To be cured would change who Leah and Anthony are, and they were not sure that God would ever ask that of them, in this life or in Heaven.

It was not only neurodivergent people who were not sure they would be required to become non-disabled in Heaven. Miranda believed that she would be a wheelchair user in the life to come:

> I'm not convinced it says in the Bible we will all be healed when we get to Heaven … Somebody said to me, 'It'll be all right when you get to Heaven.' I said 'Why?', and they said, 'Well you'll be healed!' I said, 'No I won't! Still be in my wheelchair, won't I?'

After many years with a spinal injury, disability is part of Miranda's identity and central to her experience of life. She caused a stir among non-disabled friends with her theology. They imposed on Miranda their own anxieties and hopes about 'perfect' bodies in a very normal afterlife. Guided by her lived experience, Miranda protested what Hull calls 'eschatological visions towards the singularity of the average'.[412] In traditional thinking about the life to come, we tend to imagine that we will all be non-disabled, based on Augustine's theology.[413] Yet many of our physically disabled storytellers imagined Heaven differently, in a bold new challenge to the traditional idea that we will all have perfect, idealised Risen bodies.

Isabelle also had a unique way of thinking about her impaired body in the afterlife, rooted in her disabled experience. She began to contemplate this at a retreat, early in the process of adjusting to her life as a wheelchair user as a result of MS:

> I had an image in my mind ... There was a whole load of people
> and there was Jesus at the front. And they were walking towards
> him. And I was in my manual wheelchair at the time. Because I was
> quite strong in my arms at that point, I did a couple of spins of the
> wheel, and the chair shot ahead of everyone else towards him ...
> I suppose it challenged the concept that I think people think they
> will be fine in new Heaven and new earth. Is that actually right?
> What is 'fine'? ... 'Oh, you'll have a new body.' But I'm thinking, 'Yeah,
> but is that *me*, then?'

Isabelle challenged the whole premise of Heaven, pointing out that after
Christ's return, he will renew the earth, including her body. In the life
to come, Isabelle believed her body would remain an essential aspect of
herself and her identity. 'It is part of who you are,' Isabelle said of her
impairment. 'What causes more of a problem is obstacles.' Isabelle's
image of herself racing ahead of non-disabled people to meet Jesus
before them, in an afterlife where all barriers have been dismantled, is a
profound challenge to the marginalisation of disabled people in churches.
In Heaven, we will no longer be left waiting at the gates.

Stephen, who has ME/CFS that causes mobility impairments, was
another storyteller who imagined Heavenly perfection very differently
from the way non-disabled people might imagine it:

> I feel like [disability] is as much a part of my identity as it could possibly
> be, and something that would be carried on with whatever part of
> me is carried on ... I would imagine that Heaven is so accessible that
> there's no problems with whatever people are disabled with.

Stephen could not envisage an afterlife in which he would not be a
disabled person. Like Isabelle and Leah, his concept of Heaven was
influenced both by his disabled identity and the social model. He hoped
for a Heaven free of the earthly barriers that kept him from participating
in society and churches, rather than hoping for changes to his body. In
such a Heaven, when all barriers are torn down, we will have full access
to God. Influenced by normalcy, non-disabled people – like Miranda's
friends – may be fearful of a perfect Heaven where impairment can still

exist. But for many disabled people, a perfect Heaven will be perfectly accessible. That's a vision of the Kingdom, and it comes with a true promise of healing for an ableist society.

In contrast, other storytellers were looking forward to an afterlife without impairment. Rhona believed she would be sighted in the life to come. 'Yes, I think I will have a renewed body in Heaven,' she said. Rhona's *eschatology* – her theology of God's future – was rooted in a belief in God's sovereignty over impairment and pain. Even then, disabled people's beliefs about healing in Heaven were often complex, in a world where disability culture and identity are becoming more familiar to many of us. Clare believed she would be healed in Heaven, too, and yet the image of Jesus resurrected with his scars led her to reflect on all the complexities of healing, here and in Heaven:

> I think we will be healed and we'll have perfect bodies, but Jesus doesn't ... [Revelation] talks about still being able to see the scars from where he's been crucified, and that's quite fascinating.

Clare was comfortable sitting with the questions thrown up by the image of a Jesus resurrected with a scarred body, as she explored them through disability theology, together with an interpretive community of disabled people. While hoping for healing in Heaven, Clare was able to make space for the theologies of those who may believe that there is nothing wrong with them that needs a cure, now or after death; she wondered whether Deaf people might feel this way. For other storytellers, the details of their future Risen bodies were much less important than their longing to be with God there, as their most authentic selves, as Charlotte reflected:

> I think I would say that in heaven I don't know whether I will be physically healed or not but I don't think it really matters. I will be whatever is my complete self in God. So I don't know what that will look like, but it will be whatever it's supposed to be.

Faith echoed this thought, when she told us, 'Having given my life to the Lord, I'm complete in him. So that's how I'll be when I'm in Heaven.' Storytellers' impairments were no predictor of their desire to be healed, now or in Heaven. Some long-term wheelchair users were praying for physical healing, while some people with chronic illness were uninterested in cure. Disabled people's lived experiences of disability are diverse and unique to each of us; it is no surprise that our feelings about healing and cure are just as complex.

With impairments ranging from autism to chronic illness, many storytellers considered their experience of disability to be part of their identity. As such, they were reluctant to believe that their embodied experiences would simply be eradicated in Heaven. Most were not interested in exactly what their renewed bodies would be like there. They simply had a gloriously accessible vision of the Kingdom, where they will be their authentic selves in God. Some theologians have wondered whether disabled people need an 'eschatological hope' of bodily cure in Heaven.[414] But many of our storytellers had a much more expansive hope of Kingdom healing in the next world.[415] 'Risen Christians with disabilities may be identifiable as *ourselves*,' Walker writes, 'not normalized into homogeneity, but empowered by the Holy Spirit to journey toward God's dignity and love'.[416] This is a hope that goes far beyond modern cultural ideals of perfection. It is a communal, holistic vision of wholeness, that begins when we esteem all of God's creation, including our earthly bodies. In such a vision of Heaven, there will be no more barriers and no more injustice, and we will find healing from the wounds of ableism.

A Different Kind of Healing Service

At St Martin-in-the-Fields Church, a different kind of healing Eucharist was led by disabled people on St Luke's Day every year for many years. It emerged from the disabled-led Living Edge conference, which gathers disabled people 'to resource each other and the Church'.[417] The story of the healing service begins with the first weekend conference in 2012. After an exciting gathering on the Saturday, where disabled people and allies shared wisdom and experience, the next day's St Luke's Day service was a sobering reminder of how far churches still have to travel before they become places of disability justice. Fiona MacMilllan, Chair of the

FEARFULLY AND WONDERFULLY MADE

St Martin's Disability Advisory Group (DAG) and conference planning team, writes about the painful disconnect:

> The following day we joined the Sunday morning service and listened to lessons, sang hymns and heard anthems which all used the language of sickness and sin, blindness as lack of insight and choruses of the leaping lame – a rude return to reality.[418]

Over the following years, the DAG and church community worked together to shape healing liturgy that would weave the lived experience of disabled people into every part of the service. 'Developing this service has been an integral part of our learning as individuals, groups and the whole community explore ideas of disability and healing,' MacMillan writes.[419] For the next two years, the DAG wrote the Eucharistic liturgy for the service, in workshops led by vicar Samuel Wells, and went on to invite the Healing Team to join them for the annual workshops in the following years. Each year, on St Luke's Day, disabled members of the church led intercessions, helped to distribute communion and offered healing prayer.

Perhaps most radically, disabled people's own healing ministry became integral to this St Luke's Day service. Turning the Church's healing traditions upside down, they offered healing prayer to the non-disabled church majority, joining the Healing Team in their ministry. The keynote speaker from the disability conference preached the sermon, allowing them to bring more disabled people's wisdom out from the conference and into the pulpit – from the edge to the centre. Where hymns once associated blindness with ignorance, now John Hull preached a sermon on his shared experience with God, where darkness and light are the same to him. 'Looking around the table – who's not here?' MacMillan writes, of the church's efforts to centre disabled people in this healing service. 'Are we modelling belonging?'[420]

In this chapter, our storytellers have shared experiences of church healing practice that mark disabled people out as different, sinful or faithless, and in more need of healing than others. Against that background, the St Martin-in-the-Fields healing service has been a model of healing ministry transformed by disabled people's leadership and participation.[421]

As everyone receives from disabled people's ministry, the whole community challenges and is challenged on preconceptions of health, healing and disability. Ministries like the healing service at St Martin's, where disabled people's stories and lived experience are centred, have the potential to transform the whole Church's understanding of healing and cure.

Theologies of Kingdom Healing

'Disability is not just an individual predicament,' Clifton reminds us, 'but exists in the intersection of the structures of communities. It is as much or more a social problem than a medical one.'[422] When churches reduce the Gospel healing narratives to stories of individual cure, they have missed the full story. Through his ministry, Jesus announced God's Kingdom healing for whole communities, through liberation from injustice and Empire.[423] Today, Betcher tells us, normalcy and ableism are some of the oppressive forces from which our world needs God's healing.[424] Through reconciliation to God and each other, Jesus shows us how we are no longer subject to the normalising gaze that seeks to make disabled people like everyone else, to 'fix' our bodies and minds. The diversity of the Kingdom becomes a mark of God's people. Kingdom healing is lived out in communities of justice, where, called to share in the Holy Spirit's work in the world, we live out right relationship with all God's creatures – sharing God's particular concern for the marginalised – and with the earth itself.[425] As all of us, disabled and non-disabled, come to realise that we are fearfully and wonderfully made in the image of God, we find a deeper healing than cure.

As disabled Christians are empowered to tell new stories of healing, we are showing the Church a vision of a more diverse Reign of God. Disabled people's lives and ways of being have been devalued by a model of Christian healing rooted in theology that cannot imagine us as whole, just as we are. From the edge, these storytellers share a theology of Kingdom healing, for all of humanity, shaped by their lived experience of disability. They speak out against ableist theology that, unwittingly or not, threatens us with a future where God eradicates disability and neurodiversity. They call the Church to honour all our diverse created bodies, as gifts from God, and to value the experiences of embodiment that we all share with the incarnated Christ. They cry out for the healing of our communities from the social sin of ableism that divides us from each other.

Disability theologian Julia Watts Belser echoes that cry to flourish, just as she is:

> What I wish for us is a way to push back against the ableist assumptions of these healing narratives: that disability is a sign of sin or moral degradation; that we are broken, suffering, and miserable; that we have no agency until our healing comes; that healing is the center of our story and our only longing.[426]

This disabled life is a life worth living. Watts Belser's disabled body, just as it is, has much to teach others about God, and about God's healing.[427] As Clifton puts it, this flourishing can only come through Jesus, who offers fullness of life that is not dependent on an idealised state of health, and which comes 'with the promise of the presence of Spirit in the midst of hardship'.[428] Disabled people know that God does not ask us to change to be more like non-disabled people, nor to buy into capitalist, ableist values of 'perfection'. God only asks us to flourish as we were created to be.

As disabled people lead the way in honouring the image of God in ourselves, may we inspire the Church to value all God's people. As we celebrate the Spirit's work in our disabled lives, may the Church transform its understanding of the Holy Spirit from one who guarantees to 'fix' us, to one who teaches us to recognise the diversity in God's good creation.[429] She is the reason for our hope for a transformed, anti-ableist Church that can come to honour disabled people's bodies and minds, just as we are, so that Christ's healing need no longer be conflated with cure.

CHAPTER 7

Church on the Edge: Disabled Christian Community Beyond the Church Gates

Beyond the gates of the church, disabled people are meeting together, doing church differently.

Throughout this book, we have shared stories of disabled people waiting at the church gates. But the margins are not just a waiting space. There is life on the edge, where disabled people are finding new ways to do and be Church together, in communities where we can come just as we are – where we do not have to leave disability at the church door. Many of these groups meet online. The online space is a powerful place for connection, accessible to many disabled people from our beds and our homes, where many of us are already active. Other disabled-led communities come together in physical spaces, shaping communities where accessibility is integral, and not just an afterthought.

As disabled people create our own expressions of church together, we are showing the rest of the Church what it means to 'set a table without making assumptions about how to get to the table'.[430] In their own communities, storytellers are asking what an accessible, just Church really looks like, and living out the answer. These are the edge-spaces where disabled Christians are empowered to speak out against injustice, to shape living disability theology, and to minister to each other. In these days of change in the mainstream churches, disabled-led ministries have the potential to renew the whole Church from the edge, as they reach out in mission and ministry to those outside *and* inside the church gates.

Disabled People's Online Church Groups

Online Church is real Church: YouBelong

Laura Neale set up YouBelong, an online group for chronically ill and disabled Christians, after she became seriously ill in her twenties. She suddenly found herself 'unable to eat or drink, resulting in weight loss and extreme fatigue,' she told us. As her health issues persisted, Laura's theology of suffering and healing were slowly being reshaped through experience. She felt called to ministry, but completing her theology studies was a challenge in the midst of illness, and she was not sure there was any form of ministry that could accommodate her as a disabled person:

> [I] wondered why I was even there if I would not be able to use my learning in some way afterwards ... It was at this moment that I was also introduced to online church as something that I could do without needing lots of energy. I listened, but I wanted to be involved in 'real' ministry. I didn't think that online church was 'real' church.[431]

Meanwhile, Laura was struggling to find a church where she could belong. She encountered painful reactions and attitudes to her chronic illness in churches, from 'blaming and shaming,' to being ignored by fellow Christians who were uncomfortable around her. She began to realise how many chronically ill and disabled people like her were excluded from churches, through a deadly combination of inaccessible buildings and theology that kept them from belonging:

> I felt uncomfortable in many of these places, physically as a result of the hard pews or hot buildings but also because I didn't feel like I belonged there and so much of the theology required me to be physically fit and well and excluded those who weren't.

AT THE GATES

God's answer to her situation would surprise Laura, as she was called to create the change she was seeking. As she revisited the idea of online church, Laura was inspired by the stories of people on the edge of the Church who had connected digitally:

> I realised that online church could be real church ... I felt prompted to search [on Twitter] for online church and chronic illness and disability related hashtags, and within just a few clicks, I found others like me, Christians with chronic illnesses and churches online! I hadn't felt like I belonged in other churches, so I was keen to make my account a place that others could belong and where we could connect with one another, I could share encouragement and teaching and where online church could happen – YouBelong.

From a simple beginning on one Twitter account, YouBelong grew organically, as chronically ill and disabled Christians found a welcoming sanctuary in the group. Today, the group connects about 800 people. But YouBelong is still a young community, restricted by lack of staff and finances, like many lay-led grassroots disabled Christians' groups. So, for now, their focus is on nurturing community. Laura's open Twitter posts encourage those who do not yet know the group to venture near and explore disability and faith with members, while a closed Facebook page brings together a smaller, safer group where people can share their struggles and joys more openly with each other. The group comes together for video-based Bible studies, Bible journaling sessions, and creative activities. As Laura told us, these are activities 'with God at the centre, but with the hope of initiating and allowing further conversation around life more generally too'.

Laura had never known just how many disabled Christians faced this level of exclusion from churches, until the YouBelong community brought so many of them together online. Online church is not accessible to all disabled Christians. We are a community with higher levels of digital exclusion than average, especially among older disabled people.[432] Yet many of us are already connecting through the internet, a mission field full of opportunities for connection and safe conversations among disabled people, where closed groups can offer safety, vulnerability and healing from the wounds of ableism. Only an online group like YouBelong could ever have brought together so many scattered disabled Christians, some of whom can rarely or never leave their homes, while others cannot access their local churches. For many of its members, YouBelong has become their home church. For them, online church is real church. YouBelong shows how online ministry can be vital for disabled Christians, when so many have been turned away from the church gates.

YouBelong's mission does not end with their disabled members. Their vision is not just to connect, support and empower disabled Christians, but to transform the Church. In Laura's words, they aim 'to educate church leaders and enable them to make their churches more accessible, physically as well as in the language and theologies used'. They are also exploring a mission to connect local churches with those disabled people who are longing to join a church community that meets in a building, helping both sides to overcome the barriers in the way. With the benefit of their lived experience of exclusion, YouBelong's leaders hope they can help to forge relationships that can provide more spiritual support than they can offer at a distance. It's a mission of reconciliation and grace, between those who have been left waiting at the church gates, and institutional churches willing to be renewed from the edge. That reconciliation begins online.

Church where we find ourselves: Disability and Jesus

Disability and Jesus is a conscious online ministry. Its founders, who are all disabled, know that the online space is often far more welcoming to disabled people than physical spaces. But it was in a pub, in 2014, that disabled priest Kt Tup and colleagues conceived of Disability and Jesus. Together with fellow disabled minister Bill Braviner and blind advocate Dave Lucas, who now runs The Ordinary Office, another online group, Kt had a vision for a Christian community by disabled people, for disabled people. Through experience, they knew that disabled Christians' voices are missing from churches. 'How could a ministry bring together those who had been excluded and silenced?' they asked. The online world was the ideal setting, where technology would help them put disabled people front and centre in their ministry.[433] It was on Twitter that the community first took root. '[Twitter] just happened to be the rich soil where the seed fell and we went, 'Oh, this is the right place to be', Kt remembered. It was rich soil indeed. Within six years, Disability and Jesus was engaging with over 15,000 people.

As they grew, the group's founders felt called to shape not just an activist community, but a worshipping community. Many in the Disability and Jesus community had no 'home churches' of their own, and were longing for more than Twitter discussions, whether they were too unwell to attend church in a building, or had not found an accessible welcome in their local churches. The Disability and Jesus community now shares a regular Sunday service every week, centring disabled contributors and hosted on YouTube. Mobile technology makes it simple for members of the community to record their segments during the week, edited together by Bill. The result is a Service of the Word, in Church of England parlance. The service aims to bring church to disabled people, wherever they are:

> We keep it to 15 minutes, or 20 at most ... The same format every
> week gives a sense of familiarity, so people can then relax into
> it more, without thinking, 'What will it be this week?'... It's then
> pushed out on Sunday, which means people can join in with it when
> they choose to. When do you need church to be in your living
> room, or in your bedroom, wherever? Our YouTube channel will
> flag it up. You join when you're ready to.

This is an entirely new way to do and be Church together, together with disabled people living on crip time, often with limited energy, who in some cases cannot leave their homes or even their beds. This is church with the potential to be accessible to many more disabled people than most, as Disability and Jesus collaborate with Deaf Christians and learn from neurodivergent culture, as they work to be accessible to people with learning disabilities and those experiencing fatigue, and as they encourage disabled members to lead, rather than just talking to or about them. Community members can now access other services on the Disability and Jesus YouTube channel, from services of Nine Lessons and Carols to recorded Morning Prayer. And, as they have since the beginning, the group's leaders still share a simple, Twitter-length prayer every morning and night.

Seven years after their simple beginning in a pub in Harrogate,

Disability and Jesus celebrate the fact that they are now just one organisation in a growing movement of disabled-led church groups. In a broad network, Disability and Jesus' ministry becomes one dish in a banquet set and shared by disabled people, with something to suit everyone's tastes or access needs. 'We take it in turns to signpost each other,' Kt reflected. There is space for many disabled-led groups, offering different ways to worship and connect, so that everyone can find an accessible way to Jesus.

Kt sees Disability and Jesus as true *online church,* doing very different work from parish churches that stream their services:

> 'Church online' [is] a building-based act of worship that connects to the online space ... An online church is, 'We, the community already online, will create church where we find ourselves'.[434]

Organised by ordained disabled priests, Disability and Jesus is an unusual 'online church' movement, with links to the Church of England. But they are still a fully online expression of church. They have no buildings; their community life is lived entirely on the internet, and they provide a full experience of worship in the online space. This is mission, but it is not the traditional outreach of building-based churches streaming their services to an unexplored mission field beyond their gates. This is church where disabled people find themselves. The group's leaders preach a message of disabled-led renewal from the edge, and they are taking that message out to the wider Church. But their most important work is still with and by disabled people. Through their online services, and on Twitter, they show that disabled Christians can participate and lead in the Church, especially in new forms of church that are designed by and for us. Disability and Jesus is a community of disabled people on the edge, reaching disabled people on the edge.

Discovering God together with disabled people: Struggling Saints

As a disabled pioneer minister with a Church Army background, Tim Rourke consciously set out to minister online. His mission has been to go where disabled people already are. As Tim told us:

> I think pioneering is an attitude of, we go out into the place. We
> learn from the culture of that place. And we discover God together
> with them. And that mindset, which I learned [in my ministry] on
> the estates, works for what I'm doing online.

Online disabled communities were a particular inspiration for Tim's
ministry with disabled Christians. In many ways, Tim feels that the disability
movement is ahead of churches, not only in its work for justice, but in
building community among disabled people. Seeking to learn from them,
Tim spent time with online disabled groups like the Staying Inn, a virtual
pub that has been drawing together disabled people during COVID-19
lockdowns, creating a space for mutual support and activism.[435] 'You do
realise that's ministry, don't you?' Tim reflected. 'It's really serving that
community.' As Tim got to know these online disabled communities,
he felt called to form a Twitter-based ministry – Struggling Saints. Tim
imagined it as an online setting that could bring conversations about God,
faith and disability to disabled people, bursting into life in the midst of the
vibrant disabled community and culture that exists in the digital space.

Online church groups have the potential to help the Church reach
disabled people who do not engage with churches, and just as importantly,
for disabled people to reach out in mission to the Church. That's why
Tim set up Struggling Saints as a group where anyone could contribute,
whether Christians or not. We live in a society where the Church has
given damaging messages to disabled people, Tim told us. Online, disabled
Christians have opportunities to share more loving relationships with
disabled people outside the churches. Struggling Saints' discussions about
disability and faith are held on Twitter, a very public forum:

> I really want [disabled non-Christians] to hear that there are
> Christians who don't believe the stuff you've been told. I mean,
> the reason we do the Twitter Bible study on Twitter, is because
> [disabled people] that I've connected with, will see that we're taking
> the Bible seriously and trying to work out what it actually means.

Non-disabled Christians are welcome to participate in Struggling Saints'
discussions, but disabled people lead the conversation. That flips the

traditional dynamic of church and disabled people upside down. In a community by and for disabled Christians, Struggling Saints' insights come from the whole group's shared disabled experience. The group brings disability theology alive through real-time discussion, aiming to be more accessible and experiential than academic books:

> The idea is that I ask questions that come out of my experience
> and saying to people who have the experience, with disability
> specifically, 'What can we learn as a group that will be useful for
> the church to know, because it's an aspect of God that they may
> have missed?' It's not saying we've got all the right answers. It's just
> saying that when we look at God from a different angle, i.e. the
> angle of people who are disabled, which is a wonderfully diverse
> group anyway ... we will learn stuff about God that we might not
> ordinarily see. So let's write that down and work out what it is
> ... One of our key things is trying to get some good theology out
> there.

Tim's ideas echo the theologies of Eiesland and Watts Belser, who believe that their disabled experience can teach non-disabled people truths they have missed about God.[436] Struggling Saints is sharing disabled people's knowledge of God with the rest of the Church. This is living disability theology, brought to life in a community where disabled people are leading the conversation about us. It's a contrast with the world of academic and church theology, where the gates are closed to most of us. Through the disabled people whose voices are heard in the group, the Church can be renewed from the edge, Tim believes:

> If you look at the revival movements, that's where they happened.
> They didn't happen from the centre, getting bigger. They happen
> from the edges, exploding out ... As a Church Army officer, [the
> edge] is where I'm most comfortable.

As a pioneer minister, Tim has deliberately set out not to make Struggling Saints feel 'churchy'. That means the group has been able to engage with those who have very little interest in church, but are willing to talk about the places where God, faith and disability meet. If churches measure growth by traditional metrics, online groups like Struggling Saints may not lead to increased numbers in the pews. 'If the way you count is those who attend, those who don't attend don't count,' is how Tim put it. That doesn't stop this work from being Kingdom ministry, reaching disabled people outside the churches. Yet Tim is longing for disabled people on the edge to *count* to the rest of the Church. They matter, whether they are disabled Christians looking for community in exile, disabled former churchgoers who have been alienated from churches, or disabled non-Christians with whom the Church has failed to share a Christ who loves them, just as they are.

Struggling Saints - Bible Reflections
@Strgl_St_Bible
...

Pray 3 - Healing & Cure

Meeting with God and experiencing healing happens regularly - Being cured is very rare. Hoping for the miracle can be more exhausting than living with God as disabled people

Disability Inclusion Advent thought : Day 18

10:06 AM · Dec 18, 2021 · Twitter Web App

Image description: A tweet from the Struggling Saints Twitter account, dated 18 December 2021. Text reads: 'Pray 3 - Healing & Cure. Meeting with God and experiencing healing happens regularly - Being cured is very rare. Hoping for the miracle can be more exhausting than living with God as disabled people. Disability Inclusion Advent thought: Day 18.'

There are many other disabled-led Christian communities, meeting God where two or three are gathered, often without publicity, funding, or acknowledgement from the institutional church. We spoke to disabled leaders of smaller digital church groups, from Emma's safe, closed online space where disabled people hurt by the churches can explore faith together, to Faith's group, where those who cannot leave their homes are creating a space for prayer ministry together. The value and power of self-organised, disabled-led spaces has been recognised in disability activism for many years. In our own groups, disabled people discover how to speak after we have been silenced; we empower ourselves; we find spaces for healing.[437] Disabled people's online church groups, in all their forms, have the potential to be just as liberatory for marginalised disabled Christians. These are communities making the most of the online space, whether groups feel called to the mission field of public discussion, or are seeking to create safe, closed spaces where they can heal the wounds of ableism together.[438] For these groups, the online world can be good soil for prophetic communities, where disabled people can call from the edge for justice.[439] Together, these online groups are called to a mission of reconciliation and outreach *from* disabled people *to* the churches.

Disabled-led Churches and Communities

'With, not for': Wave Church

Wave Church is a Christian community of people with and without learning disabilities, worshipping together. Jess Hardie has Down syndrome. Her family's church had always been welcoming of Jess, but when she turned 18 and left the supportive youth group, she suddenly found herself facing barriers to participating in services. 'Being at St James was like being with my family,' Jess told us, 'because I grew up at that church, but all the talks were too grown up for me!' When Jess stopped wanting to go to church altogether, her mother Bernice Hardie realised she needed to help her daughter find other ways to explore her faith:

> That's what prompted me to start Wave, because I realised she still wanted to carry on learning and growing in her faith but wasn't able to do that, in mainstream services, because it was all too

AT THE GATES

cerebral. The main thing is the length of the service. The fact that
it's all auditory. The fact that the language is quite difficult. And the
fact that in a large congregation, it's very easy to be ignored.

Without access, Jess could not belong. That meant she was missing out
on friendship and fellowship, too. The answer, for Bernice and her family,
was to listen to God's call to them to help transform the Church – *with*,
not *for*, people with learning disabilities. With the support of Christian
learning disability organisation Prospects,[440] Bernice co-founded Wave
Church, with a friend who also had a daughter with learning disabilities.

Today, Wave Church is a community of people with and without
learning disabilities, worshipping together in Muswell Hill. The church
group, whose name stands for We're All Valued Equally, does far more
than just telling members they are valued. The community makes it
possible for members to participate and belong. Accessible worship and
community is at the core of their monthly Sunday afternoon gatherings
in Muswell Hill, London. Every month, leaders with and without learning
disabilities open the gathering by telling members the most important
things they need to know: that Jesus loves them, and that everyone
is welcome here. A visual timetable shows what will happen, so that
everyone knows where they are in the service. Makaton signing and
symbols are an integral part of the service, not just an added extra.
Simple, familiar songs are signed from the front; the service always opens
with the song 'We Are Here Together', as members sing out that we
are all God's family. Tea and cake is always the last activity shown on the
screen, ending the service with fellowship. Wave Church is a community
designed to include people with learning disabilities, where they can fit
and where they are valued, just as they are. 'It feels like being part of
something for everyone – like I belong', one member told Bernice. 'I
think I am one of God's children', another member said, 'and I like going
to church. I am a sure believer that God is looking after us.'[441]

Most importantly, worship at Wave Church is embodied, creative and
interactive. 'The acronym that I use with the planning team is to make sure
that things are *short, simple, interactive and visual*,' Bernice says. 'We "SSIV"
any teaching that we do.' Instead of long sermons, the service is divided
into short segments, as members respond to the Bible through drama,

200

creative activities and sensory experiences. At one service, the story of the woman who anointed Jesus is told, as oils are passed around; members remember and retell the story at the following month's gathering. At other services, dramatised Gospel narratives bring the Bible to life. Even complex theological concepts can be made interactive and accessible. Bernice remembers a service that explored the idea of 'holy', as members came up with words to describe holiness, some grasping the concept in a way they never had before. She believes the Wave approach can help all Christians to encounter God in new ways:

> There was one Christmas when I was preparing a visual aid [to show] that Mary was the mother of God, and I showed an outline of a pregnant woman and then the Makaton symbol for God in her stomach. I realised, 'You were the almighty God, and you were a foetus, and you relied on this woman to feed you, to take care of you, to nurture you: you were completely powerless in the womb ...'. When we think of him as just all-powerful or all-perfect, that image always comes back to me.
>
> The idea that simple isn't powerful, or that it is something only relevant to people with learning disabilities, is the hurdle to overcome, I think ... If you look at Jesus, he told simple stories. And he did that because that's the way in which people could understand ... If we have the right heart and intention, I think the Holy Spirit can work through whichever way in which we try to convey his message.

As they are enabled to worship and belong, Wave Church members are enabled to serve. They have seen the impact of their ministry at their link church, St James' Muswell Hill, where congregants are blessed by the services that Wave Church members lead. Wave's ministry of interactive worship and accessible teaching is a gift they are sharing with the wider Church, as their model ripples out beyond Muswell Hill. Their newest initiative, 'Wave in a Box', is a toolkit that uses stories and resources to help grow more community groups like Wave. It's making an impact. Wave Church Little Ilford opened their doors in July 2021, the latest of several groups inspired by the first Wave Church.

Helen, who has a learning disability, comes to Wave Church with her mother, Christa, and leads the Makaton singing at some services. Interviewed with Christa's support, Helen shared how much she enjoys the interactive activities at Wave. 'I like the worship,' she told us. 'We do drama.' The accessible service 'helps me to be confident,' especially the Makaton symbols and pictures that guide members through worship. Unlike churches with long sermons, Helen is never bored or disengaged at Wave. 'I know why', she said. 'If you don't feel bored then that means you have fun.' And Helen has found fellowship and friendship at Wave. 'At Wave, what I think about is that I see somebody thinking about me', Helen reflected, as she named all the friends she enjoys seeing there. 'I'm happy if the people come.' Helen shared a little about her faith, too, as we talked about the cross she keeps at home, which reminds her of Jesus. 'It means Jesus died and came back to life', she said. Christa is delighted that Helen can continue to explore her faith at Wave, especially now that she no longer lives with her Christian family. Church exclusion of people with learning disabilities affects whole families, and Wave is designed to include families like Christa and Helen. But, even more radically, Wave's philosophy is to bring those with and without learning disabilities together. That has the potential to transform church and community. The Wave team have long been aware that people with learning disabilities are often isolated, in a society where they face barriers to friendship, and where there are few opportunities for those with and without learning disabilities to spend time together. Bernice Hardie's research has found that mixed-ability friendship and social connection can transform non-disabled people's attitudes towards those with learning disabilities.[442] Wave for Change aims to create those transformative chances to connect.

Wave's leaders are calling mainstream churches to work more closely with grassroots movements of disabled people and their families, like Wave. Writing in the Church Times, Bernice says that churches are often ill equipped to become more accessible, not least because many leaders have a poor understanding of learning disability. But transformation can be led by those with learning disabilities and their families and carers – the 'LD community,' as Bernice calls them:

> Church leaders may feel inadequate and fearful of doing significant work in this area … The focus, rather, should be on encouraging

and enabling the LD community to help churches. This approach relies on forging connections in the community, and growing mixed-ability teams.[443]

Without churches' support, there is always a risk that community groups like Wave will remain separate ministries from the rest of the Church. Social segregation is inevitable when we avoid those we perceive as different,[444] as we saw in Chapter 2 and 3, in stories of disabled people who were pushed to the edge of churches by those who feared disruption. Wave's vision is the opposite. Wave Church embraces disruption and difference, encouraging people with and without learning disabilities to live out new ways of doing and being Church together. Vulnerability, struggles and difference are welcome at Wave Church, where members bring their authentic selves to worship and community.[445] Groups like Wave Church can bring this transformative ministry *from* people with learning disabilities and their families, *to* a non-disabled majority Church. Through their leadership, every church could learn how to show that they truly value people with learning disabilities and those who share their lives.

As Jess reflected on Wave's mission, she reminded the Church how important it is to put inclusion and access at the centre. 'Wave Church is different from usual church,' she told us. 'It is more free and casual – you can let go and have fun. It feels more like a community gathering or social than a church service. I like it! I also like the fact that I can share it with my parents.' Jess sometimes misses the lively band and songs from her family's church. 'But I realise that we need songs that everyone can join in with.' That's the heart of Wave's mission. Wave Church shows us that when everyone can join in, the Church becomes a richer community, where we know that every part of the Body is needed.

'Resourcing each other and the Church': The 'Living Edge' conference and community

A decade ago, in 2012, co-author Naomi was privileged to be at the first gathering of disabled Christians for a conference on disability and church at St Martin-in-the-Fields Church, London. Hosted in partnership with Inclusive Church, this unique conference may have been the first in the UK organised *by* disabled Christians, *for* disabled Christians. As delegates listened to and worshipped among other wheelchair and walker-using, chronically ill, blind, D/deaf, neurodivergent and other disabled Christians, we had a rare moment of realisation that we were 'not the only one'. Fiona MacMillan, Chair of the conference planning team, remembers the sense of wonder she shared with many other delegates that day:

> It was as though we'd envisaged something, and then we were suddenly living it. And I felt such a sense of solidarity and homecoming, and belonging, that it was worth all the work.

Back then, disabled congregants were scattered among a Church of England whose disability ministry was led by non-disabled people, praying for a Church that would listen to our own voices. For many of us, the conference was a sign that God was already working through disabled people to answer our prayers.

The story of the conference begins with the Disability Advisory Group (DAG) at St Martin-in-the-Fields Church, also chaired by Fiona MacMillan. Fiona takes up the story:

> The disability work at St Martin's began in 2011 when, amidst wider austerity, the Church of England cut its own funding for work with disabled people. Disability Advisors in dioceses were made redundant or became voluntary roles. At a time of fear and anxiety at government policy and rising disability hate crime, there was a sense that disabled people, already excluded in terms of access and participation, were even further excluded from the Church – the one place which you'd hope would speak up and act. This became a catalyst for our disability work at St Martin's – because if not us, then who?

The DAG began with an open meeting where about two dozen members of the congregation, with experiences from acquired brain injury to chronic illness, shared their frustrations at the barriers getting in the way of their access and participation in the church. 'What worked well was listening to people's lived experience,' Fiona says, 'and becoming a place where people could bring their experience, with the wisdom and understanding that grows from it.' Now meeting once a term, the core of the DAG's work is 'fixing and dreaming', as Fiona calls it: first, making space for people with experience of disability to bring their experience of exclusion, and then together shaping a dream of access and participation enabled in the church. St Martin-in-the-Fields Church lives out a witness of 'listening even unto rebuke',[446] as the church takes the group's direct experience of disability seriously, listens to their lament, and works to create change with them.

At the same time, St Martin's began to ask how they might also resource other disabled Christians, and the wider church. Through discussions with Inclusive Church, an idea formed of a disabled-led conference on disability and church. At that first conference in 2012, titled 'Opening the Roof', speakers called the Church to two urgent tasks. The Church should be a prophetic voice in an era of social oppression of disabled people, calling for justice in society, they said. But before it is ready for that mission, the Church must deal with its own marginalisation of disabled Christians. That call for justice has echoed down through a decade of conferences.

This has always been a disabled-led event, where a majority of speakers and contributors are disabled and/or neurodivergent. That should not be as radical and unusual as it is. As the conference ethics statement puts it, 'We prioritise the voices and experience of disabled people at this conference. This is because they are rarely heard in church contexts.'[447] A culture of accessibility is woven into everything the community does, carefully planned over many years by an experienced access team, who bring their own lived experience of (in)accessibility. By its fourth year, the conference had become a whole-weekend event, with the first day bringing together disabled people, their families and supporters to share gathered wisdom on disability access and participation, through theology, teaching, storytelling, discussion, Godly Play, art, a silent space, and disabled-led worship. At a marketplace, delegates bring news of disabled Christians' groups, events and resources from across the country, reminding each other that they are far from 'the only one'. The Sunday explores conference themes through the creative arts, including film screenings and discussion with filmmakers. For many years, the Sunday after the conference was also the setting for the St Luke's Day healing liturgy; today, the Sunday service shares conference themes with the wider church community. It's just one way that the conference community ministers to the church that has been supporting their work for a decade.

The conference's work has been 'rippling out' ever since that first year, in Fiona's words, as they live out their mission to resource the wider Church. Two early books brought together wisdom from the first two conferences, sharing stories by members of the DAG and conference community. [448] Five years later, a booklet, *Calling from the Edge*, shared reflections drawn from the first half-decade of conferences. [449] And from 2018's conference, themed 'Something Worth Sharing,' came a booklet offering practical advice on 'getting in and joining in' for disabled people and their churches. [450] There, Fiona reflected on how the conference community has heard and shared the cry of disabled delegates who are desperate to see change in the Church:

> As [conference delegates] have told us, 'This once a year is wonderful but where I live it's really hard.' 'I want to be part of church but I can't do it the usual way so I can't do it at all.' 'I'm told I'm being demanding – I want to challenge this but don't know where to start.' 'How on earth do we change the church?'... It is our duty and our joy to share what we know – about access and language, communication and structure, about getting in and joining in. We hope it may enable others to unlock gates and open gifts – because we all have something worth sharing. [451]

Today, a growing conference community is a living witness to the truth that, in accessible communities where we are accepted as we are, disabled and neurodivergent people can participate and lead. Rachel is a priest in the Church of England, and describes herself as late diagnosed autistic and ADHD. In 2019, Rachel was invited to be a storyteller at the conference. Themed 'Thinking Differently About God: Neurodiversity, Faith and the Church'; it was to be a year when the conference doors would be flung open to more neurodivergent people than ever before. As Rachel shared her story of neurodivergence and mental health struggles with a community she did not yet know, she had a transformative experience of acceptance. A few days later, Rachel wrote:

Blown away at the sense of belonging and welcome in the room, of spending the day with so many others that I have ND [neurodivergent] traits in common with, of shared language and understanding. A place where all were honoured, where it was safe to be me, each of us, children of God. The sense of each person being valued, of inclusive liturgy, of access instructions being written with pictures. I don't think I've ever felt so safe to be me and to be seen to be me in a public setting … I know every church says that they are welcoming, and that all are welcome. I experienced a radical depth to that welcome today that I've never experienced before.

As Rachel reflected, it is only when neurodivergent and disabled people are accepted, just as we are, that we can come to see others as God's good creation too. In a gathering where neurodivergent ways of being were celebrated, and a commitment to justice was lived out through integral disability access, Rachel knew that her whole self was welcome. Such liberation and transformation, beginning with ourselves and rippling out into the rest of the Church, is at the heart of this conference.

Ten years on from that first event, in 2021 the tenth anniversary conference explored disabled people's calling, 'as challenge, lament and vocation'.[452] Disabled people are still crying out for justice from the edge, conference speakers and storytellers reminded the Church. It's one reason why the gathering is now informally known as the 'Living Edge' conference. As the conference community has often reflected, the edge of the forest is a place where new growth takes root; life that would be vulnerable in the centre finds light and shelter on the edge. The increasingly ecumenical conference has been held entirely online since 2020, as the community responds to its lived understanding that, in a pandemic, many disabled people are still not safe to gather in buildings. Moving online has created new opportunities to make the conference accessible to people who could not attend before, because of disability or distance. Today, delegates attend from their beds, with cameras on or off as they choose, communicating through the chat function, with the support of captions, and through BSL interpretation. 'Come as you are', Fiona says – and that's exactly what delegates do. It can feel like a stark contrast with the way delegates are often expected to leave disability at the church. The conference is a glimpse of the kin-dom of God, where disabled people are made welcome, just as we are, and where we are valued as a source of transformation.

For some conference delegates, one annual experience of access and acceptance is no longer enough. A close community of disabled people has formed around the conference, meeting regularly online for coffee, discussions and discipleship groups. For Lucy, who is neurodivergent, the community's culture of access has opened up the time and space she needs to process information, reflect, and discuss her faith:

> [It's] an hour or so of hope a month. The Sunday Zoom coffees are great. The ethos of, it doesn't matter if we are still in pyjamas or haven't washed our hair for weeks, or there is washing behind you, which there almost always is with me! It is a space that it feels like we can bring our whole selves to, a really empowering and comforting space. It's a good place to be able to know it is safe to share that stuff isn't going well, or to celebrate when stuff is going well. [These groups] have been a lifeline, really.

Lucy's confidence as a disciple and leader has grown in these disability-affirming, disabled-led spaces, where she has been empowered to serve and be served. Inspired by Nadia Bolz-Weber's *Shameless*, Lucy has felt bold enough to lead a series of community discussions on sexuality, disability and Christian faith. 'It definitely wouldn't have happened if it wasn't a space that I felt safe in, with people that I would be happy to share some quite personal stuff with', Lucy told us.

It is no accident that, just as institutional church support for disability was at an all-time low, space was made for grassroots, lay- and disabled-led movements to emerge, like the Living Edge conference. But renewal from the edge needs support from the centre. In his introduction to the conference booklet *Calling from the Edge*, Samuel Wells, Vicar of St Martin-in-the-Fields, reminds us that 'The stone the builders rejected has become the cornerstone.'[453] The life of the Church is renewed when, through grace, it is reconciled with those it has rejected, Wells tells us. In the words of disabled priest Rachel Wilson, reflecting on the work of the conference in the same booklet:

208

I believe that if disabled people were allowed to truly flourish in the service of the church, in whatever capacity, then the effect would be transformative.[454]

Through lament, celebration and a call for justice, the Living Edge conference community is calling the Church to transformation together with disabled and neurodivergent people, as they dream renewal into being.

Sarah's story: Lee Abbey

Not all our storytellers were looking for groups aimed at disabled people. Some were seeking diverse communities, where they could fit, just as they are. As we saw in Chapters 2 and 3, this is no easy prospect for disabled people, but some found church on the edge in ways that worked for them. Sarah found spiritual community beyond the gates of the church, at a centre she attended once or twice a year. Parish church life has always been a challenge for Sarah, who is autistic. During years of misdiagnosis and disruption to her life, Sarah fondly remembered going with her parents to clergy weeks at Lee Abbey, a Christian community and retreat centre in Devon.[455] Seeking a place to heal, she returned to Lee Abbey. It became an accessible sanctuary for Sarah. The flexible, familiar environment was a good fit for her sensory and social needs, one week at a time:

> There is fellowship going on there. I think it's been the one constant, when I had problems about not being able to get to church, or especially when everything fell apart with this new heating system, Lee Abbey has been the thing that I've continued to do ... You're taking people as you find them [at Lee Abbey], because you don't know them long term ... Your past matters less, because you're taken as you present ... Particularly with a disability that perhaps varies, or a disability that you come to later in life, [it's good] to be somewhere where people take you as you are now ... People are reacting to me as I am. There is something so powerful in that.

AT THE GATES

As a Christian community, Lee Abbey worked for Sarah both because she was encouraged to participate there in the same way as anyone else, and because a more accessible environment *enabled* her to participate.

More than that, Lee Abbey was a place where Sarah was accepted and enabled as her autistic self. Sarah remembered church settings where leaders' perceptions of her health and access needs had kept her from playing a full role in community, when she was not seen as someone who could serve others. But Lee Abbey made it possible for Sarah to serve and be served. No matter what she was capable of offering, Sarah was valued as a contributing member of the community:

> You can go there at a low ebb, and you're probably giving less than other people are giving to you, or you can go there at a high ebb, when you've got a variable condition, and you're giving to people who are at *their* low ebb. So you can be as useful, or not, as you are. And again, that's something you can't get necessarily in a weekly church situation ... In a sense, you can go [to Lee Abbey] and offer nothing ... You can go along utterly exhausted. And the idea is that they help you refresh.

It was no accident that Lee Abbey was also the first environment where Sarah felt able to be open as an autistic person. The transient community there made it easier than having to 'out' herself to a church, where she knew there might be a risk of being stigmatised in the long term. Through Sarah's openness and visibility, she found herself in a position where she could serve others, just as she had been served by other disabled people at Lee Abbey:

> I've been on the receiving end of wisdom from people who've been there. And then I've also been there as the one who other people have asked questions of... What I found was because I was open about [being autistic], other people then sought me out to talk about things ... There was a girl [who] came and had a long discussion with me ... She was struggling. Basically, she thought she was probably autistic ... She needed to talk it through with someone who was older, but who wouldn't rubbish what she was saying, because I didn't

know anything about her, other than what she said to me. I wasn't 'official' … [At Lee Abbey] they have what they call pastoral helpers … I wasn't doing that role. I was just being a human. But the fact that she approached me made me realise that, otherwise, she wouldn't have approached anyone who – That was why she approached me. I think I had made something that she was struggling with visible, and I'd made it visible in a positive way.

Sarah's confidence to be openly, authentically herself was bolstered by a community that valued the embodied wisdom that disabled people can share from lived experience. There, she did not have to leave disability at the door. Disabled Christians' service is distinctive and irreplaceable, in communities where we can show each other that we are 'not the only one', as we reflected in Chapter 4. It was important to Sarah that she was an active, serving member of a Christian community, rather than someone on the edge who simply received from a parish church's pastoral outreach:

> As part of the week [at Lee Abbey], there will be quite a lot of worship, but there will also be a communion service. There have been years when, apart from Easter and Christmas, where that's the only communion I've had. Because I haven't been able to get to church. And yes, I could initiate getting [communion] another way, but that is me initiating something special. Whereas this is me being part of a fellowship. And there's something in that.

As Sarah returned again and again to the stable, familiar setting, she had all the information she needed to participate at Lee Abbey, and some control over her sensory and social environment there. At the same time, in a fellowship of edge-walkers,[456] relationships at Lee Abbey were transient as Sarah needed them to be. Today, Lee Abbey is still church on the edge for Sarah, a community of 'misfitting and belonging',[457] where she is enabled to participate in mutual hospitality, where she is valued and accepted as a disabled person, and where she can share her needs and her service alike. She knows she can come just as she is, bringing her whole self to the community. For Sarah, that's a unique experience.

Theologies of Revival and Renewal on the Edge

In our own self-organised, empowering communities, disabled people are doing church differently. The edge can be a creative space, where marginalised people come together to build something new. In spaces on the thresholds of churches,[458] disabled Christians are creating alternatives to old, ableist ways of doing church. This is dangerous, prophetic work. In bell hooks' words:

> This space of radical openness is a margin – a profound edge. Locating oneself there is difficult yet necessary. It is not a 'safe' place. One is always at risk. One needs a community of resistance.[459]

As all these groups have found, there are disabled Christians outside the church gates who are hungry to explore faith in community with those who share their lived experience. Disabled-led groups have responded to this gap, creating spaces where disabled Christians can recover the truth of who we are.[460] Until churches are transformed of their ableism, self-organised and closed groups may be the only places where some disabled Christians feel safe to be Church together.

Yet these groups are far from insular. Disabled Christians are reaching out to those inside the church gates, who have not always seen how the Holy Spirit is moving beyond them. Whether disabled-led church groups meet online or in buildings, or as a hybrid of the two, they are showing that ministry does not flow in only one direction. Disability and Jesus have seen how the Spirit is at work in the online disabled Christian movement, which they call 'church on the margins'. They write:

> These 'marginal' communities are where the Holy Spirit is working. It is these communities that are on the rise, breaking new ground, exploring new theologies. We see these groups as having the power, drive, openness and creativity to revive the broader church. These are groups of people who are hungry for meaning, for welcome, for inclusion, for genuine belonging.[461]

In our experiences of injustice, exclusion, lament and longing, disabled Christians are reaching out to each other, right where we are – on the edge. Some disabled leaders are calling this a revival, one that can renew the wider Church. Looking at the stories that they and their members tell, it is hard to disagree.

At the same time, there may be danger lurking in our retreat to our own groups on the edge. Critical neurodiversity scholar Krysia Emily Waldock has written about how many benefits she has gained from more accessible online worship during the COVID pandemic. And yet, she warns, online church groups could easily shift from *safe* spaces to *segregated* spaces. If the mainstream Church is content with asking disabled people to worship 'over there', it will never have to transform what it is doing 'here', Waldock reflects:

> People have often described this as the way I should partake
> in church: if you listen online, you'll be over there and we can
> continue to act and practise as we were. It's felt as if it's been
> promoted for a dual way of doing church, but with neither side
> touching. 'Doing Church' online has such potential, but we must
> ensure that we do not end up inadvertently segregating people
> based on their needs, and therefore dividing a community.[462]

Though she is excited by disabled people's transformative new expressions of church on the edge, Waldock dares to ask why there is an edge at all. 'The fact that there are margins disconcerts me, even more so when small adjustments which could help the church be so accessible are seen as an inconvenient add-on.'[463] Disabled-led groups expose the reality of the disabled people waiting at the gates, for whom church on the edge is both a blessing among our community and an indictment of the ableist churches that exclude us. As we will argue in the next chapter, the COVID-19 pandemic has been an opportunity for change in churches, 'a true and real opportunity to re-examine what church should be'.[464] But transformation will take conscious work on the part of a Church seeking to act justly towards disabled people. As we have argued throughout this book, that starts with listening. Many disabled people have made our home in the wilderness, where the mainstream Church is often too afraid to venture. We are calling from the edge. A Church that hears the prophetic call of the edge-walkers can be transformed, if it can come to see disabled people not just as an opportunity for outreach, but as practitioners and partners in the art of doing and being Church differently.

CHAPTER 8
Church in COVID-19 and the Prophetic Witness of Bed-Based Prophets

'I had somebody yesterday on Zoom church, saying, "It has been so amazing to see your ministry really flourish. We need to make sure that we keep having it flourishing."' Emma

COVID-19 changed the landscape of church and, indeed, of wider society. Its rapid onset forced many churches to rethink the ways we gather, worship and support each other. The accessibility issues discussed in this book suddenly became tangible for our non-disabled fellow parishioners who were all of a sudden shut out of the building. Nobody could access the pews or the altar rail as churches were forced to close their doors to everyone. This opened up a particular experience of many disabled people to the rest of the church. Our lived experience was being reflected back to the wider community as lack of access became everyone's problem. Maybe this would be the accidental turning point for the inclusion of those whose needs did not fit the typical 'turn up once a week on a Sunday morning for worship' model of participation in church. Maybe this would finally open up the conversation that we have been trying to initiate for years – as the stories in this book have shown.

AT THE GATES

At the 2016 Living Edge Conference, on the theme of Prophets and Seers, I (Emily) was asked to be a storyteller. After much deliberation of how I was in any way prophetic, my talk revealed itself to be an exploration of the ways my online presence, mainly on Twitter, was a prophetic calling. Tweeting has major parallels to my life with a disability in that it places limits on me. Just as I have become a master at editing my life in terms of day-to-day living, I have taken those skills to Twitter – finding new ways of saving space, reframing words as I would rearrange my day and rethink my activities. Twitter has provided me with a vital community of similar prophets who I can share my life with, especially on those harder days. Twitter has done a lot to combat the isolation that living with long-term pain and fatigue can cause. Twitter has taught many disabled and chronically ill people like me how to turn limitation into strength, create community in isolation and to exercise our ministries and share our gifts from our phones and iPads.

At the conference, it was affirming to share my social media expertise, something which my disability had equipped me for; something that was a gift rather than a deficit. But little did I realise quite how prophetic my position was. Because four years later, in 2020, it seemed as if the whole church had joined me on my corner of the internet. But they had not joined us by design, or through any influence on the part of digital disabled prophets. After COVID-19, the Church found itself in the same online space as disabled Christians, through circumstance.

COVID-19 brought with it a legal obligation for churches to close. Whether disabled or non-disabled, congregants were no longer permitted to attend services in person. At the same time, many churches made it clear that they had a responsibility to protect 'the vulnerable'. The virus presented the biggest risk to older people and those with underlying health conditions. Many disabled Christians found themselves a part of this wider 'vulnerable' group. But vulnerability is created. COVID has magnified, and indeed exacerbated, the inequalities we already see in society, for groups including those from Global Majority Heritage backgrounds, people living in poverty, and disabled people.[465] This pandemic has shown how little society values disabled people's lives, as the UK media and government have emphasised that 'only' people with pre-existing conditions are likely to become seriously ill or die from COVID.[466] Lockdowns and COVID policies have had an unequal impact on disabled people, with reports of increased health and social inequalities, from difficulties getting hold of food and medical equipment, to a lack of vital information about COVID in Easy Read and British Sign Language.[467] Many disabled people were shut out of society for many months, under the government's 'shielding' policy, barely leaving our homes.[468] Many of us continued to self-isolate for far longer, knowing that disabled people are significantly more likely to die from coronavirus than non-disabled people.[469] Yet there has been a constant push to get 'back to normal' from people at lower risk from the virus. Reflecting on her experiences of the pandemic in the USA, disability activist Imani Barbarin writes:

> Why would Americans change their behavior to save the disabled and elderly if we're presented as disposable to begin with?[470]

In a society where many people would rather be dead than disabled, Barbarin says, it is no surprise that disabled people have been made vulnerable to COVID, when we could have been protected by policy and the actions of those less at risk. In a world where a social crisis once again had an unequal impact for disabled people, disabled people were hoping for better from churches.

This was the social context in which churches had to make decisions on the suspension of communal worship: the common good and protection of those who were 'vulnerable' to the virus, versus the pressure from wider society to get 'back to normal' as quickly as possible, where disabled people's safety and lives was a lower priority.

Opening the Online Gates

❝ I think [the pandemic has] prompted people that they have to find another way. ❞ Sarah

In complete contrast to the majority lockdown experience, for many bed-based disciples, the pandemic, even with increased restrictions, was a time of freedom and expansion as more opportunities for participation opened up. The removal of existing structures brought with it the opportunity for improvisation, a skill that is particularly acute in disabled people who have had to previously negotiate access and participation. Disabled people no longer had to be up and ready on a Sunday morning to be able to do a reading or lead intercessions. Contributions could be made ahead of time in line with energy levels. I (co-author Emily) have been able to record sermons reclining on my bed on high pain days, and can now regularly lead Morning Prayer on Facebook without the pain and fatigue of travelling into a church building.

Storyteller Fern had a similarly expansive experience of online church, both during and after 2020's lockdowns. At the time she shared her story with us, Fern could no longer physically enter most church buildings, nor could she sit up for the length of a service:

> I have found a solution to this in attending church online. I found (pre-COVID) not too many [churches] offered this, or it wasn't always consistent. However, through trial and error [I] have now found a church in Australia that I feel part of, even if I never physically will be in the same room or even same country. They realise that they have an online audience and there is a special welcome for people attending this way. They also are big on issues of accessibility, from having sign language interpreters, different language interpreters, notes that can be sent out in the week if you want to virtually attend a smaller 'house' group, and Facebook groups. You can attend live online or later. This works well for me if I am particularly unwell and can take as many days or hours I need to get through a service when I don't have the stamina for sitting through a whole service. It really works well for me, though I do miss the community aspect of knowing other attendees personally sometimes too.

For Fern, online services with asynchronous access allowed her to attend church flexibly, on *crip time*, from her bed. Although the pandemic was the reason that the church had expanded its online worship, this church was offering far more than accidental access. This was a church where Fern could *fit*, in a community that made conscious provision to enable disabled people to participate. Their disability hospitality was a sign to

Fern that she was welcome at the church, *as* a disabled person. For Fern, who had once been 'very afraid' to attend church as a wheelchair user, this church's online ministry gave her both the confidence and means to return to church again. Fern was just one of many disabled people who could finally return to church when pandemic ministry moved churches online. Laura, founder of online community YouBelong, actually saw a decrease in engagement in the online church group during the early days of the pandemic, as regular users were, for the first time ever, able to participate in their 'home' church or a local church, rather than needing the alternative provision of disabled-led initiatives like hers. Through new digital access, many disabled people have found the church gates suddenly flung open to them.

Some storytellers found that their churches' online ministry opened up new opportunities not just to participate, but to lead. Pioneer minister Emma was able to serve her church community again, when disability and access issues had previously limited her ministry. When Emma's community suddenly found themselves isolated at home, they needed Emma's digital ministry more than ever:

And suddenly my ministry has just gone ba-boom! In fact, I had somebody yesterday on Zoom church, saying, 'It has been so amazing to see your ministry really flourish. We need to make sure that we keep having it flourishing.'

As the church learned to find its ways around the new online culture they found themselves in, Emma's experience was vital. 'I'm the most techie person in the church,' she said:

I've been facilitating and running services and helping other people be involved. Our retired clergy have never done video, but we managed to make it work. People record Bible readings, and get 92-year-olds on Zoom – you name it, we've done it ... We've managed to get the [recorded service] audio down and get it onto CDs. And it's gone to people who can't get online at home, and it's gone into our local nursing home. Because, why not? It's not impossible. And I think one of the things is, disability has taught me to think about things differently. So I've just said to people, anything is possible. Let's just figure out how.

Emma's leadership in online ministry was shaped by her personal experience of disability and her pioneering work among disabled people on social media. She was able to help her congregation adapt to a changing world, just as she learned to adapt when she lost her sight and mobility.

When the world changed overnight, churches had to respond in new, creative ways, finding another way to be Church together. A minority experience became a majority experience. COVID-19 led to two major changes in their churches: communities began to understand disabled people's experiences, and they began to value our distinctive gifts. That's why some storytellers had hope that a new, more accessible and empathetic Church might rise from the ashes of COVID lockdowns. Emma told us how, as her congregants experienced isolation and found themselves unable to access church, they began to empathise with her experience of disability. She told us about a congregant in her eighties whose world opened up again when Emma showed her how to use Zoom:

> And she suddenly burst into tears and she went, 'I can see everybody. I haven't seen anyone in weeks.' And she then said, 'Now I know really what it was like for you, Emma, when you became disabled …' And, you know, people suddenly are putting two and two together and going, 'We now know what it's like for people. Suddenly when someone vanishes, we'll know how hard that is, we'll know that we need to reach out. We know that we need to adapt.' It's amazing.

Storyteller Sarah had similar thoughts. When a church has to find different ways to gather, its priorities shift, she reflected. Sarah was holding onto hope that the isolating Covid experience, shared by all of us, might lead churches to think more deeply about access for disabled people:

> I think [the pandemic has] prompted people that they have to find another way. And I think with the best will in the world, people

have other priorities ... If you're disabled, or someone who is your family member is, that's when [access] becomes a priority to you ... As much as you might sympathise, empathise, until the point that it suddenly becomes your priority, other things knock it out.

In a world where COVID is changing all our priorities, perhaps Emma and other disabled Christian leaders have been formed 'for such as a time as this'.[471]

'I think you're on mute, Vicar': Moving to online worship

> ' The online space is sacred ... This is not crumbs under the table. This is genuine [worship] space for genuine people. ' Kt

When society locked down in 2020, the obvious migration for churches was to the online arena. Churches have been negotiating this space for the last decade or so, whether out of genuine interest in reaching those already engaging in social media or rather to be seen as doing the modern thing. As a social media officer for my church I (co-author Emily) initially had to argue, in the early 2010s, that joining the online space was a *good* idea and would not bring about the end of the world. Church engagement with social media has had varying degrees of impact, but in March 2020 it seemed that many in the church quickly discovered the ability to transfer their worship online. Within about a week of the UK's national lockdown, churches and individual ministers were streaming services, on YouTube, Facebook, Instagram live or over video communication services like Zoom. For the purpose of this chapter, we're focussing mainly on the Church of England, simply because, as the established church in the UK, they have had to negotiate the shape of UK church in the pandemic in the public eye. 'A Church Near You', the Anglican church's online directory, now lists over 5,000 churches offering some kind of online service, whether they are short daily prayers or larger-scale, multi-camera weekly streamed services.[472] The Church of England began an official live streamed service just before lockdown, which has continued every Sunday since. These services have come from a range of contexts which display the breadth of ministry in the Church of England, with settings from the kitchen of Lambeth Palace to HMP Stockton. Following important debates about digital exclusion, which affects disabled people as well as older people,[473] the Church of England also set up the 'Daily Hope' line, providing weekly prayers, music and reflections over the phone.

The church move online brought with it both hope and frustration to many disabled people. Hope, because finally, with a levelling of access for many, this may have been the opportunity for an honest conversation on how we include those who find it hard to physically attend, who are profoundly isolated and whose voices and talents are missing from our congregations. But on the other side of this there was frustration. Overnight, churches became adept at livestreaming, at setting up Zoom prayer meetings and providing informative online content. Those same churches which for years had been failing to provide transcripts of sermons or to keep the information on their websites up-to-date, overhauled everything so that the suddenly-limited majority could have access from home. On the whole, most churches moved online. Very fast.

This puzzled many in the disabled Christian community, who had been asking for this expanded digital access for years. As we shared in the previous chapter, many of these disabled people had set up their own Facebook, Twitter and YouTube-based groups for mutual prayer and support, from their homes and beds, when they were tired of waiting for their churches to do it. The stories in this book attest to the fact that disabled Christians have long been asking for different ways of doing church, with mixed results. Some had been listened to and found ways of 'getting in and joining in' with their church communities,[474] but many had left after facing hostility, rather than the hospitality they were hoping for. They had either formed their own communities – often, but not always, online – or had turned away from church altogether. This is certainly not to single out churches in their sudden realisation that online access was possible: many workplaces that had argued that it was impossible for disabled people to work flexibly or from home suddenly overhauled their working structures and practices to support a workforce fully participating from bedrooms and home offices. In some ways, in the pandemic, society and culture became far more accessible, but this was, to a large extent, accidental access.

After March 2020 the mainstream church was forced to join us in the online world, and sometimes that resulted in pushing out those who already occupied the space, back to the edge once again. As we saw in Chapter 7, there was a blueprint for the church to use when faced with the problem of how to gather when we can no longer gather: the disabled Christians' online church movement. The online space has long been used by disabled Christians as an alternative meeting place for those to whom the church gates are closed. As the mainstream churches moved online, they found they were not the first in this space. Kt Tup reflected on how, in the sacred online space, Disability and Jesus has always been just as much 'real' church as a church that meets in buildings. She did not feel that the mainstream church always respected that space, nor did they always prioritise disability access, as they moved online en masse. Kt called this 'the colonisation of the online space':[475]

> The mainstream church found themselves reluctantly dumped in the online space, didn't like it, but had no other option but to get used to it quickly ... There was a huge influx of hurt privilege that said, 'Well thank God it'll only be for a few weeks, and then we can clear off again.' The building-based people trained to minister in buildings were suddenly going, 'I wasn't trained to be online, I was trained to be in a building. And if I go back there, I can flourish.' And I felt torn, as a priest without a building ... saying, 'But the online space is sacred, it's just different.' There was a real dilemma for us, as Disability and Jesus, wanting to say, 'If you're going to go back [to the buildings], do it, but don't forget the people who can't come back. Don't just abandon the space as temporary ... This is not crumbs under the table, this is genuine [worship] space for genuine people.'

Like other unfunded, informal online church groups of disabled people, Disability and Jesus found their expertise ignored by churches moving into the digital world. Not all disabled people were finding online churches as accessible as Fern and Emma did. For some, inaccessibility simply followed them online.[476] Disabled people's access and participation was forgotten by some churches rushing to go digital, often without seeking to learn from church groups already meeting online. As Emma Major asked in the *Church Times*, during the early days of the pandemic:

> Why are these churches assuming that they're breaking new ground? Why are they not asking those who've been doing it successfully for years how exactly you build relationships online? Why are they not thinking about how to ensure that online is accessible for those with hearing or sight loss?[477]

We have a wealth of expertise in the disabled community, having been forced to pioneer our way into the online space. Although churches' move online was finally opening the church gates to some of us, others continued to feel left out on the edge.

Meanwhile, the institutional church was clamouring to return to church buildings. The Twitter debates raged, as clergy lamented being kept from their sanctuaries. This was particularly poignant for disabled Christians, many of whom had been kept from the sanctuaries for years, and now feared a move away from online church would close the gates to us again.

Lockdown, 'real' worship and the push to reopen churches

❝ As I can't attend a service in person on a Sunday and just make it routine, time spent with God – whether it be an online service or something else – is something I have to make a conscious effort to do and seek out with more intention.❞ Fern

Since the beginning of the online church movement, theologians and clergy have asked the question 'Is online church real church?'[478] In early March 2020 this debate intensified, as online church became the only way of meeting together when churches were closed. Even before COVID brought about the shutting of church doors to the majority, and not just a minority group, debates were already raging about the authenticity and legitimacy of online worship.[479] Much work has been done by the churches to counter the image of online worship as a 'second best' way of attending church, but there was a persistent view that the valuable members of the congregation were those who were in the pews, physically attending week after week.[480]

As lockdown moved churches online, and many disabled people were talking about how exciting it was to have the online access to church that we had long been asking for, some clergy seemed more concerned about whether church can or should happen in the private, domestic space. Can worship at home, far from the altars and robes of church buildings be an authentic expression of church?[481]

Then there were questions over whether the numbers of people watching online services were truly reflective of 'engagement' in those services[482] (even though we rarely question the 'engagement' of the daydreaming masses in our pews!) These are old arguments. As digital sociologist Tim Hutchings points out, there have been theological concerns about online ministry since the beginning of the online church movement: 'fears of online competition, disembodied relationships and uncommitted digital consumers remain just as prevalent in 2016 as they were in 1996.'[483] For disabled people, this debate can dismiss the embodied, experiential aspects of our worship from our beds and homes, in favour of gathered, institutional worship. For some non-disabled church members and leaders, legitimate worship looks like a Sunday gathering of the faithful, led by the priest at the altar. Participation means physical presence; those that matter, those who are considered most faithful, are the ones who show up week in, week out. But as we have heard over and over again from storytellers in this book, social location shapes disabled people's lived experience of faith. Which leaves the question: What does it mean when you are denied equal access to the only form of legitimate church, which takes place in buildings?

AT THE GATES

Disabled people have been asking this question for a long time. Suddenly, in March 2020, this was a question faced by the majority of the church.

Perhaps even more difficult to negotiate than the church's experimental foray into online worship were the cries of joy in summer 2020 when, as COVID restrictions eased in the UK, churches were permitted to reopen and worship could return to normal. 'Normal', here, was code for gathered, in-person worship. 'We are looking forward to being back together' was the mantra of some churches, as the promise of lifted restrictions loomed on the horizon, in an echo of debates about 'getting back to normal' in society.[484] In a survey from the National Churches Trust in May 2020, 49 per cent of those surveyed thought that places of worship should reopen. This figure grew to two-thirds amongst church goers.[485]

As disabled people have been overlooked in debates about reopening society and churches, there has been a silent echo of the old, ableist narrative that our lives are less valuable than others, as our needs are sacrificed so that others can have their freedom. Disabled people were marginalised in church communities long before coronavirus. The growing call to sing and gather in large numbers, as congregations cast off masks and other restrictions, has pushed many of us even further to the edge. Online access expanded our world; reopening churches has shut many of us out of the church gates once again. There is no doubt that, as restrictions were eased, leaders had to make difficult decisions about the safety of returning to in-building[486] worship, feeling the pressure of conflicting needs and demands from church members. But, as churches reopened, their actions were a good indicator of whose voice matters to them. Of whose bodies matter. In *how* they reopen, churches have been showing who is safe to come to church and who is left, once again, to retreat into lockdown and isolation. This will include not just many disabled people, but the 3.7 million people in the UK who were classed as Clinically Extremely Vulnerable, who since the pandemic may now be unable to go safely to church for the first time. Arguments about reopening have also assumed that 'the vulnerable' are those in the pews, passive and consuming, rather than those in positions of authority. Debates have often divided the line between leadership and 'vulnerable' laity, not taking into account the many disabled priests and servers feeling apprehensive about returning to full, face-to-face worship.[487] But in reality this ignores the needs of at-risk church leaders and volunteers who help keep our churches open and serving their local communities.

If shutting church doors was ever about protecting those at higher risk from the virus, then now that restrictions have ended, provisions should centre those same 'at risk' people, making sure that the church gates are not closed to disabled people again. In her message to churches on the eve of reopening, Sarah Mullally, Bishop of London, reminded churches of their position of power. 'In this new phase we must stand with those who continue to be disproportionately impacted, challenging the gap between the privileged and the disadvantaged', she said.[488] In response to guidance from the Church of England that allowed individual churches to make their own decisions about how to reopen, Naomi joined with other disability activists to write:

> The institutional church has abandoned many of us who are at higher risk from COVID, who will be too afraid to attend unsafe church buildings from next week onwards ... Already, those of us who have spoken out on this issue are facing criticism from other Christians and church leaders, simply for asking churches to consider safety and inclusion as they make decisions about COVID measures. We've even heard that, as 'vulnerable' people, we should not be coming to worship in church buildings. *We want to make it clear that such attitudes are ableist, and counter to the values that Jesus embodied in his ministry.* And these attitudes are at the heart of the injustice faced by disabled people during this pandemic... Now more than ever, we should be striving to create places of worship where those who have been made vulnerable to COVID are the most honoured guests at God's banquet.[489]

When society is not prioritising justice, hospitality and inclusion for all, churches can lead social transformation by modelling a different way to live in community. The pandemic has not gone away; many disabled people are still isolated at home or afraid for our lives. Unless churches prioritise justice now, more of us than ever will be missing from the pews too.

The future of online ministry and remote access for disabled people

❝ God is not constrained by pandemics or buildings, but only by people. God is always big enough. ❞ Fiona

Ever since churches reopened their doors early in 2022, disabled people have been asking questions about what happens to churches' online ministry as we emerge from the pandemic. From the beginning, many of us were worried that the church would leave the online space as quickly as it entered it in March 2020. That many disabled people, who had a glimpse of a fuller inclusion in the wider church community – albeit imperfect – during the pandemic, would have it taken from them again.

Lockdown brought with it both opportunity and challenge to the church. Overnight, physical parishes had to establish an online presence if they wanted to keep their congregations engaged and pastored, showing what many disabled Christians have been preaching for years: that adaptation and modification benefit all. Now as restrictions ease there is a fear among many disabled people that churches will go back to 'business as usual' and the eagerness to return to 'proper church' will leave many of us – who amidst lockdowns have been more engaged than ever – back where we started. As Emma Major wrote in the *Church Times*, early in the pandemic:

> Will the good intentions of accessibility still be in place in a year's time when most of your congregation are back in their seats? Or will we be the invisible again? Most people who have been excluded from churches for years have little hope that inclusivity will improve. My prayer is that lessons are learned and that improvements are made.[490]

Even while the churches talk about creating a 'new normal,' some are already returning to talk of mainstream versus adapted – or segregated – activities.[491] Instead of seeking to be renewed from the edge, churches have been falling back on the idea of bringing people from the margins into the centre. *How do we bring these people into the building?* some in the Church of England have been asking about the worshippers – nearly four million of them – who engaged with its online services in the first year of the pandemic.[492] They argue that liturgy can never be just a virtual experience, and that online worshippers might easily become spectators.[493] But the reality is that many of these worshippers will never attend central church activities in church buildings, and for many disabled people, this will be because we often can't.[494] For some of us, church buildings and policies will keep pushing us to the edge. But, like so many disabled Christians, Fiona MacMillan imagined a better way, inspired by her disabled experience and the online disabled-led church movement. Hybrid church is one answer, Fiona told us, in communities that worship together online and in the building, gathering in those who cannot join the congregation physically:

> One way to include is to make intentional space for those not present in the building. I'm suggesting that every service has something contributed by those not able to be present, a space set aside. So we model that we are gathered from different spaces – and *in* different spaces, in different ways, to be the body of Christ. God is not constrained by pandemics or buildings, but only by people. God is always big enough.

This vision of a truly hybrid church is one of many ways that institutional churches could come to value disabled people as a vital part of their communities. Other disabled people are encouraging churches to ask who is made vulnerable by the choices they make about how to worship together in a pandemic, from mask-wearing to social distancing. YouBelong's leaders recently shared guidelines on worshipping together safely, drawing on their disabled experience. They called on churches to act justly in all their decisions about how to reopen, prioritising those at risk of the virus, as they cited Matthew 25:

> '(For) I was hungry and you gave Me food, I was thirsty and you gave Me something to drink … Truly, I tell you, whatever you

did for one of the least of these brothers and sisters of Mine, you did it to Me'. (NRSV) Hospitality is at the core of our lives as disciples and of every church. God tells us to live hospitably, treating everyone as if they could be God. If, as a church, we make decisions that exclude people, we are separating ourselves from God.'[495]

Once again we have been reminded that churches are places of power where human decisions allow justice or injustice to flourish. Questions around lockdowns and reopening returned again to the central themes of this book: vulnerability and power. In a post-COVID world, churches committed to justice will need to ask who they have closed their gates to. As Fiona reminded us, God has a broader vision of the people of God. As storytellers have told us throughout this book, churches have much to learn from disabled Christians who are already active in online spaces, where we come together with other marginalised Christians to create lived theology, from our shared experience on the margins.

Theologies of Online Embodied Worship

In January 2022, as Omicron was still causing disruption in many places, particularly in the United States where the COVID death toll had just passed 800,000, the New York Times published an article entitled *Why Churches Should Drop Their Online Services*.[496] This caused a flurry of discussion, particularly on social media, as many from the disabled Christian community argued that it was another denial of their needs. In fact, criticism of this thinkpiece came not only from disabled Christians. There were responses from many who had benefited from 'the new normal' of online options, from tired families who welcomed the stress-free Sunday mornings watching from home, to people who had been separated from their home worshipping communities by geography or circumstance and had reconnected during the pandemic, as more churches offered livestreaming or Zoom church options.

Echoing other recent commentators on online worship, this article made a deeply theological argument, springing from the central concept of embodiment. We are embodied beings, the writer argued, therefore worship should be communal, in a physical gathering of bodies. Online worship just does not offer the same experience: 'offering church online implicitly makes embodiment elective.' This theology was questioned by disabled Christians, many of whom are acutely aware of our embodied existence. Am I not embodied when dialling into Morning Prayer via Zoom, nursing aching joints? Sometimes the idea of transcending my body is tempting, but whether I am sitting in a pew listening to a sermon or praying a liturgy from under my duvet, I am honouring my embodied existence. I have no other choice. As disability theologian Tanya Marlow argued, in her measured reply to the article, 'Please don't confuse geographically less proximate with disembodied'.[497]

Moreover, this vision of embodiment has certain bodies in mind. Arguments for the preference of in-building worship are often based on assumptions: that churchgoers can get out of bed, that we have access to transport, that the church community we are visiting will be accessible and that its environment will not cause us any kind of sensory overload. Recognising that some people will always be excluded from gathered worship by personal circumstance, the writer offered the alternative model of pastoral visits for those who are ill. This solution draws a line between 'healthy' people exercising ministry and passive receivers in their homes, assuming that disabled congregants are primarily objects of care and ministry, without asking whether the 'clinically vulnerable' might be members of the ministry team, even ordained leaders. Furthermore, as Marlow observed, this one-on-one model of receiving communion 'is not church – there is no Ekklesia, no gathering. That's more drive-through and consumerist than online church'.[498] Once again, this is the 'typical' model of shared gathering for the majority, with a concessionary bolt-on for those who do not fit, furthering feelings of exclusion and second-best welcome.

As Marlow argues, online church and ministry to those outside the gates is a missional issue. The pandemic offered an opportunity to reach and include an unheard community, and for the disabled community to speak to and serve the church in return:

AT THE GATES

> Around the world, people are removing barriers that keep disabled and housebound people excluded. Having online church removed a significant barrier. To reintroduce it is to re-erect the dividing walls Jesus abolished.[499]

This transformation in church life is not a new phenomenon. Churches have grown and evolved as technology and circumstances have changed. The early proclamation to witness in Jerusalem, in all Judea and Samaria, and to the ends of the earth[500] has been renewed in every generation, from the early apostles writing letters to isolated communities, to the parish church live streaming their morning mass into people's homes. Churches have always taken advantage of the latest technology to further their mission, whether through the printing press or a podcasting platform.

As many of us look forward to coming back together after the forced separation of the pandemic, we need to ask how 'together' we really were before churches closed their doors. Many disabled people were missing before the pandemic, and will still be absent from the pews for a long time. 'Togetherness' is only possible when churches are aware of these missing congregants and take meaningful steps towards making them welcome. This welcome will not always be physical.

CONCLUSION

I will lead the blind
by a road they do not know,
by paths they have not known
I will guide them.
I will turn the darkness before them into light,
the rough places into level ground.
These are the things I will do,
and I will not forsake them.
Isaiah 42:16

'I love that the Bible at some points takes
on the social model of disability – talking about
paths being made even so that people do not
stumble.' Fern

Justice in Churches for Disabled People

When the Church shuts disabled people outside the gates, it shuts Christ outside with us.

For disabled Christians, justice is urgent, if we are ever to participate in the lives of our Christian communities. We do not yet have a seat at a transformed table. Many of us are not even in the room.[501]

AT THE GATES

In their cries for justice for disabled people in churches, our storytellers echoed prophetic Old Testament images that show how God will restore us to the communities that once closed the gates to us. Fern remembered Isaiah 42, finding strength in God's promise to 'turn the rough places into level ground' – to tear down the barriers that cause disabled people to stumble. Disability biblical scholar Sarah J. Melcher shares another narrative of gates opened to disabled people, from Micah: 'I will assemble the lame and gather those who have been driven away ... The lame I will make the remnant, and those who were cast off, a strong nation; and the LORD will reign over them in Zion, now and forevermore.'[502] The Hebrew text compares these disabled people to injured sheep, Melcher says, and God to a kindly shepherd.[503] Not content to forget about the one wounded sheep in ninety-nine that has been driven away from the sheep fold,[504] the Shepherd leaves the place of safety, and goes out to the edge to pursue them. That's a vision of justice – for every disabled person waiting outside the gates.

The storytellers in this book are prophetic voices, calling from the edge for churches to be awakened. The upside-down Kingdom of God was announced by a King who rode into Jerusalem on a donkey, they are reminding the Church. Disabled people's gifts are just as unexpected, just as easily overlooked, in a Church that has honoured the powerful and strong above the rest of the Body of Christ. The kin-dom of God is liberation for disabled people, and it is liberation for a Church caught up in the ableist values of the world.

Disabled people are reaching out to the churches in mission. As we model cultures of access and radical hospitality in our own communities on the edge, we are showing churches how to transform into places of justice. Not content to wait on the edge forever, we are asking churches to enable our participation and leadership. Disabled people are asking churches to imagine and expect us in their pews and pulpits, not as objects of their mission and ministry, but as valued community members, leaders, and servants of all. We are confronting churches built on the sand of non-disabled privilege and pastoral power. We are challenging churches to embrace us *as disabled people,* and no longer to ask us to leave disability at the church door.

At the same time, these storytellers know that the values of the Reign of God can transform a Church that has been deceived by normalcy. Some are daring to speak out against traditions and beliefs that have devalued disabled people, as the Church has failed to recognise the image of a disabled God in us. Disabled people are shaping new theologies of healing that do not imagine us as mistakes waiting to be fixed, but as God's fearfully and wonderfully made creation. We are sharing untold stories of a *God like us*, glimpsed through the prism of our lived experience of disability – a disabled God, who shows a world and Church mired in ableism that disability can be godly. We are reminding the Church that the Body of Christ is not complete without all bodies and minds.[505] We are calling for *metanoia* – repentance, that leads to transformed churches. We are praying for Christian communities that embody the diverse Reign of God.

We are challenging churches to open the gates. Not for us, but with us.

In churches that talk about 'including' disabled people, are majority non-disabled congregations ready to listen to those calling from the edge for transformation? Are they ready to centre our voices in the conversation about us, allowing us to lead the Church in new directions? A biblical vision for justice could move the Church out beyond its walls, into places where the Spirit is already moving, where the Reign of God is already at hand. What new visions of justice might arise from a new kind of mission, and a deeper engagement with lived experience of ableism and disability injustice, beyond the churches? Could it transform the ways we 'do church' – for every single forgotten, exiled sheep?

Out on the edge, many disabled Christians are longing to come home. But until churches are transformed into places of access, participation and justice, many of us will be waiting at the gates.

We are waiting for the churches to join us in calling for justice.

Disabled People's Messages to the Church

We close this book with some messages that our disabled, Deaf and neurodivergent storytellers asked us to share with the Church.

First, they called churches to listen to the lament and ministry of the disabled Christians in their midst – and then to transform:

' Go out and meet disabled people and ask them what stops them coming to your church. ' Emma

' Have an actual conversation. By talking with disabled people, learn what works for them, and don't make assumptions. ' Jemma

' Don't assume anything. Don't look at somebody and think that you know something about them because of their disability... Everybody is different. So, ask. Have a conversation about it. ' Nicki

They called churches to create cultures of access, participation and radical, mutual hospitality, where disabled people can flourish:

' Churches could take the time to find out more about our disabilities, and then they could understand where we're coming from. ' Faith

' I would encourage church leaders to study disability theology and to learn about the social history and culture of disability, to be aware of issues like ableism, for example... Whilst many churches have mission statements and statements about equality, I want to see more churches with statements about disability accessibility and inclusion. ' Jemma

They called for churches where, no longer just objects of others' ministry, disabled people are empowered to participate, serve and lead:

❛ The Church isn't complete until disabled people can actively contribute and take part, not just as objects of pity and charity but as active participants whose experiences are seen as important too. ❜ Fern

❛ I think the summary for me is most churches now are reasonably good at basic access, but that's [all] they consider. Can you get into the building? Rather than, can you serve in all capacities in the church as a full member? ❜ Isabelle

They called churches to make room for difference, accepting us just as we are.

❛ You have to invite people into your [church] as a whole person. You cannot say, 'You come to me and you leave your disability at the door, you leave your colour, you leave your heritage, you leave your opinions at the door ...' My value and my worth comes from God ... It is about accepting people based on how much God values them, not how much you think they are worth. ❜ Mariam

‘ When you open your arms, and the Church, to people who look, and behave and experience the world differently, not only are you opening yourself up to discovering the most amazing wisdom, fun, and [different] perspectives, but you also can relax and start to really accept yourselves … What disabled people can teach [the Church] is that it’s okay to be who we are, to interact the way we do, and to see things differently and experience God differently. ’ Esther

‘ Include individuals. When people come to your church, that’s the person you’re including. When people want to come to your church and can’t, that’s the person you’re [not] including… If you embody loving Christian values, and you have an awareness of the barriers… you would be addressing those barriers. ’ Sarah

‘ Open hearts as well as open doors. ’ Jane

And they called churches to justice, for all disabled people, in the Church and in society.

‘ If they listened to what we need, as a whole, the Church would be much more empathic and it would be a real force for good in society. ’ Andrew

❝ We should be making churches places of refuge, accessible in different ways. We should be going out and seeing what the needs are and meeting them. ❞ Fern

And then there was Tim's message to the churches: a story of eleven lost sheep. Some years ago, Tim took part in a patients' programme to help people with long term conditions manage their symptoms. There, he brought up the subject of faith. All eleven of his fellow patients had been to church since becoming chronically ill or disabled, he learned. None of the eleven had stayed. Tim was the only one who had not left, and he had a very good reason to stay – he was paid by the diocese. Tim believed the Church had failed these eleven disabled people. Seeking answers in the Church, they had not found them. Perhaps they had not found hospitality, access and acceptance that would allow them to participate fully in the body of Christ, just as they are.

❝ There's no point in building a ramp so that people can leave easier. ❞ Tim

Tim called churches to pursue disabled people like those eleven, as relentlessly as the Shepherd pursues the lost sheep. Learn what is keeping disabled people from your churches, Tim and other storytellers told churches. Care about each disabled person missing from the pews and the pulpits – that love will motivate you to learn about the barriers that keep us out of your community. When churches truly value disabled people, and can imagine us among them, the rough ground will be levelled and the gates will be opened to all.

In an ableist society, churches must seek to be anti-ableist.[506] Injustice does not just arise out of nowhere; there is human sin behind it.[507] But Jesus came to liberate us from the 'principalities and powers' of the world – from ableism.[508] It is the Holy Spirit that empowers us all to repent of ableism, Lamar Hardwick tells us. The Spirit makes space for us to imagine and realise a diverse Church, one that fulfils God's word: 'I will pour out my spirit on all flesh.'[509]

AT THE GATES

For that vision to become a reality, the Church must change. A disability-positive Church will question its unspoken ableist assumptions about human value. It will declare, in actions as well as words, that disabled people are a vital part of the Body of Christ. From access barriers to ableist traditions, churches must confront the ways they close the gates to disabled people. That will only happen together with disabled people. With the benefit of lived experience, we have a first-hand insight into the barriers that keep us from participating in Christian communities. The storytellers in this book are just a few of the disabled people whose stories – whose Kingdom theology – are lighting the way. We are calling from the edge for churches to transform into places of justice.

There is no ableism in the Kingdom of God.

' An accessible and inclusive Church is possible. I remain hopeful that these changes will happen. ' Fern

APPENDIX I
Storytellers' Stories

Andrew

Andrew was born with a hearing impairment. He began attending church at the age of 18 and developed a passion for church planting in the inner city, taking on a number of church leadership roles. However, as Andrew's hearing loss deteriorated, he began to be excluded from his church community due to its hearing-centred culture. Everything about the way they 'did church' made it difficult for Andrew to participate and lead – from informal sharing without microphones, to house groups where people prayed with their faces bowed, which prevented lipreading. When Andrew asked if his church's sermons could be subtitled, he was told it was too expensive to provide that facility for one person. Even sermon notes were too difficult for speakers to provide, in a church where preaching was informal and spontaneous.

Eventually, Andrew left the church altogether, giving up on his ministry. 'I couldn't cope anymore,' he reflected. 'It wasn't that they didn't want me. I just didn't fit into the way that they did church. I just didn't fit into the way that Christians did things when they got together.'

From the Deaf community, Andrew has learned sign language and to accept his deafness as a gift from God, but he has not found his way back to a church community. Today, Andrew occasionally attends Church of England services, as well as the Greenbelt festival, when there is a BSL interpreter available. Andrew was in his forties when we interviewed him, and he used a BSL interpreter to access his focus group interview.

Anthony

Anthony is autistic – he also uses the older term Asperger syndrome. He shared his story through a one-to-one interview. Now in his thirties, when he was younger he attended a liturgical, 'high' Anglican church, where he was once discerning a call to ordination. Over time, the social culture of church became increasingly difficult for him to cope with, in a church where he was intimidated by what he calls the ' "everyone must join in" brigade'. Instead, Anthony saw church as a place to worship. Today he no longer attends any church, but he still has a strong faith. While he regrets not being able to attend church anymore, Anthony has accepted that he does not fit with most churches' ways of doing and being church.

Anthony celebrates his neurodivergent ways of being; he does not believe autistic people need healing from autism. He worries that well-meaning people in churches often have poor understanding of autism, and believes that more accepting attitudes towards neurodiversity could help. He hopes Christians are praying not for the eradication of autism, but for strength for autistic people in a neuronormative world. In the end, Anthony believes God understands and values autistic people, even if well-meaning church members do not always accept us as we are.

Brianna

Brianna is a part-time wheelchair user, as a result of multiple sclerosis. She is in her sixties. When we interviewed her, she had been worshipping at the same cathedral church for 15 years. She is actively involved in the cathedral community, running the Sunday school and events. But access to the cathedral is difficult for Brianna, and she has been left feeling 'invisible and violated' by her experiences as a disabled person in church. Improving the experience for disabled people who come to the cathedral is a ministry and a cause for Brianna. She describes her disability advocacy as a 'fight', one that she is determined to continue, even though her activism on behalf of all disabled people there has often been dismissed as mere complaining.

Communion can be a 'humiliating' experience for Brianna, especially when the inaccessible high altar is used for liturgical reasons. Wheelchair users at the cathedral are segregated into a separate area away from their families. Brianna and other disabled people have been physically moved 'out of the way' during services, giving Brianna the painful sense that she is always *in the way,* and less than a full part of the Body of Christ. She finds herself at the mercy of vergers and cathedral staff, having to negotiate her access needs carefully with people she must 'keep on side' if she wants their help to access the altar or nave in the future. Brianna has considered leaving the cathedral, especially after a welcoming experience at another local church where there were wheelchair spaces among the congregation, but she is determined not to give up on the cathedral's disabled visitors and members who are less able to speak out for justice than she is. Brianna shared her story in a one-to-one interview.

Charlotte

Charlotte, who is in her thirties, has a fatigue condition. She took part in a focus group interview. Charlotte is in lay ministry. She attends a Church of England congregation, and she is inspired by many expressions of spirituality, from contemplative, to sacramental, to liberation theology, to charismatic. She enjoys finding creative ways of engaging with God.

Charlotte's lived experience of illness has given her a nuanced view of healing and cure. She has experienced God's healing in the midst of disability. As for many of our storytellers, her disabled identity has had a hand in shaping her healing theology. On a retreat, when a fellow retreatant prayed for Charlotte without asking her, Charlotte challenged their assumptions that because she is disabled, she must be seeking a cure from her impairments. Our cultural beliefs that disabled people always need cure may distract us from those – disabled or not – who are longing for healing prayer, Charlotte reflects.

Clare

Clare, who is in her thirties, has ME/chronic fatigue syndrome. She took part in a focus group interview. After becoming unwell and meeting with some difficult attitudes to her chronic illness, Clare moved churches several times. She remembers one especially painful experience when a pastor doubted whether her chronic fatigue syndrome was real. When we interviewed her, she had just started attending an evangelical Church of England congregation where she felt more welcomed, although she told us it can be hard for her to get to know people at church, when she is usually too tired to attend evening home groups. Clare has found that disability-aware leaders can make a difference to her inclusion as a disabled congregant, in the simple things, right down to phrasing that shows they don't expect everyone to stand.

After attending some churches where she felt disabled people were often under a 'spotlight' for prayer, Clare believes that God can cure through healing prayer, but she affirms through lived experience that *not* finding that cure does not mean a disabled person lacks faith. 'If God chooses to heal you, that's wonderful,' she says, 'but if he doesn't, it doesn't mean that you're not praying hard enough. It doesn't mean that you're not being a good Christian.' As a disabled person, Clare's faith gives her strength in a disabling society. 'The Bible says the world will be frustrating,' she reflects, but sins of ableism are no surprise to her, in a world that needs Jesus.

Deirdre

Deirdre, who is in her sixties, is a member of an evangelical Baptist church. We interviewed her through instant message and email exchanges, to make the interview more accessible to her. When we spoke to her, Deirdre had been ill with severe ME/chronic fatigue syndrome for 18 years. She had been unable to leave her home for most of that time.

Illness has kept Deirdre from attending her church in the building, where she has been a member for nearly 20 years. But, with the support of fellow church members, she has stayed involved with her church remotely. Friends send her tape recordings of sermons, since the church does not routinely record their teaching. Deirdre has been very grateful for the church's pastoral support during her illness, although she feels that they are often focused on doing things for her, to the exclusion of spending time with her. Participation at a distance has sometimes been a challenge, when churches tend to focus on their members who can be physically present. At times, Deirdre has felt forgotten by her community.

Although many years of illness have not been easy for Deirdre, she has experienced God's healing in the midst of chronic illness. 'God has transformed me through it', she told us. But Deirdre has not been able to find Christian teaching that reflects her lived experience of illness and healing. Unable to hold a physical book, Deirdre enjoys listening to the limited selection of Christian audiobooks she can find, but she has been frustrated by the focus on relentlessly praying for cure, in the books she has read about illness and healing. She has sought out books on living with illness and seeking God's blessing in the midst of it, but has found nothing. Eventually, 'I stopped listening to any teaching [on illness and healing],' Deirdre told us.

Emma

Emma is in her forties. She shared her story in a one-to-one interview. Emma trained as a lay pioneer minister – a lay role within the Church of England with a ministry of preaching, teaching and pastoral care. After six years in lay ministry, Emma suddenly became blind and mobility impaired. The rapid onset of her condition saw her taking a year out of ministry, as she came to terms with a new way of living out her vocation.

Emma faced barriers to her ministry after she became disabled, when she was at first told that the Church of England would not be renewing her licence. She was relieved when she appealed to her bishop and he rejected this line of thinking, affirming that Emma had been called both before *and after* her change of circumstances.

Emma has learnt to practise needs-based ministry, adapting to the situations of those she is serving. She credits her disability as a gift in learning to be flexible and to look at ministry differently. Emma has a ministry on Facebook, where her closed group for disabled and chronically ill people offers a safe place to explore faith and spirituality. It has organically become a place of prayer and mutual support for those on the edge of church.

Esther

Esther is in her thirties and is currently serving a curacy in the Church of England. She has mental health problems and fibromyalgia; she shared her story in a one-to-one interview. Esther grew up with a sense of calling to ministry. Her experiences with disability began as she saw her church's response to her mother's mental health problems and MS. 'I didn't like what I saw', she told us.

In the midst of developing mental health problems herself, Esther felt called to ministry. Applying for a course at Bible college, she encountered hesitancy and barriers when being open about her mental health diagnosis. After a further diagnosis of fibromyalgia and chronic fatigue, Esther initially gave up on her call to ministry, as she could not see a place for 'people like me' within the Church. It wasn't until an encounter with a woman with mental health issues who had just been ordained that the possibility of a place in ministry became real for Esther.

Esther entered the selection process for ordination in the Church of England. After a number of rejections and setbacks, she was finally accepted to train for ministry. There was a purposeful emphasis on inclusion at her theological college, which she found refreshing. However, Esther was required to attend a medical which returned the conclusion that she could not be recommended for curacy.

After more perseverance and support from allies, Esther is now serving her curacy. She is learning that she cannot separate being called from being disabled. For Esther, the most powerful thing she brings to her ministry is her lived experience. The thing deemed most problematic about her 'suitability' for ministry is the very thing that sets her unique ministry apart. She recognises the resilience which has been formed in her through disability, amidst barriers that her non-disabled peers have not been subject to.

Faith

Faith has a condition that causes fatigue, and she is rarely able to leave her house. She shared her story through a focus group interview; she was in her forties when we interviewed her. Faith has attended churches of several denominations, from Church of England congregations to independent evangelical churches.

When we interviewed her in 2016, Faith had been unable to find a home church for several years. Morning services are too early for her, and she finds it difficult to sit upright through a service of longer than half an hour. Because, at time of interview, she was not an active member of a church, Faith often missed out on pastoral support; she did not know anyone she could ask for lifts to services or social events, and there was no minister she could ask to bring her communion. With no other choice open to her, Faith took communion herself at home, without a priest or minister.

Faith has been meeting online for prayer and Bible study with other disabled Christians for many years, beginning long before most churches were engaging in the online space. Faith's prayer ministry has developed as she has had more time to pray; she is active in a large prayer network. More recently, Faith has found a church with a daytime Bible study; although she is only rarely well enough to attend services, the community is understanding of her situation.

Faith feels that she has grown closer to God since she has been ill. 'I see my weakness as a strength because God has strengthened me in so many ways,' she said. Despite attitudes from some fellow Christians that Faith calls 'condemning,' she believes enduring illness does not mean a disabled person lacks faith – only Jesus heals.

Fern

Fern is in her twenties and currently lives in Scotland. She has attended a wide variety of churches, from traditional settings to cafe churches. She shared her story with us in writing and through email discussion.

As an autistic person, Fern's early memories of church included distressing experiences of loud worship and flashing lights, which meant she had to be taken out of the main service. Sitting outside, she got to know others with epilepsy and other conditions who had also been excluded from the main service. Fern told us that being disabled in the church often leads to feeling 'extremely alone and othered', and yet those people she encountered in 'the other room' were extremely important to her faith, as people who occupied the same outside space as her. Much of Fern's difficulty in church settings is in navigating the 'social side' of gatherings. She has found many unwritten rules hard to understand, from post-church chit-chat to hugging and enforced eye contact during the Peace. Hearing that autism is 'a punishment and a curse' caused Fern profound shame and, for a while, led her to leave churches altogether.

Since becoming a wheelchair user, Fern has encountered more access issues and negative attitudes surrounding healing and wholeness. She relates the feeling of being 'pounced' on for healing when she attended churches which, while probably well-intentioned, made her feel 'othered' and reduced her to an object of pity and charity. Ultimately, Fern wanted 'someone to sit with me and be there and listen', but this was not what she found in churches.

Now often unable to leave her bed, during COVID lockdowns, Fern has found a church in Australia where she can participate remotely. The church is attuned to meeting access needs through sign language and written notes, while the 'watch later' features have enabled Fern to participate in her own time, depending on her stamina.

Fern told us that she now has a personal faith, one on her own terms, rather than one that is entirely connected to and dependent on church. 'It has made me think and find things out for myself. I feel I know a bit more about what the Bible means when it talks about rejoicing in weakness and relying on God.'

Hazel and Victor

Hazel and Victor are both blind; they are a married couple. When we interviewed them together, Hazel was in her sixties and Victor was in his fifties. They are long-term members of their evangelical church, nominally Baptist. Outside of churches, Victor has been active in Disabled People's Organisations and the disability movement for many years, while Hazel has worked in access consultancy.

Hazel said that she and Victor were 'not very well included' in their church, although they enjoy the worship and evangelical teaching there.

New songs used to be taught to the whole church; now it is assumed that everyone will be able to read the words on the screen. Hazel and Victor have asked for worship song lyrics to be sent to them by email, so that they can read them via accessible computer software, but the worship team would rather choose songs spontaneously during the service. Barriers have been placed in the way of the couple's leadership and service at the church, especially for Victor, who was discouraged from leading an Alpha course when church focused on the ways they imagined blindness would limit Victor's ability to lead. Church social life is also difficult for the couple to participate in, thanks to inaccessible booking systems and social events organised around sighted people's needs. Hazel and Victor now rarely attend events in the church's community calendar. While there is much they appreciate about their church, their access needs are often forgotten, pushing them to the edge of church life.

Isabelle

Isabelle is a full-time wheelchair user as a result of multiple sclerosis; she is in her fifties. She attends a charismatic, evangelical Church of England congregation. When she shared her story in a one-to-one interview, Isabelle had recently been accepted to train as a non-stipendiary minister in her church, where she has been a member since before she was disabled.

Isabelle feels very included at her church, although she continues to face some access barriers. She thinks being well-known in a community has made a difference for her participation and leadership there. 'My church family has known me for a long time, so they see me as a person', she told us. She was delighted when her community burst into applause when it was announced that she had been accepted to train for ordination. Access to the church building has been far from perfect for Isabelle, after her offers of help with redevelopments have been turned down. She has been left having to deal with mistakes that could have been avoided if she had been listened to, including doors that are not wide enough for wheelchairs to navigate through easily.

The church's accessible toilet is accessed from outside and kept locked, meaning that Isabelle must wait outside for someone to open it. But the most important thing for Isabelle is that her participation, service and leadership is enabled in a community, and she knows that her church family values her and recognises her gifts.

In contrast, as a wheelchair user visiting a new community, Isabelle feels she can be seen more as a problem than a person. Being regularly 'pounced on' for healing prayer at festivals has been particularly traumatic for her. Through her experience of illness and disability, Isabelle feels she is able to pray more sensitively in her own healing ministry, now that she knows how physically and emotionally intimidating healing prayer can be for people in her position. She knows very few other disabled Christians, and has wondered whether she is 'the only one' in the particular ministry role she is in.

Jane

Jane is in her sixties and has cerebral palsy; she became a regular wheelchair user in her forties. She also has a hearing impairment. Jane was confirmed Anglican in the 1990s, and now mainly attends Methodist churches. She shared her story through a text-based interview.

Access for Jane has 'not been too bad' when attending churches, with alternate entrances available and churches making it possible for her to receive communion in her seat. She finds attendance at morning services difficult; this can be an issue when there is no alternate evening service. On suggesting a Book of Common Prayer service Jane was told, 'You can get that at 8 am', which for Jane highlighted the common church mantra, *But we've always done it like this*. Jane understands many of these attitudinal barriers to be more of a denominational quirk rather than a specific rejection of her access needs.

Jane finds some aspects of healing ministries run counter to her own sense of personhood as a disabled person, especially when they are focused on cure more than healing. 'It argues that there is something wrong that needs correcting.' For Jane, healing should rather be about healing the wounds that these ableist perceptions inflict, and the healing of others' attitudes towards disability.

Exposure to the disability activist movement has informed Jane's theology. She remembers the words of a fellow disabled student: 'I used to think of myself as a failed version of a non-disabled person; now I realise I am a successful version of me.'

Jemma

Jemma is in her thirties and attends a charismatic evangelical church, after coming to faith in her twenties. She shared her story with us in writing and through email exchanges. She was born with a visual impairment, and she also has PTSD and other chronic conditions. Jemma finds that access is often 'an afterthought' in churches and at Christian events. She has had to work hard to get across that she needs to plan and have information in advance. Many of Jemma's access needs can be met with simple, inexpensive adaptations. Churches have been less responsive to her mental health access needs. She has faced barriers when churches have not given trigger or content warnings, and when changes have been implemented without warning her. However, when her access needs have been met, Jemma has been able to thrive and grow, taking on more leadership responsibilities.

Jemma has found that her conditions, particularly their more visible effects such as her use of a cane, have made her a 'target' for healing prayer. When she has asked people not to pray for cure for her blindness, her requests have often been ignored, leaving her feeling that her lived experience is not valued. Like many disabled people, Jemma has complex experiences of healing. 'My blindness is part of who I am and my identity,' she says. It has been more difficult for Jemma to accept that she has not found healing from PTSD. In her church's prayer ministry, through her own experience, she has been able to advise and train pray-ers in praying for healing in more sensitive ways.

Jemma has found a lack of Christian teaching on disability. Much of the disability theology she *has* encountered has not centred disabled voices. She is exploring theological education, but she is finding many courses inaccessible to her, whether because of transportation issues or course materials not offered in alternative formats – or which come with an added price-tag.

Kt

Kt has cerebral palsy and is in her forties. She is an ordained Church of England priest, currently working as a part time Disability Adviser for the Oxford Diocese. When we interviewed her in a focus group discussion in 2016, Kt had been looking for theologies of disability that resonated with her. When she realised how difficult it was for disabled Christians to find good teaching about disability, or to share their stories with other disabled Christians, Kt and her colleagues established Disability and Jesus. The group has grown quickly over the past few years, becoming a large, disabled-led online Christian network. Disability and Jesus reaches out to disabled Christians through online services and by connecting people through social media. Although Kt has faced ongoing barriers to her work and calling as a disabled priest, she feels that she has had more positive experiences as a disabled person in churches than negative.

Laura

Laura is in her twenties and was raised in a traditional Baptist church in a small town. She shared her story with us in writing and email exchanges. In her early twenties, Laura began to experience issues with fatigue and being unable to eat or drink. Now at a larger, youth oriented church, she was encouraged to pray for her situation. However, her faith did not seem to explain her new circumstances. This time was the beginning of a 're-shaping' of her theology around healing and suffering. She sought healing, partly for her own relief but partly for the benefit of her family and community and their perception of her faith. Moments of healing did come for Laura, but she continued to experience symptoms, which reinforced for her the difference between *healing* and *cure*.

Feeling a call to youth ministry, Laura trained at theological college. Despite her concerns about whether she had the stamina to keep up with the course, she was encouraged to stay, and the college made adaptations to make it possible for her to continue. When she was initially introduced to the concept of online church, Laura was sceptical about how online ministry could be legitimate. She persevered with what she considered 'real' church but after attending many churches she grew despondent. Physical inaccessibility and difficult attitudes of others towards her chronic illness made her feel unwelcome.

These setbacks caused Laura to rethink her attitude to online church, as she encountered other disabled and chronically ill Christians through social media. She founded YouBelong, a community to bring them together in online church. The group has grown at a rate that has surprised Laura, showing that there is an appetite for an online community of chronically ill and disabled Christians. The community has opened up a new path for Laura to exercise her ministry in a way that allows her gifts to flourish. YouBelong has become a vital place of connection and community for those who, like Laura, have found traditional churches hard to navigate.

Leah

Leah is autistic and dyspraxic, and has insulin-dependent diabetes. At the time of our one-to-one interview, Leah was in her twenties, and she was attending an independent evangelical church with a Baptist history. As an autistic person, participating in church can be a challenge for Leah. She struggles with the large size of the church and its social culture. Church coffee can be a particular challenge for her, with all its expectations of small talk and meeting near-strangers. Teaching throws up barriers for Leah, too. She finds it difficult to follow the long sermons preached from the front at her church, but even small group teaching often moves too quickly for her, and she is longing for Christian teaching that she can understand and engage with.

Overnight, access improved for Leah when her church was being redeveloped, when a smaller congregation and quieter venue opened the gates to Leah's participation. This was accidental and temporary improved access, but it helped Leah to see how churches could be more accessible to autistic and dyspraxic people. She appreciates it when churches share information in advance, on websites or in service sheets. She has thought of several ways that her church could help her to fit better, from a member list with photos of the congregation, to clearly-written directions to church from local stations and bus stops, shared on the church's website. Leah is still praying for a church where, through access that meets her needs, she can participate in the community in meaningful ways.

Leah does not feel that she needs a cure, as an autistic person. She does not wish to be changed or 'fixed' to become neurotypical. She wonders whether, in Heaven, it will be non-disabled people's attitudes to disabled people that will be healed. Not all impairments are necessarily a problem, Leah reflected. 'So if they're not a problem, why would they be fixed?'

Maria

Maria has fibromyalgia, which causes chronic pain and fatigue; she is in her forties. When she shared her story in a focus group interview, Maria was attending an independent evangelical church where there was a strong pressure to attend every week. She struggled with the morning service, held at a time when her fatigue is often at its worst. Maria often ended up in the kitchen, fighting to stay awake till the end of the service. When she began to withdraw from her church, as she became more unwell, her pastors were concerned that she was not attending regularly. They eventually supported her in taking a break 'for a season', but they expected her to return to church, and to health. They could not recognise the barriers their church culture created for someone with chronic illness.

A few months after her interview, Maria told us through follow-up emails that she had left her church and was prioritising her disability access needs in her search for a new community. Maria has increasingly found her own ways of creating church on the edge: listening to teaching on Christian television, attending evening church groups when she is well enough, and meeting with other Christians to pray together.

Maria continues to pray for healing from her chronic conditions; she hopes that, if she is not healed in this world, she will be healed in Heaven. At the same time, she thinks the assumption that we will all have 'perfect' bodies in Heaven could be a problem for disabled people.

'If you're a disabled person, it's such a part of who you are and your personality,' she reflected, wondering whether some disabled people would want to be a 'healed version' of themselves.

Mary

Mary, who is in her twenties, has long-term mental health problems; she does not personally identify as disabled, but she is covered by the Equality Act definition of disability. She has attended a number of churches, including Assemblies of God and evangelical Church of England congregations. When she shared her story in a one-to-one interview, Mary was just beginning to attend a church from an evangelical charismatic network. Mary has had a difficult history of exclusion from churches, including an Anglican church where she was an intern, where leaders shared confidential information about her health without her permission, and asked her to have counselling with an unqualified fellow church member. Mary found this approach to pastoral care inappropriate. She told us that church leaders needed training on practical inclusion of people with mental health problems in the congregation and in leadership, and that they needed to learn when to refer people to mental health services outside the church.

With the benefit of lived experience, Mary now reaches out to others with mental health problems, sharing informal peer support. It has been Mary's way of offering service on the edge, even in churches that cannot always recognise her gifts.

Mary feels more welcome at her current church, just as she is. No one puts her under pressure to attend services, but if she is ill, they remind her that they are praying for her. They honour her own decisions about what is best for her access and health. It's a 'light touch' balance of pastoral care and respect for Mary's agency, and she wishes more churches could find that balance with members who experience distress.

Mims

Mims experiences long-term mental distress. Mims is in her fifties; she shared her story in a one-to-one interview. She was brought up in an evangelical Baptist church. When she suddenly began to experience bipolar symptoms in her twenties, other members of her church struggled to understand her mental health problems. Mims took a break from churches for a while, but she began to find peace in large, liturgical churches where she could have some anonymity when she needed it.

Today Mims is an active member of a large liturgical Anglican church, where she has been a pioneer in the church's disability work, advocating for better inclusion for people who experience distress. 'It is a mission to get people to understand', she told us. Increasingly, Mims struggles with her large church and its socially-focused community life, but she enjoys the smaller evening services.

Miranda

Miranda, who has incomplete tetraplegia (paralysis), is in her sixties. Miranda has attended Church of England churches all her life, and is a Franciscan Tertiary. She has a ministry of disability inclusion; she has worked with her Franciscan order to make their documents more accessible to blind people, and she has encouraged her church to do better when it comes to including all disabled people.

At the time of her one-to-one interview, Miranda was attending a church where she enjoyed the worship and fellowship, but the building was full of barriers, and she felt that disabled people's access needs were rarely taken seriously by clergy. Miranda found it especially troubling when, during the Eucharist, she was often left waiting at the raised altar to receive last. In post-interview emails, she told us that she had left the church, after clergy decided to remove the wheelchair spaces that Miranda had argued were needed among the pews. By this point, access to the building and communion had become so difficult that she was left feeling deeply discouraged. Because she is 'just a minority', Miranda felt that no one in church leadership at the church cared about the barriers that were not just keeping her from getting through the door, but closing the gates to her participation.

Miranda believes she will still be a wheelchair user in Heaven, though she sometimes lacks confidence in arguing this position with her non-disabled fellow Christians.

Nicki

Nicki, who shared her story through a one-to-one interview, has a background in church planting. It was while living and working abroad that she developed cauda equina syndrome, which causes paralysis, nerve damage and pain. Nicki now uses a wheelchair, which allows her to live a full and active life.

On returning to the UK, finding a church to suit Nicki's access needs became a priority. She and her family found a church which was accessible, but the accessible toilet was used as a storage cupboard. The toilet became an ongoing problem as leadership continually failed to grasp how vital access to a safe and private bathroom was for Nicki. Nicki reflects that she wasn't missed after leaving the church. She questions what her presence as a disabled person meant for that community, wondering if she was an 'inconvenience' and a 'contradiction' for a church that believed in cure through healing ministry.

Nicki then found a church which, while waiting for a redevelopment, was temporarily meeting in a school. However, Nicki had to travel for an hour to get to this more accessible church. Nicki sometimes found her place in the church as a 'permanent guest' to be frustrating, observing that she 'can't be called on to just do anything' as a wheelchair user in a space that is not fully accessible to her, whether that is taking the offering or washing up the coffee mugs. Nicki reflects that, since becoming a wheelchair user, she has never been asked to serve in these ways.

In post-interview emails, Nicki updated us on how her parish church has recently created level access to the building and installed an accessible toilet. The access improvements have given Nicki the chance to start attending a local, accessible church where she can be more fully involved in community life.

Despite the setbacks of others' assumptions, Nicki is keen to make church a place where everybody can be comfortable, even though it is often 'the place where most people feel least comfortable'. Nicki's experience of parenting a neurodivergent child means that she recognises that welcoming church environments need to take into consideration a range of access needs for people with all kinds of impairments. Challenging people's assumptions is the first step in creating an accessible church, Nicki told us.

Rhona

Rhona, who is visually impaired, is in her sixties. She shared her story in a focus group interview. She is a local preacher in the Methodist Church; through this lay leadership role, she serves in her church and across the wider circuit. Rhona enjoys her charismatic church and her ministry there, but access barriers make it more difficult for her to participate and lead there. In terms of physical access, poor lighting and closed doors can make it a struggle to get around the church. Culturally, Rhona often meets with thoughtlessness or resistance from others, when she has asked for large print documents or made other access requests, so that she can worship and minister in the same way as anyone else.

Rhona's capacity for ministry has sometimes been questioned, with other leaders wondering how she can help serve communion without being able to see, although Rhona has offered imaginative solutions from her own lived experience of visual impairment. When she has used technology in church to find hymn words or readings in large print, Rhona has sometimes met with disapproval from others. Many of these barriers come from poor awareness of blindness and visual impairment in churches, Rhona reflected, and a failure to understand how interdependent we all are – not just disabled people. She told us that her experiences of church have been a mix of negative and positive: 'negative in catering for my disability, positive in the sense of growing my faith and gifts'.

Sarah

Sarah, who shared her story through a one-to-one interview, was late diagnosed autistic, after years of misdiagnosis. One of the most disabling aspects of her condition is sensitivity to noise. When her church replaced their heating system, the new 'air-blowing' system caused sensory overload, and Sarah could no longer attend worship.

Since childhood, however, Sarah has been visiting Lee Abbey, a Christian residential and retreat centre. This is a place with positive memories for Sarah, and so when she needed a place of restoration in the midst of distress, she decided to return to this familiar setting. Now the Abbey remains a constant point in Sarah's life, a place she can return to and regroup. Sometimes it has been the only place she has received communion from one year to the next. The transient nature of the community is freeing for Sarah and it has become a safe space where she can be open about being autistic.

When thinking about how churches could be more accessible for autistic people, Sarah told us that information is key. Just as many tourist and commercial buildings publish access guides online, Sarah thinks the same detailed access information is vital for autistic and other disabled people visiting a new church. She thinks there is work for churches to do on both physical and social access. Sarah has found 'shaming' attitudes unhelpful, such as comments that 'we haven't seen you for a few weeks'. But she recognises that 'it's a really hard one to change, because you need to change culture to change that'.

Shona

Shona is deaf, and has a cochlear implant. She is in her thirties. She has multiple impairments, but in her focus group interview she mainly wanted to discuss her experiences as a deaf person in churches. With a background in Anglo-Catholic churches, Shona has a theology degree and has been discerning a call to ordination.

Shona has had mixed experiences as a disabled person in churches, although she has felt more included over the past few years. Her biggest frustration is with stereotypes and a poor understanding of deafness in churches. Exploring ordination has been challenging, when church leadership has often suggested – as a 'solution' to access barriers – that Shona might want to serve in a Deaf church. But Shona is not a BSL user and has no familiarity with Deaf culture, and she has often found herself trying to explain deafness to church leaders with little knowledge of it. There have been few other solutions proposed to the access barriers that Shona foresees coming with leadership, in inaccessible church cultures and hierarchical structures.

Shona's most positive experience of deaf inclusion came when she was on a pilgrimage, in a Roman Catholic church with a ministry to deaf members and visitors. Clergy offered to interpret the service in BSL for Shona and her sister, who is also deaf. After they explained that they do not use BSL, a priest lip-spoke the entire service. Shona felt a true sense of welcome, just as she is, in a church that was creating an accessible culture for deaf members and visitors alike.

Stephen

Stephen has had ME, also known as chronic fatigue syndrome, since he was a child. Now in his thirties, he uses a mobility scooter when he leaves his house. As well as being disabled himself, Stephen is a carer for his disabled wife. Stephen has always been a member of Church of England congregations. At the time of his focus group interview, he had recently moved to a rural town and joined a small local church. The building there is not as accessible as some churches he has attended – although it is accessible enough – but Stephen feels very included by a community that has welcomed him, as a disabled person. However, he still sometimes feels forgotten when he is not well enough to go to church for a while. Being present in church tends to be essential to belonging in a community, but so many disabled and chronically ill people cannot be in the building all the time, Stephen reflected; he wondered how churches can remember and include these disabled people.

Stephen had nuanced views on healing, especially the concept of healing and perfection in Heaven. As someone who has been disabled for most of his life, Stephen has a disabled identity, and he cannot imagine a Heaven where he would become a non-disabled person. He believes some part of his experience of disability will be carried on in the hereafter.

Susanna

Susanna, who is in her thirties, has ME/chronic fatigue syndrome. When she took part in a one-to-one interview, Susanna was attending a Methodist church in her small town, but she said, 'I tend just to identify as "Christian", as I attend the church I feel is the best fit.' Susanna thinks attitudes are often the biggest barrier for disabled people in churches. She has generally felt included in churches, and puts this down in part to her personal confidence in asking for access arrangements and information. She is aware that it can be harder for some disabled people to begin conversations about access, when they do not know how their requests will be received. In her 'genuinely loving' community, members and leaders are willing to have open conversations about disability, access and participation. Susanna wishes she could attend Sunday morning services at her church, but the early start is too much of a barrier. But her home group has been church for her, offering practical support and fellowship when she has been unwell. Susanna thinks this kind of loving community is unusual for disabled and chronically ill people, who can easily become isolated and forgotten, especially in larger churches.

Susanna feels that if Jesus were living in her community today, he would be with the poorest and most oppressed people – including disabled people. She believes the Church should be working for justice with those same people. Susanna has nuanced views about healing and disability, after many years of illness, and has come to believe that praying constantly for cure can be more an expression of doubt than faith. She prefers to faithfully accept the reality of her body and illness, and to recognise God's work in her life as it is.

AT THE GATES

Talitha

Talitha, who has cerebral palsy and uses a wheelchair, is in her thirties. She shared her story in a focus group. Talitha is actively involved in her independent evangelical church, which she has attended for over a decade. On the whole, she finds the community welcoming, but sometimes she feels 'a bit on the outside'. At times she has been discouraged when her service and leadership potential has not been recognised. While serving on the welcoming team, she is still asked by church members if she is lost, even after a decade of being a member of the community. She thinks that there is sometimes a perception that disabled people are not in church to serve or lead, but to be looked after by others. Talitha is interested in disability theology, and has attempted to share it at church, although she has been discouraged by a lack of interest in the topic. With another disabled member of her church, Talitha regularly attends a Disabled Christian Fellowship group; they have found it useful to explore disability issues from a Christian perspective with other disabled Christians.

Tim

Tim is a pioneer Church Army minister, with a history of community development work and evangelism. He is in his fifties, and shared his story in a one-to-one interview. During his ministry, Tim developed a chronic pain condition caused by swelling in his spine affecting his ability to walk. He now uses a mobility scooter. Had he not been in ministry when he became disabled, Tim questions whether he would have seen the church as the 'natural place' for him, given his often difficult experiences of other Christians' responses to his pain.

Bringing up the subject of faith while he was on a long-term conditions management programme, Tim learned that all eleven of his fellow patients had visited a church since the onset of their health condition, and that all eleven had left, being put off by their experience. Tim saw this as a missed evangelistic opportunity: disabled and chronically ill seekers were not finding answers in the Church. It is these people who have subsequently inspired Tim's ministry as he has sought to include and embrace those

262

who have been marginalised by the church. His lived experience of pain and disability has become a connection point for those on the edge. As Tim worked to counter attitudes in churches that see disability as deficit, it led to the creation of Struggling Saints, a weekly Twitter Bible study centring the perspectives of disabled people, open to both disabled and non-disabled Christians. Struggling Saints is an extension of Tim's pioneer ministry into the online space where disabled people are already gathering, as Tim and his group discover God together with them.

Zoe

Zoe has a chronic pain condition, and is a part-time wheelchair user. She is an ordained Church of England minister. When we interviewed her as part of a focus group, she was in her forties, and a curate in a liberal 'high' Anglican church. Zoe has had mixed experiences as a disabled person in churches. As a priest, barriers can prevent her from serving and leading, whether those are attitudinal barriers in the form of objections when she needs to sit down to preside over communion, or physical barriers such as raised pulpits, shaping communities' expectations that a priest should stand to lead. In other churches, Zoe's leadership has been received more positively. In church leadership, Zoe's limitations become her gifts, as she models interdependence in her church communities. The whole Church works better 'when we bring what we are', she reflected.

Zoe shared a theology of the 'upside-down Kingdom of God' with us, as she spoke about justice for disabled people in churches. 'The kingdom of God is meant to look really different to a well-run organisation', Zoe reflected, reminding us that Jesus, our King, rode on a ridiculous donkey, and that he is our model of power. Zoe believes disabled people can model that challenge to power in the Church. As someone who experiences chronic pain, healing is a complex issue for Zoe, but she is concerned about society's 'pursuit of physical improvement' and perfection, and how the Church reflects that obsessive pursuit.

Other interviews and stories

We could not use stories from all our interviews in this book, but more stories are shared in Naomi's thesis. There are a few people we have quoted more briefly: Mariam, who is autistic and shared her story through a one-to-one interview; Sheila, a wheelchair user who took part in a focus group interview; and co-author Emily, whose story is shared at the beginning of the book. There were a few more interviews in the disabled-led church groups where we spent time observing and participating in community life. During the six months we spent at Wave Church, we interviewed member Helen, with her mother Christa; we also interviewed Wave's co-founder Bernice Hardie, while Jess Hardie shared her story through comments transcribed by Bernice. Alongside our ongoing involvement with the St Martin-in-the-Fields/Inclusive Church annual disability conference and community, we interviewed Fiona MacMillan, Chair of the DAG and conference planning team, along with community member Lucy, while conference planning team member Rachel sent a written story.

APPENDIX 2
Glossary

Ableism: A system of beliefs that privileges some kinds of body, mind and ability over others. This culturally constructed ideology sees disabled people as inferior or deficient.[510]

Accessible cultures or **Cultures of access**: In an accessible culture, disabling barriers are dismantled before they can become the norm for a community.

Accidental access: Access that is created through circumstance, but not specifically with disabled people in mind. For example, a church that improves its amplification may accidentally include more people with hearing impairments.

Anglo-Catholic: Churches that follow the traditions of the nineteenth-century Oxford Movement, which sought to renew Catholic aspects of faith and practice in Anglican churches. Sometimes called 'high' churches.

Audiocentricity: Cultures that centre hearing people. Audiocentric churches may privilege listening to long sermons or discussions in home group settings, above other ways of encountering the Bible.

Autistic: A *neurodivergence*, characterised by differences from the norm in thinking, feeling, sensory processing, social interaction and/or communication. The now-outdated term 'Asperger syndrome' was also used by some storytellers.

Barriers: Barriers keep disabled people from participating in society. They may be physical: heavy doors, steps or poor lighting. They are often attitudinal, including negative ideas and attitudes towards disabled people. They are imposed on top of our impairments and interact with them.

Basileia: See *Kingdom*.

Capital: In society, our capital opens doors to us. Capital is the manifestation of privilege, in the skills and assets people develop as a result of their social position, allowing them to maintain that position. Capital may be economic, social or cultural.[511]

Charismatic churches: Churches which, in common with Pentecostal churches, emphasise the gifts of the Holy Spirit, such as speaking in tongues, along with informal worship.

Circuit: In the Methodist Church, a circuit is a grouping of churches. The circuit has pastoral and administrative oversight of several local churches.

Crip theology: Crip theology is critical of ableism in the Christian tradition and celebrates the disabled body of Christ; a theology by and for disabled people and our allies, which reclaims the Christian tradition for the disabled people it has alienated. It is still an emerging theology.[512]

Crip time: Disability theorists speak of crip time as time that disabled people bend to fit our needs, rather than having to harm our bodies or minds to fit schedules designed for non-disabled people.

Compulsory non-disability: The ableist belief that disabled people must desire non-disability and seek to be 'fixed'. McRuer calls this 'compulsory able-bodiedness;' a system that asks disabled people to say 'yes' to the unspoken question, 'Wouldn't you rather be more like me?'[513]

Conditional guests and **Conditional welcome**: A *conditional welcome* is one that invites guests into a space, but only according to the goodwill of the hosts. If guests are asked to change, to fit better into the ideologies or practices of their communities, they are *conditional guests*.

Cultural models: Cultural models of disability emphasise community belonging and pride among a group of disabled people. Deaf people often hold to a cultural model of Deafness, understanding themselves as a linguistic and cultural minority. The neurodiversity movement has a growing cultural model of its own. Disability culture is emphasised by other communities of disabled people too.[514]

Cure: Seen by some theologians as distinct from holistic healing, *cure* is the removal of an impairment or condition.

Deaf/deaf: *Deaf* (with a capital 'D') is generally used to indicate someone who is culturally Deaf, uses British Sign Language and sees themselves as part of the Deaf community, a linguistic and cultural minority. Those people with hearing impairments who do not use BSL, nor consider themselves part of the Deaf community, tend to call themselves *deaf* with a lower-case 'd'.

Deanery: In the Church of England context, a deanery is an administrative grouping of parishes.

Deficit or **Deficit Model**: A deficit model of disability understands disabled people as 'less than' non-disabled people.

Deliverance ministry: Often, but not only found in neo-Pentecostal and charismatic churches, this is a ministry that prays for God's healing from the influence or indwelling of evil spirits. In some churches, such spirits are seen as the cause of illness or impairment in disabled people.

Disabled People's Organisation (DPO): Participatory, user-led organisations of disabled people, with activist aims of societal change for disabled people, especially in service provision. These organisations have been central to the history of the disabled people's activist movement. See also *user-led organisation.*

Disablism: Discrimination against individual disabled people, made possible within ableist systems.

Disability Justice: A framework for understanding ableism as connected to white supremacy, colonialism, capitalism and other systems of oppression. This framework was developed by a movement for collective struggle against ableism, led by the most marginalised disabled people, including disabled people of colour, trans and queer disabled people.[515]

Ecclesia: The Church of Christ, regardless of denomination.

Embodied welcome: We use this term to talk about a welcome not just in words or good intentions, but a welcome that disabled people experience when our bodies and minds are imagined and expected in a community – through accessible buildings and cultures of access.

267

Emotion work: Work done by marginalised people, especially, to manage and diffuse emotions in a difficult situation – either their own emotions or those of others.[516] Sometimes called *emotional labour,* though this form of emotion work is more usually expected in a paid setting, e.g. in the service industry.

Emotional dissonance: An impact of emotion work, *emotional dissonance* is the clash between the expectations that disabled people will be polite and grateful so that our access needs are more likely to be met, and the anger and stress we may feel at being expected to respond to ableism in this way.[517]

Epistemic injustice: Injustice that relates to knowledge. It can involve the silencing of a person or group, our misrepresentation, or the devaluing of our opinions – specifically because of the marginalised group we belong to.[518]

Epistemic invalidation: Disabled people's experiences of embodiment and disability are often invalidated, especially by professionals in positions of power over us.[519]

Eschatology: Christian theology relating to the end times and the afterlife.

Eucharist: The Christian service, rite or sacrament commemorating the Last Supper, also referred to as Holy Communion.

Evangelical churches: Churches, usually Protestant, which focus on personal salvation (including conversion or being 'born again'), have a high, sometimes literalist regard for the Bible, and have a missionary commitment to sharing the gospel.

Fall, the: A theological term, this concept refers to the Fall of Adam and Eve from God's grace through the first sin of disobedience, and through them the Fall of humanity from grace.

Franciscan Tertiary: A member of the Third Order of Saint Francis, a lay order, in both the Roman Catholic church and the Church of England. Several storytellers were Franciscan Tertiaries.

Gospel vs. gospel: The different capitalisation distinguishes the *Gospels,* the four books of the Bible that narrativize Jesus' life, from the *gospel* or Christian message of Christ and salvation. See also *social gospel.*

Graciosi theology: A long Christian tradition in which some disabled people have been considered *graciosi* – those with a special blessing by God, primarily for the benefit of non-disabled people.[520]

Hermeneutic(s): The field of study dealing with interpretation of the Bible and other religious texts, or a particular method or theory of interpretation.

Identity-first language: Language through which people claim their identity as part of a group, putting the identity first: 'disabled people' and 'autistic people' are two examples. Many marginalised groups speak about themselves this way.

Ideal: A social *ideal* is an aspirational example or a shared societal norm. For example, in occupational studies, an *ideal worker* is consistently present and noticed at the workplace, and seen as committed to their organisation.

Imago Dei: The image of God in human beings.

Impairment: As a simple tool to understand disability oppression, the social model distinguishes impairment from disability. Impairment is the effects of an individual's illness, injury or health condition. Disability is the loss or limitation of opportunities to participate in society as a result of social and environmental barriers.

Inclusion: An approach which advocates for disabled people to be included in society, as it is. Inclusion 'may offer only 'cosmetic adjustments' that preserve the status quo' of a community,[521] rather than seeking transformation so that all can participate, just as we are.

Inclusive language: A form of language that consciously includes a diversity of disabled people, such as 'stand if you are comfortable, able and safe to do so'.

Instrumental use (of disability): The use of (the concept of) disabled people, or disability, for other people's ends. For example, in theology that focuses on what non-disabled people can gain from ministry with disabled people. See also *graciosi theology*.

Interactional: In sociology, *interactionism* argues that meaning is created through our social interactions. *Interactional justice* is a form of justice in which everyone is treated with dignity and respect through all interactions.[522]

Kingdom healing and **Kingdom theology**: For liberation theologians, the Reign of God is a vision of liberation from oppression, poverty, and discrimination. Kingdom healing is holistic healing for all of us and the world.[523] Many storytellers shared a similar vision of the transformative Reign of God, which in this book we have called *Kingdom theology*.

Labour: Additional work that disabled people (and other marginalised groups) must do in order to increase our chances of access and participation.

Lay minister: A minister who carries out some or all of the functions of ordained clergy, but are not ordained. They are often *non-stipendiary* or volunteer ministers.

Liberation Theology: A theological movement of the twentieth century, emerging in Latin America, and going to influence other theologies, including disability liberation theology. Liberation theologies understand God as having a preferential concern for those living in poverty and oppression. They seek the transformation of unjust societies through the Reign of God.

Liminal: A liminal state is one where individuals are neither in society nor entirely out of it, without role or status.[524] In communities such as churches, disabled people may find ourselves on the edge, in liminal spaces like side aisles.

Liturgical church: A church with prescribed, formal structures or orders of service, in such denominations as Anglican, Lutheran and Roman Catholic.

Liturgy: The words, rites and ritual actions used in churches.

Lived theology and **Lived religion**: 'Everyday' religious reflection and practice, by people without training in theology or church leadership.[525]

Metanoia: A New Testament Greek term meaning repentance or conversion; a transformation of the heart.

Mental distress: The field of mad studies increasingly uses this term, because it is self-defined and in keeping with the social model of disability. The term *mental distress* has a focus on societal oppression, rather than on the individual.

Microaggressions: Behaviour that communicates hostile or negative attitudes towards marginalised groups. For disabled people, that might include staring, patronising or dismissive language, touching a person or their mobility aid without consent, interference with assistance dogs, and speaking to carers instead of directly to a disabled person.

Ministerial ideal: In churches, there is an *ideal* of a minister (or priest) – that ideal minister is non-disabled. This ideal is communicated through buildings and practices that expect ministers to lead in ways that are not accessible to all disabled people. Many of these expectations are rooted in *pastoral model* assumptions that church leaders will be non-disabled.

Ministerial marginality: In some church structures, marginalised groups, such as disabled people, are less enabled to train and serve as ministers or priests than those from dominant groups.[526]

Misfitting: A situation in which disabled people's bodies and minds meet environments not designed for us, and we become square pegs in round holes.[527]

Non-stipendiary minister: A minister who is not paid, but is authorised to serve to the full extent of the ministerial position to which they are appointed.

Normalcy: Rooted in the work of nineteenth-century statisticians who first imagined the 'normal man,' normalcy is a set of bodily and neurological norms we are all expected to measure up to, influenced by a colonialist, capitalist ideal of health. Normalcy is at the root of societal ableism.[528]

Neurodiversity and **Neurodivergence**: The *neurodiversity* paradigm sees autism, and other neurological differences, as different ways of being, rather than as 'disorders' that require cure. The term originates with autistic sociologist Judy Singer. A *neurodivergence* is a variation in thinking, feeling and/or sensory processing that is considered atypical, compared with the accepted norm. Examples include autism, ADHD, dyslexia and Tourette syndrome.

Neurotypical: Those whose neurology fits within an accepted, dominant neurotype – who fit societal norms of thinking, feeling and sensory processing.

Ordained minister: An ecclesiastically appointed minister, in some denominations called a priest, who is authorised to perform church rites and sacraments.

Partial participants: When disabled people are offered only partial or second-rate access to institutions or buildings, we become partial participants. That can affect our sense of belonging, leaving us feeling less than a full member of a community.[529]

Participatory design: A person-centred approach to access that takes into account how different disabled people's access needs may vary and even conflict, understanding that there is no 'one size fits all' approach to access.

Pass or **Passing**: The ability of a person to be overlooked as a member of a marginalised group – to *pass* as a member of the dominant group. In the case of disabled people, at times some of us may seek to be perceived by others as non-disabled, or as less impaired than we are, for a range of social reasons.

Pastoral care: The spiritual and emotional support that churches offer to their congregations, within a Christian context, focused on the salvation of souls. It is usually offered by ministers and others in a pastoral leadership role.

Pastoral model: A model of power rooted in Christianity and its history of the care of the sick and those in need. See *pastoral power* and *pastoral care*. Overlapping with the *charity model*, a Christian *pastoral model of disability* today sees disabled people as being in church to receive pastoral care, often leading churches to fail to recognise our gifts as a result. Society inherited the pastoral model from the churches, as they took over the care of those who were sick or in need.[530]

Pastoral power: A form of power that is focused on the conscience and inner life of an individual, within a Christian framework. Church leaders must have knowledge of their congregations' souls, leading to power that demands complete individual obedience to church hierarchies. Although well meaning, pastoral power can become disempowering, with those who have traditionally received pastoral support having little say in how they are received into churches.

Pastoral theology: The theory and practice of Christian ministry.

Presenteeism: The expectation that an 'ideal worker' will be physically present and noticed at work. Some scholars suggest that churches have a similar requirement to be present and active in the community, an expectation embedded in church cultures.

Preside (at Holy Communion): To lead in administering communion to a congregation. In some churches, a function only undertaken by ordained priests.

Privilege: The structural advantages that an individual gains by belonging to a socio-economic or identity group. Non-disabled people benefit from non-disabled privilege; white people benefit from white privilege.

Psycho-emotional disablism: The disempowering encounters through which structural ableism becomes personal, including microaggressions, hostility and denial of access.[531]

Radical welcome: More than a welcome in words, radical welcome is about transformation of congregations, so that those who were once excluded are welcome at church, just as they are.[532]

Religious capital or **Spiritual capital**: *Religious capital* is the skills and privilege needed to participate or lead in a religion, including theological knowledge and an understanding of ritual and shared beliefs. Also called *spiritual capital*.[533]

Resistant readings: A way of 'reading against the grain'.[534] In resistant readings of the Bible, we shift the subject of biblical interpretations, focusing on the effects of a text on marginalised groups – including its effects on disabled people.

Rhetorical welcome: A welcome in words and good intentions, rather than in actions that enable access and participation.

Safe spaces: In activist parlance, a safe space is one where marginalised groups can come together in our own communities, without the interruption of ableism (or racism or sexism, etc.). These can be spaces for healing.

Segregated spaces: Segregation is the separation of disabled people into spaces away from the rest of society; 'special schools', for example. Access barriers keep disabled people from participating community life, in a form of de facto segregation.

Site for healing: A disabled person who becomes an object and symbol of God's healing power, rather than a person in their own right.

Scarcity paradigm: When churches argue that their resources to improve access are limited, they are often working from within a capitalist *scarcity paradigm*, as different priorities compete for churches' resources.[535]

Social gospel: The Christian message of the gospel understood not just as about personal salvation, but as a call to social transformation as a manifestation of the Kingdom of God.

Social location: Our position in society, based on our intersectionality along lines of gender, race, social class, disability, age, religion and other social backgrounds, which can lead to our privilege or marginalisation in society.

Social model of disability: The social model says that, in a world designed for non-disabled people, people with impairments are disabled by *barriers* – physical, attitudinal and social barriers.[536]

Stigma: A mark – such as an obvious impairment – that 'spoils' our identity, leading to shame about who we are.[537]

Structural exclusion: In sociology, *structure* is the way society is organised. Disabled people in churches may meet with *structural exclusion*, which is not conscious exclusion on the part of church members, but arises from the way institutions work.

Theological invalidation: The exclusion of disabled people's stories and perspectives from theology, sometimes because of the pastoral model, which does not expect disabled people to speak for ourselves. See also *epistemic injustice* and *epistemic invalidation*.

Transformation: Inspired by Jesus's mission to the margins, liberation theologies seek the transformation of an unjust everyday world into the just Reign of God.

User or **Service user**: A person who uses health and/or social care services.

User-led organisation (ULO): A group that is organised and controlled by people who use support services: by disabled people, or by people with a specific impairment. A ULO is usually defined as having a minimum of 75 per cent of its board made up of disabled people, and should demonstrate a commitment to the social model.

Visiocentricity: Cultures that centre sighted people. Blind people find it difficult to fit in visiocentric churches, because these church cultures were not designed for them.

Ways of being: Some disability scholars call disability a different 'way of being'. Our different ways of being in the world give disabled people distinctive – and valuable – perspectives.[538]

Wellness: Beginning in the 1950s, a new wellness movement encouraged people to strive for healthy living and well-being. Wellness has since become a consumerist cultural value and personal project, 'now bordering on a form of religiosity.[539]

APPENDIX 3
Abbreviations

BSL: British Sign Language

DAG: The Disability Advisory Group at St Martin-in-the-Fields Church

ME/CFS: Myalgic encephalomyelitis, also known as chronic fatigue syndrome, is a condition that can cause fatigue, pain and other impairments. It varies widely in severity.

MS: Multiple sclerosis, a condition of the brain and central nervous system that interrupts the signals between the brain and the body, often causing mobility difficulties. Depending on the type, it may be progressive, or people with MS may have periods of remission.

Wave Church: A church group with, not for, people with learning disabilities. The group's name stands for We're All Valued Equally.

Resources for Churches on Disability, Access and Justice

Practical Guides

Fiona MacMillan, ed., *Something Worth Sharing* (London: St Martin-in-the-Fields Church/Inclusive Church, 2019), https://www.inclusive-church. org/wp-content/uploads/2020/05/Something-Worth-Sharing-WEB. pdf. Sharing wisdom from several years of disability conferences, with resources and guidance for churches aiming to create cultures of access for disabled people.

Ann Memmott, *Welcoming and Including Autistic People in our Churches and Communities* (Oxfordshire: Diocese of Oxford, 2019), https:// churchesforall.org.uk/wp-content/uploads/2019/12/Autism-Guidelines-2019-Oxford-Diocese.pdf. Written by an autistic advocate, this guide shares wisdom on autistic culture and communication, reflects on the impact of theology, and shares practical ways your church can be more inclusive of autistic people.

Church of England, *A Place to Belong*, https://www.churchofengland.org/ sites/default/files/2018-07/A%20place%20to%20belong%20Guide_0.pdf. An access audit guide, showing you how to assess how far whether your church is accessible – physically and culturally – to a range of disabled people, and where you can improve access.

The Methodist Church, *Equality, Diversity and Inclusion Toolkit: Disability and Impairment, https://www.methodist.org.uk/media/9015/edi-toolkit-4.pdf.* A guide helping church communities and leaders to reflect on practical and theological aspects of disability and justice in churches.

Baptists Together, *Disability Justice Hub.* Resources for discussion on disability and church, reflecting on discrimination, healing, and the image of God in disabled people, along with BSL resources. https://www.baptist.org.uk/Groups/310661/Disability_Justice_Issues.aspx

Shelly Christensen, *From Longing to Belonging: A Practical Guide to Including People with Disabilities and Mental Health Conditions in Your Faith Community* (United States: Inclusion Innovations, 2018). Written by a parent of a disabled child, this how-to guide considers disability inclusion in all areas of church life, from worship to youth groups.

Groups and Communities

Wave for Change, https://www.wave-for-change.org.uk/wave-church-muswell-hill. Wave Church brings together people with and without learning disabilities, sharing their model for mixed-ability churches and community activities with the wider Church.

St Martin-in-the-Fields/Inclusive Church Conference on Disability and Church, https://www.inclusive-church.org/disability-conferences/. Talks, reports and resources from a decade of disabled-led conferences.

Disability and Jesus, http://disabilityandjesus.org.uk/. A user-led online church and community, of and by disabled people, exploring theology and worshipping together.

YouBelong, http://www.youbelong.org.uk/. A community of people with chronic illnesses and disabled people, meeting online.

Struggling Saints, https://twitter.com/Strgl_St_Bible. Weekly Twitter-based discussions on disability and faith, led by a disabled pioneer minister. *The Ordinary Office,* https://www.anordinaryoffice.co.uk/. An online community sharing faith and life on the margins, led by disabled people.

Christian Writing by Disabled, Neurodivergent and Deaf Theologians

Nancy L. Eiesland, *The Disabled God: Toward a Liberatory Theology of Disability* (Nashville, TN: Abingdon Press, 1994).

Lamar Hardwick, *Disability and the Church: A Vision for Diversity and Inclusion* (Westmont: InterVarsity Press, 2021).

Daniel Bowman Jr., *On the Spectrum: Autism, Faith, and the Gifts of Neurodiversity* (Grand Rapids: Brazos Press, 2021).

Donald Eadie, *Grain in Winter: Reflections for Saturday People* (Wipf and Stock, 2012).

Stephanie Tait, *The View from Rock Bottom: Discovering God's Embrace in Our Pain* (Harvest House: Eugene, 2019).

Nancy Mairs, *Waist-High in the World: A Life Among the Nondisabled* (Boston: Beacon Press, 1996).

Tanya Marlow, *Those Who Wait: Finding God in Disappointment, Doubt and Delay* (Welwyn Garden City: Malcolm Down Publishing, 2017).

Shane Clifton, *Crippled Grace: Disability, Virtue Ethics and the Good Life* (Waco: Baylor University Press, 2018).

Hannah Lewis, *Deaf Liberation Theology* (Aldershot: Ashgate Publishing, 2007).

John M. Hull, *Disability: The Inclusive Church Resource* (London: Darton, Longman and Todd, 2014).

John M. Hull, *The Tactile Heart: Blindness and Faith* (London: SCM Press, 2013).

Kathy Black, *A Healing Homiletic: Preaching and Disability* (Nashville: Abingdon Press, 1996).

AT THE GATES

Sharon V. Betcher, *Spirit and the Politics of Disablement* (Minneapolis, MN: Fortress Press, 2007).

ENDNOTES

CHAPTER 1

1   Creamer writes that 'While many people with disabilities have found welcome in the church, others may still wait outside the gates' (2009:36). In the light of the stories in this book, we would state the case more strongly, but her metaphor has inspired the title of this book. Deborah Creamer, *Disability and Christian Theology: Embodied Limits and Constructive Possibilities* (Oxford: Oxford University Press, 2009), 36.

2   Nancy L. Eiesland, *The Disabled God: Toward a Liberatory Theology of Disability* (Nashville, TN: Abingdon Press, 1994), 20.

3   Lamar Hardwick, *Disability and the Church: A Vision for Diversity and Inclusion* (Westmont: InterVarsity Press, 2021).

4   Fiona MacMillan, 'St Luke's Day', in *Liturgy on the Edge: Pastoral and Attractional Worship*, ed. Samuel Wells (Norwich: Canterbury Press, 2018), 112.

5   John M. Hull, *Disability: The Inclusive Church Resource* (London: Darton, Longman and Todd, 2014), 97.

6   Eiesland describes disabled people's alienation from the Church's 'social-symbolic life' as a result. Eiesland, *The Disabled God*, 20.

7   Miriam Spies, 'From Belonging as Supercrip to Misfitting as Crip: Journeying through Seminary,' Journal of Disability and Religion 25, no. 3 (2021): 296-311.

8   This book can only speak about the UK context of our storytellers. Under the Equality Act 2010, 14 million people are disabled – 8% of children, 19% of working age people, and 46% of those over retirement age. Office for National Statistics, Family Resources Survey: Financial year 2019 to 2020 (London: ONS, 2021), https://www.gov.uk/government/statistics/family-resources-survey-financial-year-2019-to-2020/family-resources-survey-financial-year-2019-to-2020; Equality Act, 2010, c. 15 (UK); para 6 (1).

9   Nearly half of the 14 million people living under the poverty line are either disabled, or live with a disabled person: the 'disability poverty gap.' Joseph Rowntree Foundation, UK Poverty 2019/20 (York: Joseph Rowntree Foundation, 2022), https://www.jrf.org.uk/report/uk-poverty-2019-20.

10   66% of households referred to a Trussell Trust food bank in early 2020 included one or more disabled people. Glen Bramley et al., *State of Hunger: Building the Evidence*

on *Poverty, Destitution, and Food Insecurity in the UK* (London: The Trussell Trust, 2021), 11.

11   Frances Ryan, *Crippled: Austerity and the Demonisation of Disabled People* (New York: Verso, 2020); Kayleigh Garthwaite, "The Language of Shirkers and Scroungers?' Talking about Illness, Disability and Coalition Welfare Reform,' Disability & Society 26, no. 3 (2011): 369-372.

12   John Pring, 'Disability Minister Says Addressing DWP's Legacy of Distrust and Distress is a Big Priority," Disability News Service, 7 October 2021, https://www. disabilitynewsservice.com/disability-minister-says-addressing-dwps-legacy-of-distrust-and-distress-is-a-big-priority/.

13   In 2020, only 53.7% of British disabled people were employed, compared with 81.6% of non-disabled people. Disabled people earn on average £3822 less per year than their non-disabled peers – the 'disability pay gap.' Trades Union Congress, Disability Pay and Employment Gaps (London: TUC, 2020), https://www.tuc.org.uk/research-analysis/ reports/disability-pay-and-employment-gaps.

14   Disabled people face extra disability-related costs of £583 a month, on average; 1 in 5 have extra costs of more than £1000 a month. Evan John et al., *The Disability Price Tag 2019: Policy Report* (London: Scope, 2019), https://www.scope.org.uk/campaigns/extra-costs/disability-price-tag/.

15   Amy Kavanagh, 'My Harassment Got Worse When I Picked Up My White Cane,' BBC Ouch Podcast, 12 July 2021, https://www.bbc.co.uk/programmes/; Office for National Statistics, *Outcomes for Disabled People in the UK 2020* (London: ONS, 2020), https:// www.ons.gov.uk/peoplepopulationandcommunity/healthandsocialcare/disability/articles/ outcomesfordisabledpeopleintheuk/2020.

16   This includes caregiver abuse. ONS, Outcomes for Disabled People.

17   Reported disability hate crimes rose by 54% between 2016 and 2020; only a small fraction ever result in prosecution. 'Reports of Violent Disability Hate Crime Continue to Rise as Number of Police Charges Fall Again,' United Response, 2020, https://www. unitedresponse.org.uk/news-item/reports-of-violent-disability-hate-crime-continue-to-rise-as-number-of-police-charges-fall-again/.

18   An estimated 55% of female prisoners and 34% of male prisoners in the UK are disabled. Charles Cunniffe et al., *Estimating the Prevalence of Disability Amongst Prisoners: Results from the Surveying Prisoner Crime Reduction (SPCR) Survey* (London: Ministry of Justice, 2012), https://assets.publishing.service.gov.uk/government/uploads/system/uploads/ attachment_data/file/278827/estimating-prevalence-disability-amongst-prisoners.pdf.

19   In 2020, 15.1% of disabled people had no qualifications at all, compared with 5.1% of non-disabled people; only 23.0% of disabled people aged 21 to 64 had a degree, compared with 39.7% of non-disabled people. ONS, Outcomes for Disabled People.

20   As of 2021, 400,000 people in the UK were on waiting lists for social care support. About a third of care in the UK goes to disabled people aged 18-64. Omar Idriss et al, *Social Care for Adults Aged 18–64* (London: Health Foundation, 2020), https://www.health. org.uk/publications/reports/social-care-for-adults-aged-18-64.

21   Eleanor Lisney et al, *The Impact of Covid-19 on Disabled Women* (London: Sisters of Frida, 2020), https://www.sisofrida.org/wp-content/uploads/2020/05/The-impact-of-COVID-19-on-Disabled-women-from-Sisters-of-Frida.pdf.

22　Bê defines ableism 'as a system of beliefs that privileges normate notions of the body/mind and ability that are culturally constructed and views disabled people as inferior and lacking.' Ana Bê, 'Feminism and Disability: A Cartography of Multiplicity,' in *Routledge Handbook of Disability Studies*, ed. Nick Watson, Alan Roulstone and Carol Thomas (Oxford: Routledge, 2012), 373. For an in-depth analysis of ableism, see Fiona Kumari Campbell, *Contours of Ableism: The Production of Disability and Abledness* (New York: Palgrave Macmillan, 2012).

23　Lennard J. Davis, 'Constructing Normalcy: The Bell Curve, the Novel, and the Invention of the Disabled Body in the Nineteenth Century,' in *The Disability Studies Reader*, ed. Lennard J. Davis (New York: Routledge, 1997); Dan Goodley, *Dis/ability Studies: Theorising Disablism and Ableism* (Oxford: Routledge, 2014); Hannah Lewis, *Deaf Liberation Theology* (Aldershot: Ashgate Publishing, 2007), Kindle edition.

24　Patty Berne and Stacey Milbern, 'My Body Doesn't Oppress Me, Society Does,' Sins Invalid/Barnard Center for Research on Women, https://www.youtube.com/watch?v=5z6P-z8c67g.

25　Goodley, *Dis/ability Studies*.

26　Connor Sparrowhawk, who was autistic and had learning disabilities and epilepsy, died at a residential assessment centre after he was left unsupervised in the bath, under the care of an NHS trust that was eventually found not to have adequately investigated more than 1000 deaths of people with learning disabilities or mental health problems in their care. Denis Campbell, 'NHS Trust 'Failed to Properly Investigate Deaths of More Than 1,000 Patients,'' Guardian, 9 December 2015, https://www.theguardian.com/society/2015/dec/09/southern-health-nhs-trust-failed-investigate-patient-deaths-inquiry.

27　In the deadliest residential fire in the UK since World War II, in which 72 people died, 15 of the 37 'vulnerable' disabled residents living in Grenfell Tower lost their lives. A 'stay put' policy forced them to wait till they could be rescued by firefighters; that rescue never came. The Grenfell Tower Inquiry found that disabled people had been housed on high floors with no regard for their evacuation needs, in a 'systemic failure' that breached their rights to life and safe housing. Equality and Human Rights Commission, Summary of Submissions Following Phase 1 of the Grenfell Tower Inquiry (London: EHCR, 2019), 7, https://www.equalityhumanrights.com/sites/default/files/summary-of-submissions-following-phase1-of-the-grenfell-tower-inquiry.pdf.

28　John M. Hull, The Tactile Heart: Blindness and Faith (London: SCM Press, 2013), 99.

29　As Clapton argues, 'ancient belief systems of Judeo-Christian theology which view disability in a "highly negative manner" have helped to create the social construction of disability as a political state of oppression.' Jayne Clapton, *A Transformatory Ethic of Inclusion: Rupturing Concepts of Disability and Inclusion* (Rotterdam: Sense Publishers, 2009), 19, citing Avi Rose, '"Who Causes the Blind to See": Disability and Quality of Religious Life', Disability & Society 12, no. 3 (1997): 396.

30　Hull, *The Tactile Heart*, 99.

31　Eiesland, *The Disabled God*, 23.

32　Doreen Freeman, 'A Feminist Theology of Disability,' *Feminist Theology* 10, no. 29 (2002): 71-85.

33　Just a few examples are Livability, Churches for All and Through the Roof. They all do important work on disability inclusion in churches, but they are not consciously user-led, i.e. with a majority of disabled people in leadership. An emerging exception is Torch Trust, with several blind people on its board of trustees.

34   Foucault describes pastoral power as a form of power that is focused on the conscience and inner life of an individual, within a Christian framework. Church leaders must have knowledge of their congregations' souls, leading to power that demands individual obedience. Although well-meaning in its aims, those on the receiving end of pastoral power often have little say in how they are received into institutions such as churches. Society inherited the pastoral model from the churches, as they took over the care of those who were sick or in need. Michel Foucault, 'The Subject and Power,' *Critical Inquiry* 8, no. 4 (1982): 777-795. See also Sharon L. Snyder and David T. Mitchell, *Cultural Locations of Disability* (Chicago: University of Chicago Press, 2006); Gary L. Albrecht, *The Disability Business: Rehabilitation in America* (Newbury Park: Sage Publications, 1992).

35   Rachel Muers, *Keeping God's Silence: Towards a Theological Ethics of Communication* (Oxford: Blackwell, 2004), 24.

36   The slogan of the National League of the Blind March in 1920, one of the first demonstrations for disability rights in the UK. 'Justice Not Charity: National League of the Blind March, Sunday April 25th 1920,' Disability History Scotland, 2015, http://www.disabilityhistoryscotland.co.uk/.

37   Fiona MacMillan and Samuel Wells, 'Calling from the Edge,' *Plough Quarterly*, 23 November 2021, https://www.plough.com/en/topics/justice/politics/human-rights/calling-from-the-edge.

38   See, for example, Matt Edmonds, *A Theological Diagnosis: A New Direction on Genetic Therapy, 'Disability' and the Ethics of Healing* (London: Jessica Kingsley, 2011); Brett Webb-Mitchell, *Unexpected Guests at God's Banquet: Welcoming People with Disabilities Into the Church* (New York: Crossroad, 1994); Hans Reinders, *Receiving the Gift of Friendship: Profound Disability, Theological Anthropology, and Ethics* (Grand Rapids: Eerdmans, 2008).

39   See, for example, Mary McClintock Fulkerson, *Places of Redemption: Theology for a Worldly Church* (Oxford: Oxford University Press, 2007), 113.

40   See, for example, David A. Palin, *A Gentle Touch: From a Theology of Handicap to a Theology of Human Being* (London: SPCK, 1992), 31-36.

41   See, for example, Jennie Weiss Block, *Copious Hosting: A Theology of Access for People with Disabilities* (New York: Continuum, 2002) 19; John Swinton, 'From Inclusion to Belonging: A Practical Theology of Community, Disability and Humanness,' *Journal of Religion, Disability & Health* 16, no. 2 (2012): 172-190; Nicola Hutchinson, 'Disabling Beliefs? Impaired Embodiment in the Religious Tradition of the West,' *Body & Society* 12, no. 4 (2012): 1-23.

42   See, for example, Thomas E. Reynolds, *Vulnerable Communion: A Theology of Disability and Hospitality* (Grand Rapids: Brazos Press, 2008), and a growing number of disabled Christian thinkers, from John M. Hull and Nancy L. Eiesland to Shane Clifton and Sharon V. Betcher.

43   Creamer, *Disability and Christian Theology*.

44   David T. Mitchell, *The Biopolitics of Disability: Neoliberalism, Ablenationalism and Peripheral Embodiment* (Ann Arbor: University of Michigan Press, 2015), 29.

45   The question 'aren't we all a little bit disabled?' can be a way of failing to engage with the real, material inequalities experienced by disabled people. Robert McRuer, *Crip Theory* (New York: New York University Press, 2006), Kindle edition, 157.

46   See Hull, *Disability*; Sharon V. Betcher, 'Saving the Wretched of the Earth,' *Disability Studies Quarterly* 26, no. 3 (2006), https://dsq-sds.org/article/view/721/898. See also the significant body of work in liberation theologies, from mujerista theologian Isasi-Díaz on the structural sins of sexism and colonialist charity, where transformation begins in grassroots community, to Young, who argues that through Jesus's political action among the marginalised, he called God's people to shape a new vision of God's Kingdom. Ada María Isasi-Díaz, *Mujerista Theology: A Theology for the Twenty-First Century* (Maryknoll: Orbis Books, 1996). Pamela Dickey Young, *Feminist Theology/Christian Theology: In Search of Method* (Eugene: Wipf & Stock, 1990).

47   Church of England (Archbishops' Anti-Racism Taskforce), *From Lament to Action, 2021*, https://www.churchofengland.org/sites/default/files/2021-04/FromLamentToAction-report.pdf.

48   A term used in the Archbishops' Anti-Racism Task Force report, acknowledging that the UK's common social policy phrase 'Black, Asian and Minority Ethnic' is a contested term. From Lament to Action, 11.

49   See, for example, A. D. A. France-Williams, *Ghost Ship: Institutional Racism and the Church of England* (London: SCM Press, 2020); Jarel Robinson-Brown, *Black Gay British Christian Queer: The Church and the Famine of Grace* (London: SCM Press, 2021).

50   James H. Cone, *God of the Oppressed* (New York: Orbis Books, 1975), 31, cited in Robinson-Brown, Black Gay British Christian Queer, 9.

51   As we write in 2022, the Church of England post of National Disability Advisor has been empty for a year, with no commitment made to maintaining this role, while Diocesan Disability Adviser posts are increasingly being rolled into generic Equality and Inclusion roles. The Church of England has a Disability Task Group. Malcolm Brown, Director of Faith and Public Life, Church of England, email communication, 17 February 2022. The Methodist Church is moving towards Equality, Diversity and Inclusion teams that work with groups of Experts by Experience, which are largely voluntary roles. The Methodist Church is developing disability-focused Equality, Diversity and Inclusion training resources for churches and has an accessibility policy. Jill Marsh, Inclusive Church Implementation Officer, The Methodist Church, email communication, 12 April 2022; 'Equality, Diversity and Inclusion Toolkit: Disability and Impairment,' The Methodist Church, 2017, https://www.methodist.org.uk/media/9015/edi-toolkit-4.pdf. The Baptist Union of Great Britain is in the early stages of creating resources and a strategy on disability justice. Gerry Stanton, Baptists Together, email communication, 16 February 2022.

52   "Dignity and Fullness of Life': Tim Goode Speaks at the General Synod Launch of the Booklet 'Something Worth Sharing,'" Inclusive Church, 15 February 2022, https://www.inclusive-church.org/2022/02/15/dignity-and-fullness-of-life-for-all-tim-goode-speaks-to-the-general-synod-fringe-launch-of-the-booklet-something-worth-sharing/; Inclusive Church, 'Disability Conferences.'

53   Here we draw on theology emerging from the 'Living Edge' annual disability conference, a partnership between St Martin-in-the-Fields Church and Inclusive Church, whose annual themes have twice focused on disabled Christians 'calling from the edge.' We are also influenced by their conference theme of disabled people valued by God 'just as we are.' 'Disability Conferences,' Inclusive Church, 2021, https://www.inclusive-church.org/disability-conferences/.

54   'Being a humbler church... means seeking out the rejected precisely because they are the energy and the life force that will transform the church.' Samuel Wells, *Humbler*

Faith, Bigger God: Finding a Story to Live By (London: Canterbury Press, 2022), Kindle edition, 156.

55 Hull, *Disability*, 97. See also Reynolds, Vulnerable Communion.

56 Hull, *Disability*, 97.

57 A number of disability theologians write about flourishing enabled, in churches that celebrate disabled Christians as made in the image of God, including Shane Clifton, *Crippled Grace: Disability, Virtue Ethics and the Good Life* (Waco: Baylor University Press, 2018).

58 Stephanie Spellers, *Radical Welcome: Embracing God, The Other and Spirit of Transformation* (New York: Church Publishing, 2006).

59 Liberation theology does 'not stop with reflecting on the world, but rather tries to be a part of the process through which the world is transformed.' Gustavo Gutiérrez, *A Theology of Liberation: History, Politics, and Salvation* (Maryknoll: Orbis Books, 1973), 12.

60 Robinson-Brown, *Black Gay British Christian Queer*, 3.

61 Creamer, 'Toward a Theology That Includes the Human Experience of Disability.'

62 Hull, *The Tactile Heart*, 17.

63 Avi Rose, '*Who Causes the Blind to See*.'

64 Jesus is unlikely to have looked like our modern picture of health, in first-century Palestine, with limited access to medical treatment, where impairment would have been very common. Jon L. Berquist, 'Childhood and Age in the Bible,' Pastoral Psychology 58, no. 5-6 (2009): 521-530.

65 Sharon V. Betcher, *Spirit and the Politics of Disablement* (Minneapolis, MN: Fortress Press, 2007), 3, citing Lennard Davis, 'Nude Venuses, Medusa's Body, and Phantom Limbs: Disability and Visuality,' in *The Body and Physical Difference: Discourses of Disability*, ed. David T. Mitchell and Sharon L. Snyder (Ann Arbor: University of Michigan Press, 1997), 54.

66 Eiesland, *The Disabled God*.

67 'We refuse to engage with the post-resurrection body of Jesus.' Lamar Hardwick, in 'Ableism in the Church: Disabled People and Marginalization,' Episcopal Parish Network, 1 Feb 2022 (59:50-1:00:36), https://www.youtube.com/watch?v=zmz1v8g28Hs.

68 Carole R. Fontaine, 'Disabilities and Illness in the Bible: A Feminist Perspective,' in *A Feminist Companion to the Hebrew Bible in the New Testament*, ed. Athalya Brenner (Sheffield: Sheffield Academic Press, 1996), 286-300.

69 In the Christian faith, disability has long been used as a 'metaphor to think with.' Betcher, *Spirit and the Politics of Disablement*, 59. See also Warren Carter, "The Blind, Lame and Parayzed' (John 5:3): John's Gospel, Disability Studies and Postcolonial Perspectives,' in Disability Studies and Biblical Literature, ed. Candida R. Moss and Jeremy Schipper (New York, NY: Palgrave Macmillan, 2011), 129-150; Carol M. Webster, 'Paradox in the Development of the Non-Disabled Church,' *Journal of Religion, Disability and Health* 11, no. 3 (2008): 23-49.

70 Wynn calls this a normate hermeneutic. Kerry H. Wynn, 'The Normate Hermeneutic and Interpretation of Disability within the Yahwistic Narratives,' in *Disability Studies and Biblical Literature*, ed. Candida R. Moss and Jeremy Schipper (New York, NY: Palgrave Macmillan, 2011), 91-102.

71   Eiesland, *The Disabled God*, 72.

72   Disability is a modern category, but the Bible has long influenced – and continues to influence – the way we think about disabled people today. Reflecting as a blind theologian, Hull writes 'We read the Bible in the light of our cultural construct of blindness, which is at the same time replicated and reinforced by what we read.' Hull, *The Tactile Heart*, 37. See also Rebecca Raphael, *Biblical Corpora: Representations of Disability in Hebrew Biblical Literature* (London: T&T Clark, 2009).

73   See Betcher, Spirit and the Politics of Disablement; Elisabeth Schüssler Fiorenza, *In Memory of Her: A Feminist Theological Reconstruction of Christian Origins* (New York: Crossroad, 1983).

74   Betcher, 'Saving the Wretched of the Earth'; Bethany McKinney Fox, *Disability and the Way of Jesus: Holistic Healing in the Gospels and the Church* (Downers Grove: IVP Academic, 2019).

75   Nancy Mairs, *Carnal Acts: Essays* (New York: HarperCollins, 1990), 130, cited in Eiesland, *The Disabled God*, 13.

76   Disabled priest Tim Goode often expresses this theology, drawn from Psalm 139:14. 'God is telling me that I am loved, that I am perfect in his sight, that I am fearfully and wonderfully made. For I am made in God's glorious image, revealed through the Risen Body of Jesus Christ, both wonderfully divine and profoundly vulnerable.' Tim Goode, 'Lives Held in God's Hands,' Church Times, 17 December 2021, https://www.churchtimes.co.uk/articles/2021/17-december/features/features/lives-held-in-god-s-hands

77   Leviticus 21:16-23; 22:4. There is debate about how the Levitical laws may have been lived out in Temple Judaism. For disabled people today, what matters most is how these laws are remembered. Hector Avalos, 'Disability and Liturgy in Ancient and Modern Religious Traditions, in Human Disability and the Service of God, ed. Nancy L. Eiesland and Don E. Saliers (Nashville, TN: Abingdon Press, 35-54); Sarah J. Melcher, 'Visualizing the Perfect Cult: The Priestly Rationale for Exclusion,' in *Human Disability and the Service of God*, 55-71; Mary Douglas, *Purity and Danger: An Analysis of the Concepts of Pollution and Taboo* (London: Routledge, 1966).

78   Tim Goode, in 'Ableism in the Church,' Episcopal Parish Network.

79   Canons of the Church of England, C4.3.

80   Hull, *Disability*, 91.

81   Disability liberation theology, inspired by other liberation theologies, remains a minority perspective among theologies of disability. Hull, *Disability*, 9.

82   Clifton, *Crippled Grace*, 180. In this approach, disability liberation theology is strongly influenced by other liberation theologies that seek the transformation of an unjust, oppressive everyday world into the just Kingdom of God. See, for example, Ada María Isasi-Díaz, 'Lo Cotidiano: A Key Element of Mujerista Theology,' *Journal of Hispanic/Latino Theology* 10, no. 1 (2002): 5-1; Anthony Reddie, 'People Matter Too! The Politics and Method of Doing Black Liberation Theology,' *Practical Theology* 1, no. 1 (2008): 43-64.

83   Crip' is an intentionally provocative reclaimed term of abuse, designed to make non-disabled people 'wince' and to shake up their pre-existing ideas about disability, bodies and minds. It stakes a claim about our radical politics. Alison Kafer, *Feminist, Queer, Crip* (Bloomington: University of Indiana Press, 2013), 15. Crip theology centres disabled people's experience and readings of the Bible, while critiquing ableism, normalcy and inaccessibility in churches and Christian thought. Clifton, *Crippled Grace*, 178.

84   Lewis, Deaf Liberation Theology, 16, citing Walter Wink, *Engaging the Powers: Discernment and Resistance in a World of Domination* (Minneapolis: Fortress Press, 1992), 74.

85   Kafer, *Feminist, Queer, Crip*, 23.

86   'In living in and with disabled bodies, we… are often forced into a hopeful reimagination that creates alternatives for communication challenges, access issues and supported communities of care.' Heather Renée Morgan, 'Disability and Gregory of Nazianzus's Oration 14: No Body Without Our Bodies,' *Canadian Journal of Theology, Mental Health and Disability* 1, no. 2 (2020): 157.

87   A slogan of the disabled people's movement, probably first used by South African disabled people's activist groups in the 1990s. James I. Charlton, *Nothing About Us Without Us: Disability Oppression and Empowerment* (Berkeley: University of California Press, 1998).

88   Judy Hunt, *No Limits: The Disabled People's Movement – A Radical History* (Manchester: TBR Imprint, 2019).

89   Mike Oliver, 'The Social Model in Action: If I Had a Hammer,' in *Implementing the Social Model of Disability: Theory and Research*, ed. Colin Barnes and Geof Mercer (Leeds: The Disability Press, 2004).

90   Kafer, *Feminist, Queer, Crip*, 7.

91   See, for example, Liz Crow, 'Including All of Our Lives: Renewing the Social Model of Disability,' in *Exploring the Divide: Illness and Disability*, ed. Colin Barnes and Geof Mercer (Leeds: The Disability Press, 1996), 55-72; Susan Wendell, 'Toward a Feminist Theory of Disability,' in *The Disability Studies Reader*, ed. Lennard J. Davis (New York: Routledge, 1997), 260-278.

92   Rosemarie Garland-Thomson, *Staring: How we Look* (Oxford: Oxford University Press, 2015).

93   Carol Thomas, *Female Forms: Experiencing and Understanding Disability* (Buckingham: Open University Press 1999), 60.

94   Kafer, *Feminist, Queer, Crip*, 6.

95   Leah Lakshmi Piepzna-Samarasinha, *Care Work: Dreaming Disability Justice* (Vancouver: Arsenal Pulp Press, 2018), 239.

96   See, for example, Tim Goode, "Dignity and Fullness of Life'; Inclusive Church, 'Disability Conferences.'

97   See Carol M. Cusack, 'Graciosi: Medieval Christian Attitudes to Disability,' *Disability and Rehabilitation* 19, no. 10 (1997): 414-419.

98   Elisabeth Schüssler Fiorenza, *The Power of Naming: A Concilium Reader in Feminist Liberation Theology* (London: SCM Press, 1996). Power and privilege shape identity; thinking of themselves as 'just normal,' non-disabled people may fail to recognise that they have an abled identity – and abled privilege – when it is rarely questioned. See Rod Michalko and Tanya Titchkosky, eds., *Rethinking Normalcy: A Disability Studies Reader* (Toronto: Canadian Scholars' Press, 2009).

99   There are geographical variations in terminology; North Americans often prefer 'people first' language ('person with a disability'). Neither does everyone with impairments in the UK identify with the term 'disabled people,' and people with different impairments may have their own preferred terminology, e.g. 'person with chronic illness. 'Sacred Embodiment: A Conversation with Dr. Sharon Betcher' G'98 on Disability Theory/Praxis,' Drew Theological School, 9 November 2021, https://drew.edu/stories/2021/11/09/sacred-

embodiment-a-conversation-with-dr-sharon-betcher-g98-on-disability-theory-praxis/.
https://drew.edu/stories/2021/11/09/sacred-embodiment-a-conversation-with-dr-sharon-betcher-g98-on-disability-theory-praxis/.

100 As disabled activist Lisa Egan points out, no one calls her a 'person with femaleness,' and nor does she call herself a 'person with a disability.' Highly stigmatised identities are euphemised, even when marginalised groups work to reclaim them. Lisa Egan, 'I'm Not a Person With a Disability. I'm a Disabled Person,' *Everyday Feminism*, 17 December 2012, https://everydayfeminism.com/2012/12/im-not-a-person-with-a-disability/.

101 As disabled activist Lawrence Carter-Long has argued. See Barbara J. King, "Disabled': Just #SayTheWord,' NPR Cosmos & Culture, 25 February 2016, https://www.npr.org/sections/13.7/2016/02/25/468073722/disabled-just-saytheword?t=1649768519739.

102 Disabled Christians are both subject and object of disability theology. This is a risky position to speak from, as disabled scholars in disability studies have described. Kumari Campbell, *Contours of Ableism*, 122. In a Christian context, see Maria Pilar Aquino, 'The Collective Dis-covery of Our Own Power,' in *Hispanic/Latino Theology: Challenge and Promise*, ed. Ada María Isasi-Díaz and Fernando F. Segovia (Minneapolis: Fortress Press, 1996), 255.

103 Kafer warns against claiming the term 'we' too easily, to avoid homogenising a diverse community of disabled people. Kafer, *Feminist, Queer, Crip*, 19. We agree with her, but when even the most basic questions of justice have not been well addressed in theology of disability or in the churches, disabled Christians may need to start with 'strategic essentialism' that emphasises our shared experiences of ableism in churches. Rosemarie Garland-Thomson, *Extraordinary Bodies: Figuring Disability in American Culture and Literature* (New York, NY: Columbia University Press, 1997), 23.

104 Some disabled people may use cultural models to define themselves, as do many in the Deaf community and a growing neurodiversity movement. Lewis, Deaf Liberation Theology. Disability identification is a journey many of us go on, as we travel from the 'what' to the 'who' of disability. Rod Michalko, *The Difference that Disability Makes* (Philadelphia: Temple University Press, 2002).

105 Galatians 3:28.

106 There are just a few exceptions from the UK, including Waldock and Forrester-Jones on attitudes in churches towards autistic people. There is a little more research on the topic from the United States of America, often focusing on families of children with learning disabilities and/or autism. Krysia Emily Waldock and Rachel Forrester-Jones, 'An Exploratory Study of Attitudes Toward Autism Amongst Church-Going Christians in the South East of England, United Kingdom,' *Journal of Disability & Religion* 24, no. 4 (2020): 349-370; Elizabeth O'Hanlon, 'Religion and Disability: The Experiences of Families of Children with Special Needs,' *Journal of Religion, Disability & Health* 17, no 1 (2013): 42-61; Erik W. Carter, et al., 'Supporting Congregational Inclusion for Children and Youth with Disabilities and Their Families,' *Exceptional Children* 82, no. 3 (2016): 372-389.

107 Most major denominations have not, up till now, collected data on whether their ministers or priests are disabled, although some are beginning to. We discuss this further in Chapter 4.

108 Church of England (Archbishops' Council), Everyone Counts 2014: Diversity Audit Key Findings, 2015, https://www.churchofengland.org/sites/default/files/2017-11/everyonecounts_keyfindings.pdf.

109 The original 35 interviews took place in 2015-6, followed by a further 12

interviews and written stories shared in 2020-1, along with 7 interviews/written stories in communities where Naomi was observing. This was participatory activist research, aiming to centre the voices of disabled Christians, drawing on the emancipatory disability research paradigm. Naomi Lawson Jacobs, 'The Upside-down Kingdom of God: A Disability Studies Perspective on Disabled People's Experiences in Churches and Theologies of Disability,' PhD diss. (SOAS, University of London, 2019), https://eprints.soas.ac.uk/32204/.

110   Naomi was also a participant-observer for six months with Wave Church, and both Naomi and Emily have been involved for multiple years with the St Martin-in-the-Fields/ Inclusive Church 'Living Edge' disability conference; we tell the stories of these disabled-led Christian communities in Chapter 7.

111   This book is not an academic research report – that is Naomi's thesis, which can be read online. It is one of our attempts to make the research findings accessible to the Church and disabled Christians, along with speaking on panels, giving talks, and collaborating with a growing disabled Christian movement. Jacobs, 'The Upside-down Kingdom of God.'

112   With so little research existing on disabled Christians' experiences, we look at a broad range of experiences across church traditions. Participants came from Church of England, Methodist, Baptist, Pentecostal and non-denominational evangelical church backgrounds. We were not able to speak to any Roman Catholics. Many storytellers had attended churches from multiple traditions. This book mainly shares the experiences of working-age disabled Christians, but Naomi's thesis includes more stories from people impaired through age.

113   Equality Act, 2010, c. 15 (UK); para 6 (1).

114   See Chapter 7 for their stories. 'Wave for Change,' Wave, 2020, https://www.wave-for-change.org.uk/.

115   Naming 'experts' in research has precedence, as does allowing qualitative interview participants to use either first names or pseudonyms, although this is not common. From the beginning of this research project, we were aware that, in a church and world where disabled people's stories are told for us, it was important for storytellers to have ownership of their theologies and stories. We had multiple conversations with storytellers about this, showing them how we used their data and confirming how they wanted to be named, in an ongoing process of informed consent. We support those storytellers who made the informed choice to risk being identifiable; we offered them the 'dignity of risk.' Melanie Nind, and Jane Seale, 'Concepts of Access for People with Learning Difficulties: Towards a Shared Understanding,' Disability & Society 24, no. 3 (2009): 273-287; Anne Grinyer, 'The Anonymity of Research Participants: Assumptions, Ethics and Practicalities,' Social Research Update 36, no. 1 (2002): 4. Naomi's research project was approved by ethical review processes at the University of Sheffield and the Department of the Study of Religions at SOAS, University of London, and it is compliant with the ethics policies of the British Sociological Association.

116   Garland-Thomson calls this 'imagined community;' she writes that disabled identity can be useful for 'facilitating imagined communities from which positive identities can emerge.' Garland-Thomson, Extraordinary Bodies, 23

117   Here we quote storyteller Isabelle. More than one storyteller spoke of their fear, at least at some point in their lives, that they were 'the only one' – the only disabled Christian in a particular context.

118   Of the 54 people who shared their stories for the research, 47 are white British,

2 are white European, 2 are Black British, 2 are from biracial Black backgrounds, and I is from a biracial British Chinese background. Naomi made various efforts to reach out to Black disabled Christians in particular, including networking with Black-majority congregations, but this was not successful. There may have been issues arising from our different backgrounds. Future research, especially in teams led by Black and Global Majority Heritage disabled researchers, would have more scope to look at intersectional issues of race, disability and Christianity.

119 We spoke to only 6 men. Although women are a majority in churches, this is still far fewer men than we expected. On disability and gender, see e.g. Helen Meekosha, 'Body Battles: Bodies, Gender and Disability,' in *The Disability Reader: Social Science Perspectives*, ed. Tom Shakespeare (London: Continuum, 1998), 163-180.

120 This book draws on disability theology and biblical scholarship from around the world, including North America, Australia and Latin America, where interdisciplinary research between theology, biblical studies and the humanities may be more common than in the UK. See, for example, Betcher, *Spirit and the Politics of Disablement*; Clifton, *Crippled Grace*; Hardwick, *Disability and the Church*; Hector Avalos et al., eds., *This Abled Body: Rethinking Disabilities in Biblical Literature* (Atlanta: Society of Biblical Literature, 2007).

121 'Christian theology in and of itself has no cognitive or analytical tools for understanding contemporary social reality.' Stephen Pattison, Pastoral Care and Liberation Theology (London: SPCK, 1994), 48. Interdisciplinary research is not new, in theology or religious studies. One traditional role of sociology of religion has been to critique power in religious institutions. Penny Edgell, 'A Cultural Sociology of Religion: New Directions,' Annual Review of Sociology 38 (2012): 247-265.

122 Some of our storytellers still used the older term 'Asperger Syndrome,' or used this term interchangeably with 'autistic.' The term 'neurodiversity' describes human variation in neurological functioning – including different cognitive, affective, sensory and social ways of being – which in society are considered atypical. The neurodiversity movement does not see neurodivergence as 'disorder' that requires cure, but celebrates us just as we are.

123 We sometimes refer in this book to mad studies, which has grown out of the Mad Pride movement. Peter Beresford, ' "Mad", Mad Studies and Advancing Inclusive Resistance,' Disability & Society 35, no. 8 (2020): 1337-1342.

124 The term 'intellectual disability' is not commonly used in the UK. Although not all people with learning disabilities wish to be so labelled, it is the more common term in UK social policy. See, for example, Learning Disability England, https://www.learningdisabilityengland.org.uk/.

125 After reflection, we have used the term deaf (not D/deaf) to talk about deaf people as a group or deafness, to emphasise the commonalities between deaf people, as scholars in deaf studies increasingly do. Annelies Kusters et al., eds., *Innovations in Deaf Studies: The Role of Deaf Scholars* (New York: Oxford University Press, 2017).

126 The Disability Justice movement has been led since the early 2000s by trans disabled people, queer disabled people and disabled people of colour, initially in the US, who have offered an alternative to the white-dominated, single-issue disability rights movement. *Sins Invalid, Skin, Tooth, and Bone – The Basis of Movement is Our People: A Disability Justice Primer* (San Francisco: Sins Invalid, 2016).

127 'New Disability Justice Strategy for The Methodist Church,' The Methodist Church, 16 March 2006, https://www.methodist.org.uk/about-us/news/latest-news/all-news/new-disability-justice-strategy-for-the-methodist-church/.

128 The term 'kin-dom of God' comes from mujerista theology; Isasi-Díaz uses it to speak back against the hierarchy and elitism that the term 'Kingdom' can reflect. When God's kin-dom is realised, we will all be family. Other feminist theologians use the term 'Reign of God' to avoid implications of God as male. Isasi-Díaz, *Mujerista Theology*.

129 Psalm 139:14; Goode, 'Lives Held in God's Hands.'

130 WOW was a series of Christian compilation albums similar in concept to the 'Now That's What I Call Music' franchise.

CHAPTER 2

131 Architectural design marginalises disabled bodies, through its expectations of normalcy. The concept of the 'ideal' body of a worshipper or priest in churches is older than modern normalcy, and can be traced back to biblical texts such as Leviticus. But today's pews and pulpits are full of members of modern society, and normalcy and ableism also shape modern churches. Normalcy in churches, and how it impacts access for disabled people, is therefore the focus of these next two chapters. See Rob Kitchin, "Out of Place', 'Knowing One's Place': Space, Power and the Exclusion of Disabled People,' *Disability & Society* 13, no. 3 (1998): 343-356.

132 Kathy Black, *A Healing Homiletic: Preaching and Disability* (Nashville: Abingdon Press, 1996), 123.

133 Ever since the nineteenth century, when statisticians imagined the 'normal man' as someone who measured up to a colonialist, capitalist ideal of health and fitness, we have all been expected to fall within a limited range of bodily norms. Today we see evidence of this societal expectation to measure up to a 'normal' standard in everything from IQ tests to the Body Mass Index. Disability scholars call this normalcy, and it is at the root of societal ableism. Davis, 'Constructing Normalcy.'

134 The concept of misfitting is both a social and materialist theory of embodiment, showing what happens when disabled bodyminds meet normative design. Disabled people often struggle to enter or move around buildings and environments that were not designed for bodies and minds like ours. At worst, if we cannot fit at all, we are cast out into segregated spaces. Rosemarie Garland-Thomson, 'Misfits: A Feminist Materialist Disability Concept,' *Hypatia* 26, no. 3 (2011): 591-609.

135 Walker defines access as 'the accommodation of people's differences... both the ability to fulfill one's physical and spiritual needs, and having the metaphorical and physical space to share one's gifts with one's community... the freedom to move, adequate health-care and nutrition, and freedom from pain, within our communities.' Mike Walker, 'Grace in a Place' (paper presented at 'Dialogue: New Horizons for Embracing Difference' Symposium, St. Michael's College, Faculty of Theology, 7 February, 2014), https://www.academia.edu/36063308/Grace_in_a_Place_the_Sacramental_Facilitation_of_Physical_Access_for_People_with_Disabilities_in_Ecclesial_Spaces.

136 Tanya Titchkosky, The Question of Access: Disability, Space, Meaning, 2nd ed. (Toronto: University of Toronto Press, 2011), 40.

137 Margaret Price, 'Education,' in Keywords for Disability Studies, ed. Rachel Adams, Benjamin Reiss and David Serlin (New York, NY: New York University, 2017), 66, Kindle edition.

138 Walker, 'Grace in a Place.'

139 Ibid.

140   For disability theorist Titchkosky, this reflects 'an extraordinarily common belief that disability is not only rare but also nothing but limit and lack, unexpected and undesirable, or simply, 'trouble'... Disability is not normal, not imagined, not welcomed, not needed, not common, not necessary, and not going to come to mind as the type for whom buildings are built or services provided.' Tanya Titchkosky, "To Pee or Not to Pee?' Ordinary Talk about Extraordinary Exclusions in a University Environment,' *Canadian Journal of Sociology* 33, no. 1 (2008): 48.

141   See MacMillan, 'St Luke's Day', 112.

142   '[Disabled people] have been set on the margins of the Church because the Church does not know what else to do with them. In doing so, the community is no longer composed of people with all their richness, weakness, and poverty; of people who accept and forgive each other; people who are vulnerable to one another and to God.' Webb-Mitchell, *Unexpected Guests*, 79.

143   For more on how disabled people's stigmatised bodyminds are seen as 'spoiling' things for others, see Margrit Shildrick Leaky Bodies and Boundaries: Feminism, Postmodernism and (Bio)Ethics (London: Routledge, 1997). On disabled people's disruption as we misfit in Christian contexts, see Erin Raffety, 'From Inclusion to Leadership: Disabled 'Misfitting' in Congregational Ministry,' *Theology Today* 77, no. 2 (2020): 198-209; Spies, 'From Belonging as Supercrip to Misfitting as Crip.'

144   Tanya Titchkosky, 'Disability Images and the Art of Theorizing Normality,' *International Journal of Qualitative Studies in Education* 22, no. 1 (2009): 83, emphasis ours.

145   Segregating disabled people into liminal edge-spaces is often easier, for institutions, than dealing with the injustices that keep us on the edge. But it can emphasise that we are not seen as entirely human, in the communities where we are segregated away. See Colin Barnes and Geof Mercer, *Exploring Disability: A Sociological Introduction*, 2nd ed. (Cambridge: Polity Press, 2010); Garland-Thomson, 'Misfits.'

146   On 'crip time,' see Kafer, *Feminist, Queer, Crip*, 27.

147   When disabled people cannot fit in spaces that were not designed for us, it can lead to our 'literal casting out.' Garland-Thomson's choice of words highlights how storytellers' experiences echo texts in Leviticus that once cast disabled people out of the inner sanctum of the temple. Garland-Thomson, 'Misfits,' 594.

148   Yong has written about disabled people's eschatological hope for healing; many more of our storytellers had an eschatological, Kingdom hope for access and justice. See Amos Yong, 'Disability, the Human Condition, and the Spirit of the Eschatological Long Run: Toward a Pneumatological Theology of Disability,' *Journal of Religion, Disability & Health* 11, no. 1 (2007): 2-25.

149   Hardwick, *Disability and the Church*, 56; Luke 14:7-11.

150   Ibid, 51.

151   Disabled people are used to similar disempowering segregation in secular society. Jenny Morris, 'Independent Living and Community Care: A Disempowering Framework,' *Disability & Society* 19, no. 5 (2004): 427-442.

152   Misfitting can lead to disabled people's creative resistance to normalcy, when our presence calls for transformation. Garland-Thomson, 'Misfits,' 603. See also *Spies, 'From Belonging as Supercrip to Misfitting as Crip.'*

153   John 21:18.

154   See Kavanagh, 'My Harassment Got Worse When I Picked Up My White Cane.'

155   'When people come to notice that physical barriers prevent the participation of some people, comments about such exclusions erupt. One dominant type of comment is justification… justifying what is can hold at bay considerations of what is not.' Titchkosky, 'To Pee or Not To Pee?' 44.

156   Body practices – the 'physical language' of routine and ritual in churches – reveal whose bodies matter in liturgy. Eiesland, The Disabled God, 112.

157   Ibid. We explore Eiesland's image of the disabled God in more detail in Chapter 5.

158   Ibid, 112.

159   Ibid, 113.

160   Walker, 'Grace in a Place.'

161   Luke 14:15-24.

162   Critical neurodiversity scholar Waldock writes about church communities where she has experienced gaslighting, and where she has had to answer personal questions and do emotional labour to get her access needs met, because churches are not designed for her. Krysia Emily Waldock, "Doing Church' During COVID-19: An Autistic Reflection on Online Church,' Canadian Journal of Theology, Mental Health and Disability 1, no. 1 (2021): 66-70.

163   Disability theorist Rob Kitchin calls inaccessible buildings 'landscapes of power,' which maintain the privilege and power of non-disabled people. Disabled people are left negotiating for access with those in power, having to beg to come in. Kitchin, "Out of Place,' 'Knowing One's Place.''

164   Hardwick, Disability and the Church, 56-7.

165   Luke 14:1-11, our paraphrase.

166   Hardwick, Disability and the Church, 57.

167   Webb-Mitchell, Unexpected Guests, 80.

168   Nancy Mairs, Waist-High in the World: A Life Among the Nondisabled (Boston: Beacon Press, 1996), 106.

169   There is no 'one-size-fits-all' approach to access. A person-centred approach to accessible design is sometimes called participatory design. Price, 'Education.'

170   Spies, 'From Belonging as Supercrip to Misfitting as Crip,' 310.

CHAPTER 3

171   Taylor Katzel, 'Creating a Culture of Accessibility,' CBC Digital Labs, 22 Nov 2018, https://medium.com/cbc-digital-labs/creating-a-culture-of-accessibility-963bc5b468dc.

172   Vic Finkelstein and Ozzie Stuart, 'Developing Accessible Services,' in Beyond Disability: Towards an Enabling Society, ed. Gerald Hales (London: Sage, 1996), 170-187.

173   '(Still) Calling From the Edge,' St Martin-in-the-Fields/Inclusive Church Disability Conference, London, 16 October 2021.

174   A church's culture is a 'unique expression of its shared beliefs and values,' made concrete in 'the church's behavior that a visitor might observe on a typical Sunday.'

Aubrey Malphurs, *Look Before You Lead: How to Discern and Shape Your Church Culture* (Grand Rapids: Baker Books, 2013), 25.

175   Hardwick, *Disability and the Church*, 51.

176   Hector Avalos, 'Introducing Sensory Criticism in Biblical Studies: Audiocentricity and Visiocentricity,' in *This Abled Body: Rethinking Disabilities in Biblical Studies*, ed. Hector Avalos, Sarah J. Melcher and Jeremy Schipper (Atlanta: Society of Biblical Literature, 2007), 47-59.

177   Hull, *The Tactile Heart*.

178   John M. Hull, ''Sight to the Inly Blind'? Attitudes to Blindness in the Hymnbooks,' *Theology* 105, no. 827 (2002): 340.

179   Avalos identifies an audiocentric focus on hearing in the Bible, which influences audiocentric church cultures. Hector Avalos, 'Introducing Sensory Criticism in Biblical Studies.'

180   Lewis, *Deaf Liberation Theology*.

181   More specifically, this is audism: the discrimination that arises from audiocentric privilege in society. Richard C. Eckert and Amy J. Rowley, 'Audism: A Theory and Practice of Audiocentric Privilege,' *Humanity & Society* 37, no. 2 (2013): 101-130.

182   Many Baptist churches have a strong emphasis on preaching in services, a tradition shaped by their history of engaging with the Bible in depth. Helen Dare and Simon Woodman, *The 'Plainly Revealed' Word of God? Baptist Hermeneutics in Theory and Practice* (Macon: Mercer University Press, 2011).

183   John M. Hull, 'Transforming our Vision' (presentation at the St Martin-in-the-Fields/ Inclusive Church Disability Conference, St Martin-in-the-Fields Church, London, 18 October 2014). This shift in metaphor may not make the hymn inclusive of everyone, however. Jarel Robinson-Brown writes of the white supremacist origins of this hymn, by a white slave owner, and how that history of injustice creates a disconnect as he sings the line 'that saved a wretch like me.' Threads of injustice in the Church's liturgy may run deeper than simple line-rewriting can address. Robinson-Brown, *Black Gay British Christian Queer*, 14-15.

184   In writing, BSL signs are written in capital letters, hyphenated to show a single sign. In BSL, John 1:1 reads: BEGINNING, WHAT? SIGN. Lewis, Deaf Liberation Theology.

185   See, for example, Stephanie Hannam-Swain, 'The Additional Labour of a Disabled PhD Student,' *Disability & Society* 33, no. 1 (2018): 138-142.

186   An informal term used by many with lived experience of mental health problems, triggers are anything that can cause distress, from sermon topics to darkness in the church building. As Jemma told us, triggers can be managed with content warnings, and by listening to disabled people about what causes distress and working with us to minimise these conditions.

187   We draw here on more theology shaped by the Living Edge conference, where the community welcomes disabled people to 'come as we are' to Christian gatherings.

188   There are accepted ways of standing, moving and carrying our bodies, through which we communicate that we belong in a spiritual community – a religious habitus. Bradford Verter, 'Spiritual Capital: Theorizing Religion with Bourdieu against Bourdieu,' *Sociological Theory* 21, no. 2 (2003): 150-174.

189   Betcher, Spirit and the Politics of Disablement, 26. Stigma is a mark – such as an illness made visible in what we cannot do – that 'spoils' our identity, leading to shame about who we are. Erving Goffman, Stigma (Harmondsworth: Penguin, 1963).

190   In a society where disability is stigmatised, passing as non-disabled can be a necessary survival strategy for invisibly impaired people, who may worry about the consequences of revealing that they are disabled or ill. A culture that works to reduce the stigma of disability can help. The line between visible and invisible impairment is not always as clear as it may seem: some of our storytellers used wheelchairs part-time; others used white sticks or mobility aids but also had hidden impairments. Naomi Lawson Jacobs, 'Passing for Normal: The Austerity Politics of Visibility and Invisibility for Disabled People' (paper presented at 'Disrupting Visibility: The Politics of Passing,' Goldsmiths University, 12 June 2015), https://www.academia.edu/15965537/Passing_for_Normal_The_Austerity_Politics_of_Visibility_and_Invisibility_for_Disabled_People.

191   Betcher, Spirit and the Politics of Disablement, 31, drawing on Mairs, Waist-High in the World.

192   John 4:24.

193   Disability becomes a 'problem' through interactions with those who see themselves as normal, and position disabled people as different and deviant. Disability justice is also interactional, in communities that consciously choose to give a different meaning to disability in their interactions, such as in their use of language. See Tanya Titchkosky, 'Disability Studies: The Old and the New,' Canadian Journal of Sociology 25, no. 2 (2000): 197-224; Jerald Greenberg, 'Promote Procedural and Interactional Justice to Enhance Individual and Organizational Outcomes,' in Handbook of Principles of Organizational Behavior: Indispensable Knowledge for Evidence-Based Management, ed. Edwin Locke, 2nd ed. (Chichester: Wiley, 2009): 255-271.

194   Kafer, Feminist, Queer, Crip, 34.

195   Kafer, Feminist, Queer, Crip, 38; J. Jack Halberstam, In a Queer Time and Place: Transgender Bodies, Subcultural Lives (New York: New York University Press, 2005).

196   Some disabled people have claimed Donna Haraway's term 'cyborg' proudly, as we resist norms that marginalise our assistance devices and accessible technology. Donna Reeve, 'Cyborgs, Cripples and iCrip: Reflections on the Contribution of Haraway to Disability Studies,' in Disability and Social Theory, ed. Dan Goodley, Bill Hughes, Lennard Davis (London: Palgrave Macmillan, 2012), 91-111.

197   Vic Finkelstein, Attitudes and Disabled People: Issues for Discussion (New York: World Rehabilitation Fund, Inc., 1980).

198   Communities and institutions, even Christian ones, are held together by norms, reinforced by the kind of surveillance that Rhona encountered. When disabled people do not fit easily in churches, norms governed by pastoral power can be distressing or alienating for us. See Foucault, 'The Subject and Power.'

199   Waldock, 'Doing Church' During Covid-19,' 69.

200   In their views, Maria's pastors reflected theories of the sick role. Society expects people to recover from illness and return to productive roles, and sees disabled people who do not recover as deviant. Talcott Parsons, The Social System (London: Forgotten Books, 2018 [1951]).

201   Damian E.M. Milton, 'On the Ontological Status of Autism: The 'Double Empathy Problem,' Disability & Society 27, no. 6 (2012): 883-887.

202   This is presenteeism – the ableist requirement to be seen to be present in organisations, or else risk having one's commitment questioned. Deborah Foster and Jannine Williams, 'Gender, Disability and Professional Work: The Need to Question Established Norms' (paper presented at the Gender, Work and Organization 8th Biennial International Interdisciplinary Conference, Keele University, Keele, 24 June 2014), https://orca.cardiff.ac.uk/61310/3/FOSTER-%20Gender,%20disbility.pdf.

203   Churches that hope to open their gates to disabled people may need to examine the effects of church size. The church 'growth imperative,' which is common among modern churches, had a negative impact for the participation of several storytellers in their churches. See Marion Maddox, ' "In the Goofy Parking Lot': Growth Churches as a Novel Religious Form for Late Capitalism,' *Social Compass* 59, no. 2 (2012):146.

204   Some sociologists of religion suggest that the requirement to be present and active is deeply embedded in the cultures of many churches, as a normative way of assessing whether congregants are growing spiritually. David Harvey, 'Cell Church: Its Situation in British Evangelical Culture,' *Journal of Contemporary Religion* 18, no. 1 (2003): 95-10; Robert Wuthnow, *'I Come Away Stronger': How Small Groups are Shaping American Religion* (Grand Rapids: Eerdmans, 1994), 277.

205   Disabled people receive such negative reactions and microaggressions from non-disabled people every day. Reeve shares examples from research: fear of contagion, staring, accusations of not being 'disabled enough' to use accessible parking spaces or claim benefits, being left in the rain hoping someone will open an accessible entrance, and more. Donna Reeve, 'Psycho-Emotional Disablism: The Missing Link?' in Routledge *Handbook of Disability Studies*, ed. Nick Watson, Alan Roulstone and Carol Thomas (London: Routledge, 2012), 78-92.

206   Ibid.

207   Emotional dissonance comes as a result of having to do emotion work. Disabled people are expected to be polite, patient and grateful, if we would like our access needs to be met. When we really feel angry or distressed, having to respond with a show of patience can be very stressful. Donna Reeve, 'Towards a Psychology of Disability: The Emotional Effects of Living in a Disabling Society', in *Disability and Psychology: Critical Introductions and Reflections*, ed. Dan Goodley and Rebecca Lawthom (London: Palgrave, 2006), 94-107.

208   Wendell's theory of epistemic invalidation recognises the common invalidation of disabled people's experiences of embodiment, especially by professionals in positions of power over us. The mistrust of disabled people's stories and words, that we see here, has also been called testimonial injustice. Susan Wendell, *The Rejected Body* (London: Routledge, 1996); Miranda Fricker, *Epistemic Injustice: Power and the Ethics of Knowing* (Oxford: Oxford University Press, 2007).

209   Titchkosky, 'To Pee or Not to Pee?' 37.

210   Mark 10:46-52.

211   Raffety, 'From Inclusion to Leadership,' 204.

212   Betcher, *Spirit and the Politics of Disablement*, 81.

213   Erin Raffety, 'Listening Even Unto Rebuke,' *Canadian Journal of Theology, Mental Health and Disability* 1, no. 2 (2021): 117-118.

214   Ibid.

215   As early as the story of Abraham and Sarah in Genesis 18, hospitality reveals the presence and blessing of God to the people of God. Christine D. Pohl, *Making Room: Recovering Hospitality as a Christian Tradition* (Grand Rapids: Eerdmans, 1999).

216   Ibid.

217   In society, hospitality often operates on the terms of the powerful host, rather than allowing the guest to come as they are. See Sara Ahmed, *Willful Subjects* (Durham: Duke University Press, 2014), 53.

218   Spellers, *Radical Welcome*.

219   This is a welcome that 'grants differences a share of the public space only so long as they do not disrupt or cause inconveniences to a dominant group's way of life.' Reynolds, *Vulnerable Communion*, 46.

220   This is an echo of the Parable of the Banquet, says disability theologian Metzger. In the often-untold ending of the parable, the Host throws out a guest who is not wearing the right clothes. The parable (Luke 14:15-24), often championed as a model of inclusion for disabled people, may have inherited some of the ableist prejudices of its day, through which today we read a vision of inclusion that we are comfortable with, where the powerful play generous hosts to the less fortunate. This uncomfortable reading may be worth reflecting on, as we reconsider our comfortable notion of inclusion and ask whether it marginalises disabled people. James Metzger, 'Disability and the Marginalisation of God in the Parable of the Snubbed Host (Luke 14.15-24),' *The Bible and Critical Theory* 6, no. 2 (2010): 23.1-23.15.

221   Spellers, *Radical Welcome*, 69.

222   Betcher, *Spirit and the Politics of Disablement*, 87.

223   Weiss Block, *Copious Hosting*, 141.

224   On such approaches with groups that have been marginalised and shamed by churches, see Stephen Pattison, *Shame: Theory, Therapy, Theology* (Cambridge: Cambridge University Press, 2000), 287.

225   McRuer, *Crip Theory*, 112.

226   Matthew 21: 12-14, New International Version.

227   'It is no argument to suggest that just because things have always been done in a particular way this should continue whatever the cost in shame and diminishment to particular groups or individuals.' Pattison, *Shame*, 292 .

228   They imagined communities of 'belonging and misfitting,' where disabled people's different ways of being are made welcome as a source of disruption and transformation. See Spies, 'From Belonging as Supercrip to Misfitting as Crip,' 310.

229   Spellers, *Radical Welcome*, 45.

CHAPTER 4

230   1 Corinthians 12:22

231   Amanda Porterfield, *Healing in the History of Christianity* (Oxford: Oxford University Press, 2005).

232   The mission of Western Christians to the majority world often created similar forced dependency for the global majority, in what postcolonial theorists have described as 'the politics of rescue.' Betcher, 'Saving the Wretched of the Earth.' See also Lewis, Deaf Liberation Theology; Black, A Healing Homiletic.

233   Betcher, Spirit and the Politics of Disablement, 112.

234   As Wells reflects, summarising Oscar Wilde's arguments, charitable altruism can at times be 'misguided, sentimental and patronizing,' failing to challenge the status quo of oppression. Samuel Wells, A Future That's Bigger than the Past: Catalyising Kingdom Communities (London: Canterbury Press, 2019), 101-2.

235   Foucault, 'The Subject and Power.' With its roots in this Christian pastoral model of outreach to the 'needy,' a powerful secular 'disability business' now controls the lives of many disabled people, inheriting pastoral power from the churches. Albrecht, The Disability Business.

236   Fiona MacMillan, 'Introduction,' in Something Worth Sharing, ed. Fiona MacMillan (London: St Martin-in-the-Fields Church/Inclusive Church, 2019), 4.

237   This tripartite definition of ministry is Nesbitt's; she defines 'service' as 'assisting those in need either by helping individuals or by seeking social change in sources of oppression,' though it can also be seen more narrowly as service to those in the church community. Paula D. Nesbitt, 'Ministry,' in Encyclopedia of Religion and Society, ed. William H. Swatos Jr. (Walnut Creek: AltaMira, 1998), 301.

238   Mark 9:35, New International Version.

239   Betcher, Spirit and the Politics of Disablement, 112.

240   Freeman, 'A Feminist Theology of Disability,' 72.

241   See Pattison, Shame, 287. Mary's story suggests churches may need training in 'mental health first aid' and advice on deciding when to refer to professional support services.

242   A similar vision of solidarity has empowered many disabled people in the secular world. See, for example, Piepzna-Samarasinha, Care Work.

243   Yet churches often lack the training and resources needed to engage well with people in mental distress, for example. Gavin Knight and Joanna Knight, Disturbed by Mind & Spirit: Mental Health & Healing in Parish Ministry (London: Mowbray, 2009).

244   Pattison, Shame, 287.

245   Bill Hughes, 'Being Disabled: Towards a Critical Social Ontology for Disability Studies,' Disability & Society 22, no. 7 (2007): 681.

246   Under the Equality Act 2010, employers must make reasonable adjustments to accommodate disabled employees' needs. However, in the Church of England, clergy are not subject to employment law on issues including discrimination, although they have other rights under Common Tenure. The employment situation of clergy in other denominations is less clear. 'Is Your Minister an Employee?' Anthony Collins Solicitors, 17 May 2013, https://www.anthonycollins.com/newsroom/ebriefings/is-your-minister-an-employee/.

247   Eiesland, The Disabled God, 86.

248   See, for example, 'Ministers with Ill Health,' The Methodist Church, 27 September 2020, https://www.methodist.org.uk/for-churches/guidance-for-churches/wellbeing/ministers-with-ill-health/. The Methodist Conference confirmed 'good practice guidelines' for supporting disabled ministers in 2011.

249   Canons of the Church of England, C4.3.

250   Tim Rourke, The Disabling Church... And What to Do About It (report submitted to Derby Diocesan Synod, October 2021).

251   There is very little research on disabled ministers, in any denomination, especially in the UK. This may reflect the pastoral model's impact on disabled people in churches. One exception is an audit by the Church of England of its disabled clergy, in which only 3.4% of respondents to a survey declared disability – a low number, when 11% of the general workforce is disabled. This may indicate that disabled people are under-represented in ministerial roles in the Church, or it may point to an ableist institutional culture that makes it difficult for ministers to declare disability, or both – further research is needed. The study found higher numbers of non-stipendiary ministers than stipendiary clergy. The Church has not published any more recent statistics on disabled clergy. Church of England (Archbishops' Council), Church of England Clergy with Disabilities Audit 2005, July 2006, https://www.churchofengland.org/sites/default/files/2017-10/disabilityreport.pdf.

252   Lewis, Deaf Liberation Theology.

253   Pioneer ministers have a particular role in connecting with people outside the church, although they often serve within their own churches too. 'Vocations to Pioneer Ministry,' Church of England, 18 November 2020, https://www.churchofengland.org/life-events/vocations/vocations-pioneer-ministry.

254   McRuer's theory of compulsory able-bodiedness argues that society expects us all to meet physical and mental standards of productivity, enough to serve capitalist labour markets. McRuer, Crip Theory.

255   There was a frequent failure to make 'reasonable adjustments' and examples of possible disability discrimination. It is unclear whether ministers in churches can take a claim to Employment Tribunal for disability discrimination, under the Equality Act 2010, as they do not have employed status.

256   Kristin Aune, 'Singleness and Secularization: British Evangelical Women and Church (Dis)affiliation,' in Women and Religion in the West: Challenging Secularization, ed. Sonya Sharma and Kristin Aune (Aldershot: Ashgate, 2016), 57-70.

257   'I will lead the blind by a road they do not know, by paths they have not known I will guide them. I will turn the darkness before them into light, the rough places into level ground.' Isaiah 42:16.

258   See Weiss Block, Copious Hosting.

259   Jennifer Siebel Newsom, dir., Miss Representation (Sacramento: The Representation Project, 2011), DVD. Quotation from Marian Wright Edelman, Founder and President of the Children's Defense Fund.

260   This does not only mean visibly disabled people. If more invisibly impaired people are to serve as ministers, churches will need to create institutional cultures where disabled clergy and leaders feel safe to disclose that they are disabled and ask for support. Disability-affirming attitudes in the workplace can help encourage disclosure. Given the stories of barriers to leadership in this book, invisibly disabled church leaders may feel far

from safe to disclose to their denominations, although we cannot be sure without more research into their experiences. See Nadeem Khan et al, 'Diversity in the Workplace: An Overview of Disability Employment Disclosures Among UK Firms,' *Corporate Social Responsibility and Environmental Management* 26, no. 1 (2019): 170-185.

261   The lack of familiarity with mental health and distress as a disability justice issue, rather than a medical one, is common in secular society too. Julie Mulvany, 'Disability, Impairment or Illness? The Relevance of the Social Model of Disability to the Study of Mental Disorder,' *Sociology of Health & Illness*, 22 (5), 582-601.

262   There is a caveat here: not every disabled person will want to offer disability access advice to our churches, nor are we all qualified to do so. Disabled people are rarely paid for our expertise, and that is a particular problem when many of us already live in poverty. Congregations that pay for training and access auditing – from disabled consultants – are taking a stand against this economic injustice, showing how much they value disability access, and disabled people.

263   In religious ritual, bodies recede into the background of one's awareness, as Csordas argues. Disabled people's bodies rarely disappear from view in the same way. Seen as deviant or even monstrous, our bodies and differences are a challenge to the modern concept of a body-soul split. Thomas J. Csordas, *The Sacred Self* (Berkeley: University of California Press, 1997); Kevin Paterson and Bill Hughes, 'Disability Studies and Phenomenology: The Carnal Politics of Everyday Life,' Disability & Society 14, no. 5 (1999): 597-610; Margit Shildrick, *Embodying the Monster: Encounters with the Vulnerable Self* (London: Sage, 2001), Perlego edition.

264   Creamer's 'limits theology' discusses embodied limits in some depth. From a similar starting point, our storytellers went further, showing how disabled people's limits are particularly stigmatised, cast out of communities that value an ideal of perfection. See Creamer, *Disability and Christian Theology*.

265   Garland-Thomson, Staring; Shildrick, *Embodying the Monster*.

266   Susan Wendell, 'Unhealthy Disabled: Treating Chronic Illnesses as Disabilities,' Hypatia 16, no. 4 (2001): 31, emphasis in original.

267   Desmond Tutu, in *Living Philosophies: The Reflections of Some Eminent Men and Women of Our Time*, ed. Clifton Fadiman (New York: Doubleday, 1990), 235.

268   Pattison believes much pastoral care in churches today is individualistic, aimed at making suffering bearable, when churches could instead be looking at the societal causes of that suffering. Pattison, *Pastoral Care and Liberation Theology*, 208.

269   Margaret Price, 'The Bodymind Problem and the Possibilities of Pain,' *Hypatia* 30, no. 1 (2015):268-284.

270   Mia Mingus, 'Wherever You Are is Where I Want To Be: Crip Solidarity,' *Leaving Evidence*, 3 May 2010, http://leavingevidence.wordpress.com/2010/05/03/where-ever-you-are-is-where-i-want-to-be-crip-solidarity/. Cited in Price, 'The Bodymind Problem,' 279.

271   Ruth 1:16.

272   Piepzna-Samarasinha, *Care Work*, 56.

273   Ibid, 47.

274   Ibid, 65.

AT THE GATES

275   I Corinthians 12:21-25.

276   Freeman, 'A Feminist Theology of Disability,' 72.

277   Ibid.

278   In Wells' participatory theology, people are understood as assets to churches, especially those who are often disregarded as little more than problems; 'not that you have a problem to which I must find a solution; it's that you have a pearl inside you and… I must be able to help you bring that pearl into the glowing sunshine to be beheld in all its glory.' Wells, *A Future That's Bigger Than the Past*, 108.

279   Morgan, 'Disability and Gregory of Nazianzus's Oration 14,' 147.

CHAPTER 5

280   Donald Eadie, 'Prophets and Seers: Calling from the Edge,' (presentation at the St Martin-in-the-Fields/Inclusive Church Disability Conference, St Martin-in-the-Fields Church, London, 15 October 2016).

281   Maintaining control of Christian models of disability is dependent on silencing disabled voices that tell a different story. While this is not a malicious silencing, mainstream (or 'hegemonic') theologies have social power over disempowered voices, even when their aims are benevolent. Marcella Althaus-Reid, *Indecent Theology: Theological Perversions in Sex, Gender and Politics* (London: Routledge, 2010). The result is theology – and churches – shaped by a 'hegemony of normalcy.' See Lennard J. Davis, 'Disability, Normality, and Power,' in *The Disability Studies Reader*, 4th ed., ed. Lennard J. Davis (New York: Routledge, 2013), 10.

282   Fiona MacMillan and Samuel Wells, 'Calling from the Edge,' Plough Quarterly, 23 November 2021, https://www.plough.com/en/topics/justice/politics/human-rights/calling-from-the-edge. See also Shane Clifton, 'Crippling Christian Theology as I Power My Wheelchair Out the Door,' *Theology Today* 77, no. 2 (2020): 136-7.

283   Muers, *Keeping God's Silence*.

284   Deborah Creamer, 'Toward a Theology That Includes the Human Experience of Disability,' *Journal of Religion, Disability & Health* 7, no. 3 (2003): 64.

285   Muers' and Grant's concept of threshold theologies are theologies created on the margins of a church or religious community's institutional life. Some disabled people are shaping theologies on the edges of churches. Others are telling their stories from outside of the gates of the church entirely, because their voices are not heard inside institutions. See Rachel Muers and Rhiannon Grant, 'Theology at Thresholds: Learning from a Practice in Transition,' *Ecclesial Practices* 4, no. 1 (2017): 45–62.

286   Clifton, 'Crippling Christian Theology,' 136.

287   See, for example, Mairs, *Waist-High in the World*; Emma Major, *Little Guy: Journey of Hope* (Glasgow: Wild Goose Publications, 2020); Fiona MacMillan, ed., *Calling from the Edge* (London: St Martin-in-the Fields Church/Inclusive Church, 2017), https://www.inclusive-church.org/wp-content/uploads/2020/05/Calling-from-the-Edge-printers.pdf.;   Fiona MacMillan, 'Shut In, Shut Out, Shut Up,' HeartEdge, 30 April 2021, https://www.youtube.com/watch?v=rkjSYVqQ-a4.

288   Meredith B. McGuire, *Lived Religion: Faith and Practice in Everyday Life* (Oxford: Oxford University Press, 2008); see also Kathryn Tanner, 'Theology and Popular Culture,'

in *Changing Conversations: Religious Reflection and Cultural Analysis*, ed. Dwight N. Hopkins and Sheila Davaney (New York: Routledge, 1996), 101-122.

289   As explored in the Introduction, disabled people are more likely to live in poverty, to leave school with fewer academic qualifications, and to be unemployed than non-disabled people. Ordination and leadership in churches is dependent on theological education, while clergy roles are linked with economic and educational capital, or privilege. Roger Finke and Kevin D. Dougherty, 'The Effects of Professional Training: The Social and Religious Capital Acquired in Seminaries,' *Journal for the Scientific Study of Religion* 41, no. 1 (2002): 103-120.

290   In the UK, only 4.3% of academic staff declared a disability in 2020, and only 3.2% of senior academics are disabled. Advance HE, Equality in Higher Education: Statistical Report 2020 (York: Advance HE, 2020). Disabled people have begun to write about structural barriers to seminaries and other theological education. See, for example, Benjamin T. Conner, "How Do You Think You Are Going to be a Pastor?': Vocation and Disability,' *Theology Today* 77, no. 2 (2020): 138-153; Spies, 'From Belonging as Supercrip to Misfitting as Crip.' See also work in disability studies on barriers to higher education for disabled people, e.g. Damian Mellifont et al., 'The Ableism Elephant in the Academy: A Study Examining Academia as Informed by Australian Scholars with Lived Experience,' *Disability & Society* 34, no. 7–8 (2019): 1180-1199.

291   In response, critical disability theory has called for emancipatory disability research that speaks with disabled people, not for us. See also critical neurodiversity studies and critical autism studies, where neurodivergent people are speaking back to neurotypical-dominated research that focuses on deficit. Participatory Autism Research Collective, 18 November 2021, https://participatoryautismresearch.wordpress.com/; Gerry Zarb, 'On the Road to Damascus: First Steps towards Changing the Relations of Disability Research Production,' *Disability & Society*, 7 (2), 125-138.

292   Fricker, *Epistemic Injustice*.

293   Freeman, 'A Feminist Theology of Disability.'

294   Much of this theology is written by non-disabled theologians, who may have a professional interest in disability, or a personal interest through disabled friends or family members. Nonetheless, such pastoral theology of disability has given us important insights, as it has challenged a Church that has seen those with learning disabilities or mental distress as less than human, and has asked what disability can teach us all about embracing our vulnerability. See, for example, John Swinton, *Resurrecting the Person: Friendship and the Care of People with Mental Health Problems* (Nashville: Abingdon Press, 2000).

295   Raffety, 'Listening Even Unto Rebuke,' 121. Graciosi theology has long made instrumental use of disabled people, representing us as blessed by God for the benefit of non-disabled people; echoes of this theology persist to this day. Cusack, 'Graciosi.'

296   In one more example, disability theologian Shane Clifton has written that the dean of his college used Clifton's book on disability and Christianity as one reason for a ban on his teaching there. 'The accusation against me for asserting that Leviticus 21:16–23 revealed ancient prejudice against disability... was 'you seem to think that disability theologians know more about the entailments of image [of God] than Scripture." Clifton, 'Crippling Christian Theology,' 125, 127. As Black theologian James Cone tells us, the privileged majority often fail to recognise the One from Nazareth, when marginalised people speak of our experience of an oppressed Jesus. James Cone, 'Jesus Christ in Black Theology,' in *Liberation Theology: An Introductory Reader*, ed. Curt Cadorette et al. (Eugene: Wipf & Stock, 2004), 153.

297   Eiesland, *The Disabled God*, 104. Other theologians have been concerned that Eiesland's idea of a disabled God might exclude non-disabled people, even though we ourselves have long been excluded by the Church's gospel for non-disabled people. See, for example, Frances Mackenney-Jeffs, *Reconceptualising Disability for the Contemporary Church* (London: SCM Press, 2021).

298   More specifically, this silencing involves testimonial injustice and hermeneutical injustice. See Fricker, *Epistemic Injustice*.

299   Resistant readings are a feminist theological approach to the Bible, a way of 'reading against the grain,' in Schüssler Fiorenza's words. J. Cheryl Exum, *Fragmented Women: Feminist (Sub)versions of Biblical Narratives* (Valley Forge, PA: Trinity Press, 1993); Elisabeth Schüssler Fiorenza, *I Peter: Reading Against the Grain*. (London and New York: Bloomsbury T&T Clark, 2017).

300   'As theologians listen to the stories of people with disabilities and begin to see the world through this 'new' perspective, they will notice the ways in which traditional theology has not had meaning for people with disabilities.' Creamer, 'Toward a Theology That Includes the Human Experience of Disability,' 64.

301   Tanner argues that 'elite theologies' are privileged in churches over the 'theologies of ordinary people,' which are often shared by disempowered people 'without formal training in theology.' Theologians and church leaders are more likely to be speaking from the centre, not the edge. Kathryn Tanner, 'Theology and Popular Culture,' 101.

302   Fish writes that we understand the Bible through interpretive communities; for Fulkerson, biblical reading is always situated in communities. Stanley Fish, *Is There a Text in this Class? The Authority of Interpretive Communities* (Cambridge: Harvard University Press, 1980); Mary McClintock Fulkerson, "Is There a (Non-sexist) Bible in This Church?' A Feminist Case for the Priority of Interpretive Communities,' *Modern Theology* 14, no. 2 (1998): 225-242.

303   On such experiences of 'imagined community,' see Garland-Thomson, *Extraordinary Bodies*, 23.

304   Kt Tupling et al., *Pilgrims in the Dark* (Disability and Jesus, 2018).

305   See, for example, Lewis, *Deaf Liberation Theology; Black, A Healing Homiletic*.

306   Theology currently denies justice to disabled people, Eiesland argues, both in its ableist concepts of disability, and in the ways it operates to keep us out of the conversation. Eiesland, The Disabled God.

307   Stephanie Tait, *The View from Rock Bottom: Discovering God's Embrace in Our Pain* (Harvest House: Eugene, 2019), 163.

308   Resistant readings shift the subject of biblical interpretation to marginalised groups, such as onto the untold stories of unnamed women in the Bible. Exum, *Fragmented Women*. Here, storytellers focused on silenced disabled characters, as part of what Eiesland calls resymbolisation: the search for Christian symbols that represent our authentic experience of disability. Eiesland, *The Disabled God*.

309   Storytellers used three of Schüssler Fiorenza's resistant reading strategies: imaginative identification with disabled characters in the Bible, a critical examination of ableist biblical readings, and making disability the subject of biblical interpretation to resist normative readings. See Elisabeth Schussler Fiorenza, *But She Said: Feminist Practices of Biblical Interpretation* (Boston: Beacon Press, 1992).

ENDNOTES

310   Mark 10:46-52.

311   Betcher, *Spirit and the Politics of Disablement*.

312
313   We cannot escape our social location when we do theology, for '[t]he world we know is the world projected by our bodies.' Hull, *The Tactile Heart*, 62.

314   For a theology of being with those in pain and distress, see Samuel Wells, *Incarnational Ministry: Being With the Church* (Norwich: Canterbury Press, 2017).

315   Anthony F. McClelland, 'No Longer Victims But Liberators' (Hugh Price Hughes Lecture, Hinde Street Methodist Church, March 2018), 6. http://www.hindestreet.org.uk/uploads/3/2/1/3/32133699/hph2018_no_longer_victims.pdf

316   Julia Watts Belser and Melanie S. Morrison, 'What No Longer Serves Us: Resisting Ableism and Anti-Judaism in New Testament Healing Narratives,' *Journal of Feminist Studies in Religion* 27, no. 2 (2011): 163.

317   Erin Raffety et al., 'Lonely Joy: How Families with Nonverbal Children with Disabilities Communicate, Collaborate, and Resist in a World that Values Words,' *Journal of Pastoral Theology* 29, no. 2 (2019): 101-115.

318   MacMillan and Wells, 'Calling from the Edge.'

319   Thomas Merton, *New Seeds of Contemplation* (New York: New Directions, 2007), 15.

320   For reflection on the impact for marginalised groups – especially Black women – of images of God that only represent white men, see Chine McDonald, *God Is Not a White Man* (London: Hodder & Stoughton, 2021), 34.

321   'The most astonishing fact is, of course, that Christians do not have an able-bodied God as their primal image. Rather, the Disabled God promising grace through a broken body is the center of piety, prayer, practice, and mission.' Rebecca Chopp, 'Introduction,' in Eiesland, *The Disabled God*, 11. There has always been a Christological understanding of an incarnate God who suffers with us, but this image has always competed with transcendent images of God. Creamer, 'Toward a Theology That Includes the Human Experience of Disability.'

322
323   Eiesland, *The Disabled God*, 13.

324   Anton T. Boisen, 'What did Jesus Think of Himself?' Journal of Bible and Religion 20, no. 1 (1952): 7-12. We are grateful to Amy Panton for drawing our attention to Boisen's interpretation of a mad Christ, in 'Crip and Mad Spaces and Leadership in Canadian Churches,' Centre for Spirituality, Disability and Care, Martin Luther College, 3 Dec 2021, https://www.youtube.com/watch?v=0_p0-yB7Tdo.

325   Serene Jones, *Trauma + Grace: Theology in a Ruptured World* (Louisville: John Knox Press, 2019).

326   Burton Cooper, 'The Disabled God,' *Theology Today* 49, no. 2 (1992): 179. Cooper's analysis of Eiesland's theology is written from a non-disabled, pastoral perspective (and uses some stigmatising language about disability), but it explores interesting implications of the disabled God in the light of Christian tradition.

327 Mad theology – which centres the voices or hermeneutics of people who experience distress – is still a small field, but it is growing. See the Canadian Journal of Theology, Mental Health and Disability, and its related podcast, 'Mad and Crip Theology,' hosted by journal editors Amy Panton and Miriam Spies; Richard Arrandale, 'Madness, Language and Theology,' Theology 102, no. 807 (1999): 195-202; Anthea June Colledge, 'Grounding Theology in Experience: A Theological and Grounded Theory Exploration of the Narratives of People with Lived Experience of Altered Moods and Christianity,' PhD diss. (University of Leeds, 2021), iv.

328 The crucified and resurrected Christ also bears witness to those with invisible impairments, Eiesland points out; his body would have suffered pain and internal damage through crucifixion. Eiesland, The Disabled God, 101.

329 Autism is 'a fully embodied experiential' difference, not just a neurological difference. Rorie Fulton et al., 'Sensory Trauma: Autism, Sensory Difference and the Daily Experience of Fear' (position paper, 17 September 2020), https://www.researchgate.net/publication/351918786.

330 Paterson and Hughes, 'Disability Studies and Phenomenology.'

331 Creamer's vision of the incarnated Christ is 'an image of God as one who neither exaggerates nor denies limitation, but rather lives authentically as a fully grounded and real self.' Creamer, 'Including All Bodies in the Body of God,' 65.

332 Julia Watts Belser, 'God on Wheels: Disability Liberation and Spiritual Leadership,' Yale Divinity School, 24 October 2019, www.youtube.com/watch?v=tjq7sWgwsQk, cited in Erin Raffety, 'From Depression and Decline to Repentance and Transformation: Receiving Disabled Leadership and Its Gifts for the Church,' Theology Today 77, no. 2 (2020): 122.

333 Hardwick, Disability and the Church, 84.

334 See Shildrick, Embodying the Monster; Garland-Thomson, Staring.

335 John 20:26-28. Storytellers almost always focused on Christ's physical and relational disabled body, more than a distant resurrected Christ in Heaven. Like Nancy Eiesland's meditation on a Jesus who allows the disciples to experience his resurrected body, storytellers shared grounded, contextual reflection on the human-divine connection through our bodies. Eiesland, The Disabled God, 100.

336 Betcher, Saving the Wretched of the Earth.

337 Eiesland, The Disabled God, 101.

338 Zoe was drawing on Donald B. Kraybill, The Upside-Down Kingdom (Harrisonburg: Herald Press, 2011).

339 Eiesland, The Disabled God, 31.

340 1 Corinthians 1:27.

341 In Susanna's call to the Church to be in solidarity with the poorest in society, she echoed Wells' theology of being with. Wells, Incarnational Ministry.

342 See Althaus-Reid's concerns about theology's instrumental use of 'the poor' and other marginalised groups, when it does not engage with the experiences of people living in poverty. Althaus-Reid, Indecent Theology.

343 Gutiérrez, A Theology of Liberation.

344 Matthew 25:40.

345   Eiesland, *The Disabled God,* 31.

346   Watts Belser, 'God on Wheels,' in From Depression and Decline to Repentance and Transformation,' 122. On 'pain as a path to knowledge,' see Mayra R. Rivera, 'Unsettling Bodies,' *Journal of Feminist Studies in Religion* 26, no. 2 (2010): 121.

347   Jane S, Deland, 'Images of God Through the Lens of Disability,' Journal of Religion, *Disability & Health* 3, no. 2 (1999): 48.

348   Disabled people often resist ableist norms, in inaccessible cultures or environments. Our resistance can be transformative – we would say prophetic – revealing a 'resourcefulness and adaptability that can emerge from the interactive dynamism between world and body.' Garland-Thomson, 'Misfits,' 604.

349   Raffety, 'From Inclusion to Leadership,' 204.

350   Hull, *Disability,* 91.

351   Bingo Allison, 'Thinking Differently About God' (presentation at the St Martin-in-the-Fields/Inclusive Church Disability Conference, 14 October 2019), https://www.inclusive-church.org/wp-content/uploads/2020/05/TDAG2019-Bingo2.pdf.

352   Storytellers understood liberation as a uniquely Christian answer to ableism, in the context of God's love. They almost always contextualised liberation and justice through the kin-dom of God, echoing Nancy Eiesland, who speaks of 'Emmanuel, God for us, who indicts not only deliberate injustice, but unintended rituals of degradation that deny the full personhood of marginalized people.' Eiesland, *The Disabled God,* 103.

353   As Eiesland reminds us, the disabled Christ must not be allowed to become just another name for the same old ideas about God, but must transform theology and the Church. Eiesland, The Disabled God, 105.

354   Fricker, Epistemic Injustice.

355   Al Barrett and Ruth Harley, *Being Interrupted: Reimagining the Church's Mission from the Outside, In* (London: SCM Press, 2020), 183, emphases in original.

356   Clifton, 'Crippling Christian Theology,' 137.

357   Emma Stone and Mark Priestley, 'Parasites, Pawns and Partners: Disability Research and the Role of Non-Disabled Researchers,' British Journal of Sociology 47, no. 4 (1996): 699-716; Sherry R. Arnstein, 'A Ladder of Citizen Participation,' Journal of the American Institute of Planners 35, no. 4 (1969): 216-224.

358   A phrase used by Wave Church, who are church 'with not for' those with learning disabilities. See Chapter 7.

359   Disability theorist Fiona Kumari Campbell has challenged the commonly-asked question of whether non-disabled people 'can' or 'should' research disability. This is the wrong question, she says. Instead, disability studies has a responsibility to enable more disabled researchers and centre more disabled voices. We would argue that theology of disability has a similar responsibility. Kumari Campbell, *Contours of Ableism.*

360   Donald Eadie, in MacMillan, *Calling from the Edge,* 23.

CHAPTER 6

361 Kathy Black, *A Healing Homiletic*, 11, emphasis in original. Kelley also writes of a man with epilepsy who died when his seizure inspired violent 'healing' ministry. Nicole Kelley, 'The Punishment of the Devil was Apparent in the Torment of the Human Body': Epilepsy in Ancient Christianity,' in *Disability Studies and Biblical Literature*, ed. Candida R. Moss and Jeremy Schipper (New York, NY: Palgrave Macmillan 2011), 205-221.

362 'There is so much cultural emphasis on health that it is now bordering on a form of religiosity.' Stephen J. Hunt, *Alternative Religions: A Sociological Introduction* (London: Taylor and Francis, 2017), Perlego edition.

363 Barbara Ehrenreich, *Smile or Die: How Positive Thinking Fooled America and the World* (London: Granta, 2010); Sara Ahmed, *The Promise of Happiness* (London: Duke University Press).

364 James Matheson et al, *Tackling Causes and Consequences of Health Inequalities: A Practical Guide* (Boca Raton: CRC Press, 2020).

365 In an effect called the 'disability paradox,' disabled people constantly report having a good quality of life, although this is only a paradox to those who assume that disability is an entirely negative experience. Clifton, *Crippled Grace*, 95-6.

366 Carol Thomas, *Sociologies of Disability and Illness: Contested Ideas in Disability Studies and Medical Sociology* (London: Palgrave Macmillan, 2007), 66.

367 Marcia H. Rioux, 'When Myths Masquerade as Science', in *Disability Studies: Past, Present and Future* ed. Len Barton and Mike Oliver (Leeds: Disability Press, 1997), 99–112.

368 Robert Crawford, 'Sickness as Sin: A Health Ideology for the 1970s,' Health PAC Bulletin 80 (1978): 10–16; Rose Galvin, 'Disturbing Notions of Chronic Illness and Individual Responsibility: Towards a Genealogy of Morals,' Health 6, no. 2 (2002): 107-137.

369 Eiesland, *The Disabled God*, 72. The Bible represents what we would now call disability in many different ways, in texts written across centuries and in many cultures, but links between disability and sin can be found throughout the ancient near eastern world. Raphael, Biblical Corpora; Nicole Kelley, 'Deformity and Disability in Greece and Rome,' in *This Abled Body: Rethinking Disabilities in Biblical Studies*, ed. Hector Avalos, Sarah J. Melcher and Jeremy Schipper (Atlanta, GA: Society of Biblical Literature, 2007), 31-45. Researchers have found threads of the sin-sickness conflation in modern Christian teaching. Lewis, Deaf Liberation Theology; Linda L. Treloar, 'Disability, Spiritual Beliefs and the Church: The Experiences of Adults with Disabilities and Family Members,' *Journal of Advanced Nursing* 40, no. 5 (2002), 594-603.

370 Disability theologian Walker calls this Augustinian theology 'a subtly ableist paradigm of Heaven, a reading of the Last Judgment grounded in beauty and symmetry rather than in the diversity of God's image-bearing creatures.' Mike Walker, 'Persistent Pain and Promised Perfection: The Significance of an Embodied Eschatology of Disability,' *Journal of Disability & Religion* (2021): 2.

371 Disability theologian Betcher writes, 'Modern theologies have read miracle stories as healing accounts such that persons with disabilities tend miraculously to be disappeared into the law of the average,' as readers confuse healing with modern values of normalcy. Betcher, 'Saving the Wretched of the Earth.'

372 Raffety, 'Listening Even Unto Rebuke.'

373 Schüssler Fiorenza, *But She Said*; Betcher, 'Saving the Wretched of the Earth.'

374   Questions of the imago Dei in disabled people have often started with a limited concept of humanity as defined by rationality; theologians have explored the impact of this limited image of God for people with learning disabilities. There has been less discussion of the ways the divine image has been associated with a limited social construction of physical perfection, and the impact of this for disabled people. For discussion of the imago Dei and learning disability, see C. F. Goodey, A History of Intelligence and 'Intellectual Disability': The Shaping of Psychology in Early Modern Europe (London: Routledge, 2016).

375   Betcher, Spirit and the Politics of Disablement.

376   Pattison, Shame.

377   Lewis, Deaf Liberation Theology.

378   Shane Clifton, 'The Dark Side of Prayer for Healing: Toward a Theology of Well-Being,' Pneuma 36, no. 2 (2014): 204-225.

379   Psalm 139:14; Goode, 'Lives Held in God's Hands.'

380   Healing miracles have been one of the 'main attractions' of charismatic churches in particular, but healing ministries that emphasise miraculous cure can today be found in every Christian denomination. Jorg Stolz, "All Things are Possible': Towards a Sociological Explanation of Pentecostal Miracles and Healings,' Sociology of Religion 72, no. 4 (2011): 456. See also J. Keir Howard, The Healing Myth: A Critique of the Modern Healing Movement (Eugene: Cascade Book, 2013).

381   Robert McRuer calls this 'compulsory able-bodiedness.' In this book, we call it compulsory non-disability, to acknowledge that all disabled people encounter the ableist ideal that we should become non-disabled. McRuer, Crip Theory, 2.

382   Black, A Healing Homiletic; Tupling et al., Pilgrims in the Dark; Lewis, Deaf Liberation Theology.

383   Clifton, 'The Dark Side of Prayer for Healing,' 214.

384   For Stolz, discarded crutches and hearing aids function as symbolic reconstitution of healed communities, showing that disorder and sin have been cast out. Stolz, 'All Things are Possible.'

385   Clifton shares more first-hand stories of disabled people who, in churches that sought miraculous cure through healing prayer, were physically and emotionally harmed. Clifton, 'The Dark Side of Prayer for Healing.'

386   Black, A Healing Homiletic.

387   Naomi Lawson Jacobs, 'The Cult of Health and Wholeness: Normalcy and the Charismatic Christian Healing Movement,' in Theorising Normalcy: Precarious Positions, ed. Rebecca Mallett et al. (Chester: Chester University Press), 202-227.

388   Csordas, The Sacred Self. Only a few storytellers shared experiences of deliverance ministry from 'spirits of disability;' they were all from charismatic church backgrounds. Critical disability research into deliverance ministry would be useful for understanding how widespread this healing practice is, and its impact for disabled and neurodivergent people and those experiencing distress.

389   See Lewis, Deaf Liberation Theology.

390   Clifton, 'The Dark Side of Prayer for Healing,' 215. Society has not yet moved on from the 'non-disabled gaze' that the freak show encouraged; its ongoing impact is evident in some of these storytellers' experiences of healing. See Garland-Thomson, Staring.

391   Storyteller Kt shared a resistant reading of Mark 8: 22-26, which she reclaimed for disabled people who experience gradual or partial healing:'Jesus didn't heal everybody he met. And in fact [with] one guy he had to have several goes at it because something wasn't right.'

392   McKinney Fox, Disability and the Way of Jesus.

393   John M. Hull, In the Beginning there was Darkness: A Blind Person's Conversations with the Bible (London: SCM Press, 2001). 51. See also Lewis, Deaf Liberation Theology.

394   Lewis, Deaf Liberation Theology. Measuring disabled people against an impossible standard of health, these theologies and practices of healing necessarily associate impairment with deficit. See also Stephen Pattison, Alive and Kicking: Towards A Practical Theology of Illness and Healing (London: SCM Press, 1989).

395   Stephen Arterburn, Healing is a Choice (Nashville: Nelson Books, 2005), 13-14. See also Francis MacNutt, Healing (London: Hodder & Stoughton, 1988); Morris Maddocks, The Christian Healing Ministry (London: SPCK, 1995).

396   On the impact of the health and prosperity gospel for disabled people, see Tait, The View from Rock Bottom.

397   In Pattison's terms, this is an example of idealisation. When communities believe in physical cure as a central aspect of God's healing, but disabled people remain impaired, victim-blaming and scapegoating may be an attempt to resolve cognitive dissonance. The result, for the 'victim,' is alienation, shaming, and even casting out of the community. Pattison, Shame, 287.

398   The teleology of disability has been debated in theologies of disability, but most storytellers were far more interested in how God could use disability than in the reasons why it had happened. See, for example, Amos Yong, Theology and Down Syndrome: Reimagining Disability in Late Modernity (Waco: Baylor University Press, 2007).

399   Lewis, Deaf Liberation Theology.

400   Eiesland, The Disabled God, 72–73.

401   Mary Elise Lowe, "Rabbi, Who Sinned?' Disability Theologies and Sin,' Dialog 51, no. 3 (2012): 187.

402   Sarah Anne Long, 'Seeking the Intrinsic Quality of Life,' Journal of Disability & Religion 19, no. 3 (2015): 209.

403   These beliefs about healing and cure, which implicitly desire the eradication of disabled people, are also an inheritance of eugenics, which has 'catastrophically diminished the very essence of what it is to be human – our inherent diversity and creative variety.' Jane Wallman, 'Disability as Hermeneutic: Towards a Theology of Community,' PhD diss. (University of Birmingham, 2001), 67.

404   John 9:3. Jane chose to focus on biblical texts where the link between sin and disability is rejected. Hull and Lewis both remind us that even Jesus in the Gospels is ambivalent about the link between sin and impairment. What mattered more, for some storytellers, was their liberatory, 'redemptionist' reading of the Gospels, finding hope in the moments where Jesus dismantles the connection between sin and disability. Hull, In the Beginning there was Darkness, 49; Lewis, Deaf Liberation Theology; Hector Avalos, 'Redemptionism, Rejectionism and Historicism as Emerging Approaches in Disability Studies,' Perspectives in Religious Studies 34, no. 1 (2007): 91-100.

405   MacMillan and Wells, 'Calling from the Edge.'

406   See, for example, Mark 10:51.

407   MacMillan and Wells reflect on Job's difficult situation transformed into a mystery, as he sees it in the context of God's vast, unfathomable creation. MacMillan and Wells, 'Calling from the Edge.'

408   Some theologians have explored the Bible's concept of shalom as holistic healing. Schüssler Fiorenza's concept of basileia healing – Kingdom healing – brings this concept together with Jesus's fulfilment of Isaiah's prophecy of healing for all of creation, in the Reign of God. Schüssler Fiorenza, But She Said. Clifton uses the word 'well-being' for this broader, holistic concept of healing, but the secular wellness movement may give this word negative connotations for some disabled people. Clifton, 'The Dark Side of Prayer for Healing,' 221.

409   Walker, 'Persistent Pain and Promised Perfection,' 14. Walker draws here on the work of Betcher, who affirms that illness can bring our attention back to the body's relationship to the world. Betcher, Spirit and the Politics of Disablement.

410   Deanna Thompson, Glimpsing Resurrection: Cancer, Trauma, and Ministry (Louisville: Presbyterian Publishing Corporation), Kindle Edition, citing Frederick J. Gaiser, Healing in the Bible: Theological Insight for Christian Ministry (Grand Rapids: Baker Academic, 2010), 250.

411   Hanna Bertilsdotter Rosqvist et al, Neurodiversity Studies: A New Critical Paradigm (Abingdon: Routledge, 2020).

412   Hull, The Tactile Heart, 68.

413   Walker, 'Persistent Pain and Promised Perfection.'

414   Yong, 'Disability, the Human Condition, and the Spirit of the Eschatological Long Run.'

415   Walker calls this an 'embodied eschatology of disability,' a perspective that grows from disabled people's diverse embodied experiences of health and healing. Walker, 'Persistent Pain and Promised Perfection,' 2.

416   Ibid, 12.

417   Fiona MacMillan, Something Worth Sharing, 4.

418   MacMillan, 'St Luke's Day', 113.

419   Ibid.

420   Ibid, 115. MacMillan's chapter includes a how-to guide for churches seeking to create similar disabled-led healing services, from avoiding hymns that use impairments as spiritual metaphors for deficit, to using liturgy that emphasises all of humanity's need for wholeness and healing.

421   In recent years, the church has separated out the healing service from the conference, so that healing is less closely associated with disability. Disabled people continue to take a leading role in the annual healing service.

422   Clifton, 'The Dark Side of Prayer for Healing,' 215-6.

423   In the society of the Gospels, impairments were often the result of oppressive imperial Roman rule, where slaves had their eyes put out, and many people faced conditions of poverty that led to illness. Jesus's Kingdom healing was liberation from the destructive forces of Empire. Betcher, 'Saving the Wretched of the Earth.'

424 Betcher, 'Saving the Wretched of the Earth.'

425 A holistic vision of healing inspired by ecotheology comes 'in the context of a global society characterized by social inequality and injustice, the marginalization and exclusion of powerless humans, violence and conflict, and the exploitation and degradation of the earth.' David N. Field, 'Stewards of Shalom: Toward a Trinitarian Ecological Ethic,' Quarterly Review 22, no. 4 (2002): 393.

426 Watts Belser and Morrison, 'What No Longer Serves Us,' 163-4.

427 Ibid, 160.

428 Clifton, 'The Dark Side of Prayer for Healing,' 221.

429 Betcher, 'Saving the Wretched of the Earth.'

CHAPTER 7

430 Waldock, ' "Doing Church" During COVID-19,' 69.

431 We think more about online church as 'real church' in Chapter 8, where we look at the debates inspired by churches' move online in response to the coronavirus pandemic.

432 There is a digital divide for disabled people, although that divide is closing. In 2018, 23.3% of disabled people were internet non-users, compared with 6% of non-disabled people. There is a higher digital divide among older disabled people and those living in poverty. For institutional churches, the digital divide highlights the need to make buildings and church cultures more accessible to disabled people who cannot engage in church online. Office for National Statistics, Exploring the UK's Digital Divide (London: ONS, 2019), https://www.ons.gov.uk/peoplepopulationandcommunity/householdcharacteristics/homeinternetandsocialmediausage/articles/exploringtheuksdigitaldivide/2019-03-04#what-other-patterns-are-there-in-internet-usage.

433 'Disability and Jesus is a user-led organisation, stemming from the lived experience of disability rather than an 'outside-in' standpoint.' 'A Church Without Disabled People is a Disabled Church,' Disability and Jesus, 2020, http://disabilityandjesus.org.uk/.

434 As digital sociologist Tim Hutchings has said, there is a difference between grassroots 'online church', where community and worship life all happens on the internet, and 'church online,' the digital outreach of churches that usually meet in buildings. There can be tensions between grassroots' groups ways of doing online church and the digital outreach of institutional churches, tension which Disability and Jesus has sometimes felt. Tim Hutchings, Creating Church Online: Ritual, Community and New Media (London: Routledge, 2017), 254-5.

435 'The Staying Inn,' 2020, https://www.thestayinginn.org.uk/.

436 Watts Belser, 'God on Wheels,' in Raffety, 'From Depression and Decline to Repentance and Transformation'; Eiesland, The Disabled God.

437 The vibrant disability arts scene in the UK is one example, with its empowering spaces where disabled people can speak 'about the value their lives have gained through the experience of impairment, of an enhanced understanding of life.' Colin Cameron, 'Disability Arts: The Building of Critical Community Politics and Identity,' in Politics, Power and Community Development, ed. Rosie Meade, Mae Shaw and Sarah Banks (Bristol: Policy Press, 2016), Perlego edition. But as Young argues, such spaces must be self-organised and led by marginalised people, or they become spaces of segregation, where we are shut

away, rather than empowering spaces. Iris Marion Young, 'The Ideal of Community and the Politics of Difference,' *Social Theory & Practice* 12, no. 1 (1986): 1–26.

438   Struggling Saints – a public group – and Emma's private group are two contrasting examples of what Hutchings calls the 'dual nature' of online churches. Groups can exist publicly, and 'be integrated into users' social networks.' Or they can be 'kept separate as private space for exploration of new ideas… or existential vulnerabilities.' Tim's group is more suited to mission; closed groups like Emma's have opportunities to create safe space, for vulnerability and healing. Hutchings, *Creating Church Online*, 256.

439   The 'third space' of the online world can be a space for critique; it offers 'the potential for digital media to provide spaces that are separate from the institutions and structures of daily life, within which individuals can critique those structures and reflect on their own vulnerability.' Hutchings, *Creating Church Online*, 257.

440   Causeway Prospects was an organisation that supported people with learning disabilities to participate in churches. It merged with the Christian disability charity Livability in 2016. 'Our Story,' Livability, 2021, https://www.livability.org.uk/about-us/our-story/.

441   Quotations from Wave members, taken from Bernice's research. Bernice Hardie, Wave Church, email communication, 4 January 2022.

442   Bernice Hardie's research has found that mixed-ability social connections can transform attitudes to people with learning disabilities. Bernice Hardie, 'We're All Valued Equally: Researching the Potential for Community Change,' Wave, 2019, https://www.wave-for-change.org.uk/.

443   Bernice Hardie, 'It is Time to Value All Equally,' Church Times, 15 January 2021, https://www.churchtimes.co.uk/articles/2021/15-january/comment/opinion/it-is-time-to-value-all-equally

444   Hardie, 'We're All Valued Equally: Researching the Potential for Community Change.'

445   Hardie, 'It is Time to Value All Equally.'

446   Raffety, 'Listening Even Unto Rebuke.'

447   HeartEdge, *(Still) Calling from the Edge* [publicity leaflet] (London: HeartEdge, 2021).

448   Hull, Disability; Jean Vanier and John Swinton, *Mental Health: The Inclusive Church Resource* (Norwich: Darton, Longman & Todd, 2016).

449   MacMillan, Calling from the Edge.

450   MacMillan, Something Worth Sharing, 4.

451   Ibid.

452   HeartEdge, *(Still) Calling from the Edge.*

453   Samuel Wells, 'Introduction,' in MacMillan, Calling from the Edge, 3; Psalm 118:22, NIV.

454   Rachel Wilson, in MacMillan, *Calling from the Edge*, 6.

455   Lee Abbey granted permission to be named in connection with this story, after a request by storyteller Sarah.

456 Waldock writes about hearing the term 'edgewalker' – meaning one who walks on the edge and between worlds – in a disabled-led Christian community, and how it gave her agency in her experiences of church on the margins. Waldock, '"Doing Church" During COVID-19,' 69. See also Judi Neal, Are You an Edgewalker? Edgewalkers, 2016, https://edgewalkers.org/edgewalkers/are-you-an-edgewalkers/.

457 Spies, 'From Belonging as Supercrip to Misfitting as Crip.'

458 For a discussion of threshold theology, formed on the margins of institutional churches, see Muers and Grant, 'Theology at Thresholds.'

459 bell hooks, 'Choosing the Margin as a Space of Radical Openness,' Framework: The Journal of Cinema and Media 36 (1989): 19.

460 '[T]hat space in the margin that is a site of creativity and power, that inclusive space where we recover ourselves, where we move in solidarity to erase the category colonised /coloniser. Marginality as site of resistance.' hooks, 'Choosing the Margin,' 36.

461 Disability and Jesus, 'A Church Without Disabled People is a Disabled Church.'

462 Waldock, '"Doing Church' During COVID-19,' 68.

463 Ibid, 68.

464 Ibid, 69.

CHAPTER 8

465 House of Commons Women and Equalities Committee, Unequal Impact? Coronavirus and BAME People (HC 2019-20 384); House of Commons Women and Equalities Committee, Unequal Impact? Coronavirus, Disability and Access to Services (HC 2019-20 1050).

466 'All the way through this pandemic there has been a narrative to the wider population: don't worry, it only affects older people, and those with pre-existing conditions – as if, somehow, the value of those people's lives was less.' Lucy Webster, 'Why Disabled People are Calling for a Covid-19 Inquiry,' BBC News, 4 July 2020, https://www.bbc.co.uk/news/uk-53221435.

467 John Abrams, Abandoned, Forgotten and Ignored: The Impact of the Coronavirus Pandemic on Disabled People (London: Inclusion London), https://www.inclusionlondon.org.uk/disability-in-london/coronavirus-updates-and-information/campaigns-news-during-coronavirus-crisis/abandoned-forgotten-and-ignored-the-impact-of-covid-19-on-disabled-people/; Eleanor Lisney et al, The Impact of Covid-19 on Disabled Women.

468 'Shielding' was the UK government's policy of advising those who were classified as Clinically Extremely Vulnerable (CEV) not to leave their homes. There were several months of shielding policy in 2020 and again in 2021. Katherine Runswick-Cole, 'A (Brief) History of Shielding,' i-Human, University of Sheffield, 4 November 2020, https://www.sheffield.ac.uk/ihuman/news/brief-history-shielding; Karen Hodgson and Sebastien Peytrignet, Who was Advised to Shield from COVID-19? Exploring Demographic Variation in People Advised to Shield (London: Health Foundation, 2021), https://www.health.org.uk/news-and-comment/charts-and-infographics/exploring-demographic-variation-in-groups-advised-to-shield.

469 6 in 10 Covid-related deaths have been of disabled people; death rates vary by groups of disabled people, but are disproportionate, with a particularly sharp increase in deaths of people with a learning disability during the pandemic. Office for

National Statistics, Coronavirus (COVID-19) Related Deaths by Disability Status, England and Wales: 2 March to 14 July 2020 (London: ONS, 2020), https://www.ons. gov.uk/peoplepopulationandcommunity/birthsdeathsandmarriages/deaths/articles/ coronaviruscovid19relateddeathsbydisabilitystatusenglandandwales/2marchto14july2020; 'CQC publishes data on deaths of people with a learning disability,' Care Quality Commission, 2 June 2020, https://www.cqc.org.uk/news/stories/cqc-publishes-data-deaths-people-learning-disability.

470   Imani Barbarin, 'Death by a Thousand Words: COVID-19 and the Pandemic of Ableist Media,' Refinery29, 30 August 2021, https://www.refinery29.com/en-us/2021/08/10645352/covid-19-and-the-pandemic-of-ableist-media.

471   Esther 4:14

472   'A Church Near You,' The Church of England, 2022, https://www.achurchnearyou. com/.

473   Office for National Statistics, Exploring the UK's Digital Divide.

474   Fiona MacMillan, *Something Worth Sharing*, 4.

475   Hutchings calls this 'the co-opting of online religion by religion online.' Hutchings, Creating Church Online, 255.

476   In one study, a third of respondents said they had faced access issues in church's online ministry, including disabled, neurodivergent and Deaf people. Krysia Waldock, 'Inclusive Online Church Consultation: What Did We Find Out?' Inclusive Church, 18 January 2022, https://www.inclusive-church.org/2022/01/18/inclusive-online-church-consultation-what-did-we-find-out/.

477   Emma Major, 'Isolation and the Church: Online and Offline,' *Church Times*, 1 May 2020, https://www.churchtimes.co.uk/articles/2020/1-may/audio-video/video/isolation-and-the-church-online-and-offline.

478   The question has been debated since the earliest days of online churches, with some commentators arguing that online church is 'real, but it's not real enough,' and that 'A full church experience requires flesh-and-blood people to share physical space together.' Karl Vaters, 'Is Online Church Real Church?' *Christianity Today*, 12 September 2017, https://www.christianitytoday.com/karl-vaters/2017/september/online-church.html.

479   Neil Thompson wrote in 2021 that he hoped the Church of England's online ministry would not grow 'at the expense of 'real' visits by 'real' people... I suggest that this would be more than unfortunate; for it would mean the abandonment of the heart, experience, and meaning of worship – and the Church as God's gathered people.' Neil Thompson, 'Liturgy is Not Just a Virtual Experience,' Church Times, 6 August 2021, https://www.churchtimes. co.uk/articles/2021/6-august/comment/opinion/liturgy-is-not-just-a-virtual-experience.

480   See, for example, 'Supporting Congregations and People Exploring Faith Online as Churches Begin to Reopen,' Church of England, 3 July 2020, https://www.churchofengland. org/resources/digital-labs/blogs/supporting-congregations-and-people-exploring-faith-online-churches; Bill Braviner, 'Top Tips for an Accessible Online Service,' Church of England, 6 July 2020,
https://www.churchofengland.org/resources/digital-labs/blogs/top-tips-accessible-online-service.

481   In the *Tablet*, under an iconic picture of Justin Welby presiding over the Eucharist in his kitchen, Anglican bishop Peter Selby expressed concern that lockdown online church

has meant a retreat of Anglicanism into private space, when the legitimacy of the Church of England comes in part from its buildings and parish structure. Peter Selby, 'Is Anglicanism Going Private?' The *Tablet*, 30 April 2020, https://www.thetablet.co.uk/features/2/17973/is-anglicanism-going-private-.

482   'Much has been made of the numbers 'attending' online services, although it is impossible to know the extent to which everyone watching is engaging with the worship.' Here, Trott was one of many commentators who argued that only in physical churches could worshippers have a full experience of liturgy. Stephen Trott, 'The C of E Needs to be Leaner and Fitter,' Church Times, 10 July 2020, https://www.churchtimes.co.uk/articles/2020/10-july/comment/opinion/the-c-of-e-needs-to-be-leaner-and-fitter.

483   Hutchings, *Creating Church Online*, 257.

484   Harriet Sherwood, 'Clergy up in Arms as Pressure Mounts on Bishops to Reopen Churches,' The *Guardian*, 31 May 2020, https://www.theguardian.com/world/2020/may/31/clergy-up-in-arms-as-church-of-england-archbishops-resist-move-to-reopen-churches.

485   'Churches and COVID-19 Opinion Poll,' National Churches Trust, 30 May 2020, https://www.nationalchurchestrust.org/news/churches-and-covid-19-opinion-poll.

486   We use the term in-building as opposed to 'physical' or 'in-person'. The congregant joining in with worship from their home is no less physical or in-person. All worship is, by nature of the incarnation, embodied and in-person.

487   At-risk clergy responded to the risk of church reopening in the press. Pat Ashworth, 'Don't Forget Us, Say Vulnerable Clergy,' *Church Times*, 28 August 2020,

https://www.churchtimes.co.uk/articles/2020/28-august/news/uk/don-t-forget-us-say-vulnerable-clergy. For more of the stories of clergy at high risk of Covid, see 'Shielding Clergy,' Kt Tupling, 2020, https://www.youtube.com/watch?v=5iicixX4ljw.

488   'A Message from Bishop Sarah,' Bishop of London's Newsletter, 16 July 2021, https://newsletters.london.anglican.org/linkapp/cmaview.aspx?LinkID=pageid100729555qjt~jqfx htq~nhh9h~qfzrz9~z~x~f~jqnj9f~f&fbclid=IwAR1NrcwRaRWn9BqLPPB-7weiUjl2gaNro bVpo85ZwAuTrLozOAQ0nlMaheg.

489   Naomi Lawson Jacobs, Emma Major and Kt Tupling, 'Statement on the Church of England's Covid Guidance to Churches (July 2021),' At The Gates, 17 July 2021, http://naomilawsonjacobs.com/statement-on-the-church-of-englands-covid-guidance-to-churches-july-2021/, emphasis in original.

490   Major, 'Isolation and the Church: Online and Offline.'

491   Church of England, 'Supporting Congregations and People Exploring Faith Online as Churches Begin to Reopen,' Digital Labs, 3 July 2020, https://www.churchofengland.org/resources/digital-labs/blogs/supporting-congregations-and-people-exploring-faith-online-churches.

492   Church of England, 'Millions Join Worship Online as Churches Bring Services into the Home in Pandemic Year' (press release), 16 March 2021, https://www.churchofengland.org/news-and-media/news-releases/millions-join-worship-online-churches-bring-services-home-pandemic.

493   Thompson, 'Liturgy is Not Just a Virtual Experience.'

494   There is, of course, a diversity of voices and opinions in the debate about churches and online access. We should also note that some Church of England representatives

have acknowledged this, and are asking how the church can nurture online congregations who will never enter church buildings. See, for example, Church of England, 'Millions Join Worship Online.'

495   Emma Major and Laura Neale, 'Worshipping Together Safely,' YouBelong, 7 July 2020, http://youbelong.org.uk/blog/july-2021-(1)/worshipping-together-safely.

496   Trish Harrison Warren, 'Why Churches Should Drop Their Online Services,' New York Times, 30 Jan 2022, https://www.nytimes.com/2022/01/30/opinion/church-online-services-covid.html.

497   Tanya Marlow, Twitter post, 31 Jan 2022, https://twitter.com/Tanya_Marlow/status/1488206616138854400.

498   Ibid.

499   Ibid.

500   Acts 1:8.

CONCLUSION

501   With thanks to Fiona MacMillan for applying D. L. Stewart's reflections on justice in institutions to a Christian context. 'Diversity asks, "Who's in the room?" Equity responds, "Who's trying to get into the room but can't?..." Inclusion asks, "Has everyone's ideas been heard?" Justice responds, "Whose ideas won't be taken as seriously because they aren't in the majority?" D. L. Stewart, 'Language of Appeasement,' Inside Higher Ed, 30 March 2017, https://www.insidehighered.com/views/2017/03/30/colleges-need-language-shift-not-one-you-think-essay.

502   Micah 4:6-7.

503   Sarah J. Melcher, 'I Will Lead the Blind by a Road They Do Not Know: Disability in Prophetic Eschatology,' Society of Biblical Literature (2004): 55-72. These texts are not always straightforward for disabled people, Melcher argues, with some associating disability with deficit and sin, because of the cultural context they emerge from. Yet resistant readings can uncover narratives of justice for disabled people in the Old Testament eschatological texts.

504   As other Old Testament texts suggest, the sheep do not just wander away – they are driven away from the sheep fold through the actions of poor shepherds. 'My sheep were scattered over all the face of the earth, with no one to search or seek for them.' Ezekiel 34:6.

505   Morgan, 'Disability and Gregory of Nazianzus's Oration 14,' 157.

506   We are inspired here by the powerful statement attributed to Angela Davis: 'In a racist society, it is not enough to be non-racist, we must be anti-racist,' cited in Vivetha Thambinathan and Elizabeth Anne Kinsella, 'Decolonizing Methodologies in Qualitative Research: Creating Spaces for Transformative Praxis,' International Journal of Qualitative Methods 20 (2021): 1-9.

507   Gutiérrez, A Theology of Liberation, 175.

508   Ephesians 6:12, King James Version; Hannah Lewis, 'Shut In, Shut Out, Shut Up,' HeartEdge, 29 May 2021 (13.12), https://www.youtube.com/watch?v=XabBygamdFw.

509   Lamar Hardwick, Disability and the Church, 157-9; Acts 2:15-18.

APPENDIX 2

510 Ana Bê, 'Feminism and Disability: A Cartography of Multiplicity.'

511 Pierre Bourdieu, *Distinction: A Social Critique of the Judgement of Taste* (London: Routledge, 1984).

512 Clifton, *Crippled Grace*.

513 McRuer, *Crip Theory*, 9.

514 Lewis, Deaf Liberation Theology; Cameron, 'Disability Arts: The Building of Critical Community Politics and Identity.'

515 Sins Invalid, Skin, Tooth, and Bone.

516 Arlie Russell Hochschild, 'Emotion Work, Feeling Rules, and Social Structure,' American Journal of Sociology 85, no. 3 (1979): 551-575.

517 Reeve, 'Towards a Psychology of Disability.'

518 Fricker, *Epistemic Injustice*.

519 Wendell, *The Rejected Body*.

520 Cusack, 'Graciosi.'

521 Margaret Price, 'Education.'

522 Greenberg, 'Promote Procedural and Interactional Justice.'

523 Schüssler Fiorenza, *In Memory of Her*, 123.

524 Barnes and Mercer, *Exploring Disability*, 52.

525 McGuire, *Lived Religion*.

526 Aune, 'Singleness and Secularization.'

527 Garland-Thomson, 'Misfits.'

528 Davis, 'Constructing Normalcy.'

529 Titchkosky, 'Disability Images.'

530 Foucault, 'The Subject and Power.'

531 Reeve, 'Psycho-Emotional Disablism.'

532 Spellers, *Radical Welcome*.

533 Verter, 'Spiritual Capital.'

534 Schüssler Fiorenza, *I Peter: Reading Against the Grain*.

535 Webb-Mitchell, *Unexpected Guests*, 80.

536 Oliver, 'The Social Model in Action.'

537 Goffman, *Stigma*.

538 Wendell, 'Unhealthy Disabled,' 31; Rosemarie Garland-Thomson, 'The Story of my Work: How I Became Disabled,' Disability Studies Quarterly 34, no. 2 (2014).

539 Hunt, *Alternative Religions*.